# THE NAVARRE BIBLE

## Saint Paul's Captivity Letters

*Ephesians, Philippians, Colossians, Philemon*

in the Revised Standard Version and New Vulgate
with a commentary by members of the
Faculty of Theology of the University of Navarre



FOUR COURTS PRESS • DUBLIN
SCEPTER PUBLISHERS • NEW YORK

Typeset by Carrigboy Typesetting Services for
FOUR COURTS PRESS LTD
7 Malpas Street, Dublin 8, Ireland
e-mail: info@fourcourtspress.ie
http://www.fourcourtspress.ie
*Distributed in North America by*
SCEPTER PUBLISHERS, INC.
P.O. Box 211, New York, NY 10018–0004
e-mail: general@scepterpublishers.org
http://www.scepterpublishers.org



The translation of introductions and commentary was made by Michael Adams.

A catalogue record for this title is available from the British Library.
First edition 1992; reprinted many times
Second edition (reset and repaged) 2005; reprinted 2010

*Nihil obstat*: Stephen J. Greene, *censor deputatus*
*Imprimi potest*: Desmond, Archbishop of Dublin, 9 January 1992

ISBN 978–1–85182–908–8

*Library of Congress Cataloging-in-Publication Data* [for first volume in this series]

Bible. O.T. English. Revised Standard. 1999.
The Navarre Bible. – North American ed.
p. cm
"The Books of Genesis, Exodus, Leviticus, Numbers, Deuteronomy in the Revised Standard Version and New Vulgate with a commentary by members of the Faculty of Theology of the University of Navarre."
Includes bibliographical references.
Contents: [1] The Pentateuch.
ISBN 1–889334–21–9 (hardback: alk. paper)
I. Title.
BS891.A1 1999.P75 99–23033
221.7'7—dc21 CIP



ACKNOWLEDGMENTS
Quotations from Vatican II documents are based on the translation in *Vatican Council II: The Conciliar and Post Conciliar Documents*, ed. A. Flannery, OP (Dublin 1981).

The New Vulgate text of the Bible can be accessed via
http://www.vatican.va.archive/bible/index.htm

Printed and bound in Great Britain by MPG Books, Bodmin, Cornwall.

# Contents

*Preface and Preliminary Notes* 7

*Abbreviations* 9

*The Captivity Letters* 11

*Introduction to the Letter to the Ephesians* 13
The city of Ephesus 13
Readership and date of the letter 13
Pauline authorship 14
Structure 15
Doctrinal content 18

*The Letter to the Ephesians: English version, with notes* 21

*Introduction to the Letter to the Philippians* 81
The city of Philippi 81
Paul's authorship of the letter 82
An amalgam of letters? 82
The reason for the letter 83
Place and date of composition 83
Structure 84
Doctrinal content 85

*The Letter to the Philippians: English version, with notes* 89

*Introduction to the Letter to the Colossians* 121
The city of Colossae 121
Place and date of composition of the letter 122
Pauline authorship 123
The reason for the letter 124
Structure and content 125
Principal doctrinal topics 127

**Contents**

*The Letter to the Colossians: English version, with notes* 131

*Introduction to the Letter to Philemon* 161
Date and reason for the letter 161
Pauline authorship 161
Content and message 162

*The Letter to Philemon: English version, with notes* 163

*New Vulgate Text* 171
Ephesians 171
Philippians 173
Colossians 175
Philemon 177

*Explanatory Notes* 179

*Headings added to the Biblical Text* 181

*Maps* 183

*Sources quoted in the Commentary* 185

# Preface and Preliminary Notes

**The Commentary**

The distinguishing feature of the *Navarre Bible* is its commentary on the biblical text. Compiled by members of the Theology faculty of the University of Navarre, Pamplona, Spain, this commentary draws on writings of the Fathers, texts of the Magisterium of the Church, and works of spiritual writers, including St Josemaría Escrivá, the founder of Opus Dei; it was he who in the late 1960s entrusted the faculty at Navarre with the project of making a translation of the Bible and adding to it a commentary of the type found here.

The commentary, which is not particularly technical, is designed to explain the biblical text and to identify its main points, the message God wants to get across through the sacred writers. It also deals with doctrinal and practical matters connected with the text.

The first volume of the *Navarre Bible* (the English edition) came out in 1985—first, twelve volumes covering the New Testament; then seven volumes covering the Old Testament. Many reprints and revised editions have appeared over the past twenty years. All the various volumes are currently in print.

**The Revised Standard Version**

The English translation of the Bible used in the *Navarre Bible* is the Revised Standard Version (RSV) which is, as its preface states, "an authorized revision of the American Standard Version, published in 1901, which was a revision of the King James Version [the "Authorized Version"], published in 1611".

The RSV of the entire Bible was published in 1952; its Catholic edition (RSVCE) appeared in 1966. The differences between the RSV and the RSVCE New Testament texts are listed in the "Explanatory Notes" in the end-matter of this volume. Whereas the Spanish editors of what is called in English the "Navarrre Bible" made a new translation of the Bible, for the English edition the RSV has proved to be a very appropriate choice of translation. The publishers of the *Navarre Bible* wish to thank the Division of Christian Education of the National Council of the Churches of Christ in the USA for permission to use that text.

**The Latin Text**

This volume also carries the official Latin version of the New Testament in the *editio typica altera* of the New Vulgate (Vatican City, 1986).

## PRELIMINARY NOTES

The headings within the biblical text have been provided by the editors (they are not taken from the RSV). A full list of these headings, giving an overview of the New Testament, can be found at the back of the volume.

An asterisk *inside the biblical text* signals an RSVCE 'Explanatory Note' at the end of the volume.

References in the biblical text indicate parallel texts in other biblical books. All these marginal references come from the *Navarre Bible* editors, not the RSV.

# Abbreviations

## 1. BOOKS OF HOLY SCRIPTURE

| | |
|---|---|
| Acts | Acts of the Apostles |
| Amos | Amos |
| Bar | Baruch |
| 1 Chron | 1 Chronicles |
| 2 Chron | 2 Chronicles |
| Col | Colossians |
| 1 Cor | 1 Corinthians |
| 2 Cor | 2 Corinthians |
| Dan | Daniel |
| Deut | Deuteronomy |
| Eccles | Ecclesiastes (Qoheleth) |
| Esther | Esther |
| Eph | Ephesians |
| Ex | Exodus |
| Ezek | Ezekiel |
| Ezra | Ezra |
| Gal | Galatians |
| Gen | Genesis |
| Hab | Habakkuk |
| Hag | Haggai |
| Heb | Hebrews |
| Hos | Hosea |
| Is | Isaiah |
| Jas | James |
| Jer | Jeremiah |
| Jn | John |
| 1 Jn | 1 John |
| 2 Jn | 2 John |
| 3 Jn | 3 John |
| Job | Job |
| Joel | Joel |
| Jon | Jonah |
| Josh | Joshua |
| Jud | Judith |
| Jude | Jude |
| Judg | Judges |
| 1 Kings | 1 Kings |
| 2 Kings | 2 Kings |
| Lam | Lamentations |
| Lev | Leviticus |
| Lk | Luke |
| 1 Mac | 1 Maccabees |
| 2 Mac | 2 Maccabees |
| Mal | Malachi |
| Mic | Micah |
| Mk | Mark |
| Mt | Matthew |
| Nah | Nahum |
| Neh | Nehemiah |
| Num | Numbers |
| Obad | Obadiah |
| 1 Pet | 1 Peter |
| 2 Pet | 2 Peter |
| Phil | Philippians |
| Philem | Philemon |
| Ps | Psalms |
| Prov | Proverbs |
| Rev | Revelation (Apocalypse) |
| Rom | Romans |
| Ruth | Ruth |
| 1 Sam | 1 Samuel |
| 2 Sam | 2 Samuel |
| Sir | Sirach (Ecclesiasticus) |
| Song | Song of Solomon |
| 1 Thess | 1 Thessalonians |
| 2 Thess | 2 Thessalonians |
| 1 Tim | 1 Timothy |
| 2 Tim | 2 Timothy |
| Tit | Titus |
| Wis | Wisdom |
| Zech | Zechariah |
| Zeph | Zephaniah |

## 2. OTHER ABBREVIATIONS

| | |
|---|---|
| ad loc. | *ad locum*, commentary on this passage |
| AAS | *Acta Apostolicae Sedis* |
| Apost. | Apostolic |
| can. | canon |
| chap. | chapter |
| cf. | *confer*, compare |
| Const. | Constitution |
| Decl. | Declaration |
| *Dz-Sch* | Denzinger-Schönmetzer, *Enchiridion Biblicum* (4th edition, Naples & Rome, 1961) |
| Enc. | Encyclical |
| *Exhort.* | Exhortation |
| f | and following (*pl.* ff) |
| ibid. | *ibidem*, in the same place |
| in loc. | *in locum,* commentary on this passage |
| loc. | *locum*, place or passage |
| par. | parallel passages |
| Past. | Pastoral |
| RSV | Revised Standard Version |
| RSVCE | Revised Standard Version, Catholic Edition |
| SCDF | Sacred Congregation for the Doctrine of the Faith |
| sess. | session |
| v. | verse (*pl.* vv.) |

"Sources quoted in the Commentary", which appears at the end of this book, explains other abbreviations used.

# The Captivity Letters

From very early on it has been customary to distinguish four of St Paul's letters—Ephesians, Colossians, Philippians and Philemon—as the "Captivity Letters" because they were written when the Apostle was in prison (cf. Phil 1:7, 12–17; Eph 3:1; 4:1; 6:20; Col 4:3, 10, 18; Philem 9, 13, 23).

Given that St Paul suffered imprisonment in Ephesus, Caesarea and Rome, we do not know for certain whether these letters were all written from the same place. The most common and best argued opinion has it that he wrote Colossians, Ephesians and Philemon in Rome during his first imprisonment there (in the years 61–63), and, to be more precise, towards the end of that period, given that in Philemon 22 he refers to his hope of an early release. As regards Philippians, some scholars argue in favour of its having been written in Ephesus (cf. 1 Cor 15:30–32; 2 Cor 1:8–10) on the grounds that this better explains the Apostle's relationship with the faithful at Philippi.

Whichever of these theories is correct, Philippians was written before Colossians and Ephesians; and Ephesians came shortly after Colossians, dealing with the same themes in a more elaborate way. The Letter to Philemon, although written during the same period as the others, is of quite a different type, being a short note about the return of a runaway slave.

In spite of the chronology we have just described, in the present edition of the Captivity Letters we follow the traditional order in which they appeared in the Vulgate and which the New Vulgate has maintained, namely, Ephesians, Philippians, Colossians and Philemon.

In the introductions to the individual letters we discuss the arguments in favour of Pauline authorship, as also the structure of each letter. Here it is sufficient to point out that tradition is unanimous and explicit in identifying all of them as written by St Paul; St Justin, to name just one source, gives Paul as their author.

As regards the content of the letters, two factors should be borne in mind in order to situate and understand them, particularly Colossians and Ephesians. The first is that St Paul is dealing with new problems caused, apparently, by views imbued with a certain Gnosticism, that is, an excessive desire for arcane, salvation-bringing "wisdom", and a readiness to reduce the absolute primacy of Christ to the level of other forces or "powers" regarded as salvific. The second feature of these epistles is the fact that as time goes on and the Church develops, the Apostle is delving deeper and deeper into the mystery of Christ and the Church, discovering, with the help of the Holy Spirit, aspects which were only barely discernible in earlier letters.

# Introduction to the Letter to the Ephesians

## THE CITY OF EPHESUS

In the time of St Paul, Ephesus was the leading city in Asia Minor, situated between Miletus and Smyrna, about 5 kilometres (3 miles) from the Aegean Sea. It had been conquered by Alexander the Great in 334 BC and later (133 BC) came under the dominion of Rome, acting from then on as the administrative and religious centre of the Roman province known as "Asia".

From ancient times the city gave its religious allegiance to the oriental goddess of fertility, whom the Greeks identified with Artemis and the Romans with Diana and whose magnificent temple was regarded as one of the seven wonders of the world. The temple that St Paul knew had been built around the year 334 BC at the time of Alexander's conquest.

The city of Ephesus was also famous for magic and occultism, and its inhabitants were notoriously superstitious. The city's jewellers did enormously profitable business through the manufacture of statuettes of the goddess—which explains why the people rioted, at the instigation of Demetrius the silversmith (cf. Acts 19:24ff), against Paul and his companions, who naturally preached against superstition and the worship of idols.

From the Acts of the Apostles we know that St Paul stayed at Ephesus towards the end of his second apostolic journey, around the year 52 (cf. Acts 18:19ff), and that he went back there at the start of his third journey in 54–57. At that time he spent more than two years in the city and preached so much that Jews and Gentiles throughout the province learned about his message (cf. Acts 19:1, 8–10). In his preaching to the Ephesians he must have been helped a great deal by Apollos (cf. Acts 18:24–35).

However, this period was marked by all kinds of setbacks and difficulties, so much so that he eventually had to leave Ephesus on account of the riot caused by Demetrius. He left behind him, as head of the church, his disciple Timothy (cf. 1 Tim 1:3), who, tradition has it, died there confessing the name of Christ.

## READERSHIP AND DATE OF THE LETTER

St Paul may have had to leave Ephesus in a hurry, but he did not forget the faithful in that city. In the course of his imprisonment in Rome he sent them the letter now described as the Letter to the Ephesians.

It is not known for certain whether the Ephesians were the first recipients of the letter which bears their name. We do know that the title "To the Ephesians" appears in all the Greek manuscripts and all the translations from the end of the second century onwards. However, the words "who are at Ephesus" (Eph 1:1) do not appear in the earliest and most important Greek manuscripts; papyrus 46 does not contain them and seemingly the manuscripts available to Tertullian and Origen did not carry them. The New Vulgate, like the Vulgate, includes Ephesians in the Captivity Letters, along with Philippians and Colossians. There is a close parallel between Ephesians and Colossians, in form as well as content, which leads one to think that the Apostle wrote Ephesians to develop the teaching contained in Colossians.

If this was in fact the case, one would need to explain the impersonal character of Ephesians: the letter contains no allusion to the personal circumstances of people with whom the Apostle had lived for three years, nor even the slightest reference to his hurried departure from that city. In the form that has come down to us, the letter is addressed to the saints who are at Ephesus (cf. Eph 1:1), but some scholars are of the view that this local reference may have been added later to what was originally a circular letter sent to all the churches of the region. Others, however, think that the letter was originally addressed to the faithful of Laodicea and that it was the letter the faithful of Colossae were told by Paul to read (cf. Col 4:16). Neither of these theories can be proved, either from tradition or from internal analysis of the text.

The best solution may be to agree that the letter was addressed to the faithful at Ephesus, but that these were not the only ones it was written for. Given that other churches were dependent on Ephesus—Colossae, Laodicea, Hierapolis etc.—there would have been nothing unusual about the Apostle's writing it with the intention of its being read in each of these communities. The original letter would then have been conserved at Ephesus, hence its name.

As far as the date of the letter is concerned, in view of its close similarity in style and content to Colossians, the likelihood is that it was written towards the end of Paul's first imprisonment in Rome, that is, very shortly before the spring of 63.

## PAULINE AUTHORSHIP

The Fathers of the Church and ecclesiastical writers always attributed the authorship of this letter to St Paul;[1] however, since the middle of the nineteenth century some scholars have queried this, arguing that certain literary features of the letter (vocabulary, style, approach, etc.) are different from those of other Pauline letters. Others have supported Paul's authorship,

**1.** For example, Clement of Alexandria, Tertullian, Origen and the Muratorian Fragment.

with certain reservations: the letter is authentic, they say, that is, it was written by Paul, and written around the same time as Colossians, but it contains interpolations from Colossians, introduced some ten or twenty years later. These views, however, are mere conjecture.

It is quite obvious that the vocabulary of Ephesians is different from that of the other Pauline letters. In fact as many as 83 words used in Ephesians are not to be found in the rest of the Pauline corpus. But this does not prove it was not written by Paul. Also, the fact that the literary style of the letter is laden with tautological expressions and long sentences full of relative clauses and participles, is not unusual if one compares it with Romans, Corinthians and, particularly, Colossians.

Therefore, the most logical and best-grounded solution is to maintain that St Paul wrote this letter shortly after Colossians, in order to combat heresy, and that he meant it to be read by all the churches in the Ephesus region.

## STRUCTURE

Like all St Paul's letters, Ephesians starts with an *initial greeting and blessing*, in which the name of the author is given and the addressees are identified (cf. Eph 1:1–2). The *body of the letter* then follows, and the text finishes with mention of the bearer, who brings news of the Apostle (cf. Eph 1:3—6:22) and *words of farewell* which, like the start, take the form of a blessing (cf. Eph 6:23–24).

In the body of the letter two parts are clearly distinguishable. The first focuses on the mystery of the saving work of Christ and the Church. This section, which is very much concerned with expounding doctrine, is normally described as the dogmatic part of the letter. It is introduced by an ornate hymn praising God for his plan of salvation, and it concludes with a doxology or short exclamation in praise of God for the way he has effected his design (cf. Eph 1:3—3:21). The second part, on the other hand, consists of a series of exhortations to the faithful to make progress in the Christian life in keeping with the teaching given in the first part. It is therefore considered to be the moral section of the epistle (cf. Eph 4:1—6:22).

### 1. *Dogmatic section: God's plan for salvation*

In this section the Apostle expounds, in various ways, the greatness of Christ's work of salvation. That work is the fulfilment of God's eternal design—that is, a plan he made before time began—which is brought about in history by Jesus Christ through the Redemption and through the founding of his Church. Gentiles as well as Jews are called to join that Church and become one with

Christ: the Church thus makes present to people and offers to them the salvation achieved by Jesus Christ; this Redemption extends beyond mankind to all creation; Christ is "the head over all things" (cf. Eph 1:22–23).

In ecstasy at the scale of this mystery, St Paul presents it now in the form of praise of God, now in words of supplication, sometimes by emphasizing Christ's call to men, sometimes by contemplating his own role as apostle. The following sections can be distinguished in this part of the letter:

1. *A hymn of blessings* (1:3–14). This is a hymn of praise to God for all the spiritual blessings he has bestowed on those called to the Church. It shows his plan of salvation—the predestination of the sons and daughters of God (cf. Eph 1:6), then the redemption worked by Christ (cf. Eph 1:7–9), and the eventual revelation of the last part of God's design, "to unite all things in him" (Eph 1:10). Gentiles as well as Jews enjoy these blessings (cf. Eph 1:11–14).

2. *St Paul's prayer* (1:15–23). He gives thanks to God and prays that the Christians may grow in the knowledge of God and his salvific work: he asks God to enlighten them, to strengthen their hope (cf. Eph 1:15–18) and enable them to recognize God's power at work in his exaltation of Christ (cf. Eph 1:19–23).

3. *Salvation a free gift* (2:1–10). Prior to their conversion Christians were dead because of their sins. Now God's mercy gratuitously saves them through faith in Christ.

4. *Reconciliation of the Gentiles in Christ* (2:11–21). Those Christians who had been pagans and therefore distanced from the promises, from hope and from the true God who had made himself known to Israel, now—along with Christians of Jewish origin—form part of the one body of Christ; they have become "fellow citizens with the saints and members of the household of God".

5. *St Paul's mission* (3:1–13). Paul is God's minister in the plan of salvation. His ministry is part of the mystery of Christ, a mystery revealed to the prophets, to the apostles, and finally to Paul himself. Paul's specific ministry is to preach to the Gentiles, telling them that they too are called to be members of Christ's body, for that is part of God's mysterious plan.

6. *The Apostle's prayer* (3:14–19). This prayer really begins at 3:1 but Paul interrupts it to describe his own ministry. He prays that God may strengthen the Christians, that Christ may dwell in their hearts and that they may come to recognize how much Christ loves them; they will be filled with the fullness of God.

7. *Doxology* (3:20–21). This prayer ends with a short prayer of praise, or doxology, lauding God's power for effecting his plan of salvation in a manner far beyond anything men could expect or envisage.

### 2. *Moral section: New life in Christ and in the Church*

Spiritual and moral consequences derive from being saved by Jesus Christ and becoming members of his Church. Christians can and should reflect in their behaviour what they have become through grace, that is, through their insertion in Christ and their incorporation into his body which is the Church. The Apostle exhorts his readers about different aspects of Christian life, pointing out the profound changes grace effects in them and the practical steps they must take.

1. *A call to unity* (4:1–16). What he has said in the earlier part of the letter means, first and foremost, that Christians must stay united in the body of Christ; this calls for humility and perseverance. The unity of the Church is based on the fact that there is only one God, one Lord, one faith, one baptism; this unity is made possible by Christ, the head of the Church, who causes the various ministries to arise, ministries which enable the individual to reach his or her maturity in the formation of that one single body to whose growth they contribute.

2. *Interior renewal* (4:17–24). Every Christian needs to lead a new life in Christ in order to contribute to the growth of the body. This means one must shed the life of vanity and sin which one led before one's conversion and put on Christ, the new Man.

3. *Christian virtues* (4:25—5:2). The first consequence of this new life is the practice of virtue: virtues make it possible and pleasant for Christians to live together as members of the one body of Christ. The practice of virtue enables them to live together in love, imitating Christ who gave himself up for love of us.

4. *The chaste life of the children of God* (5:3–21). Being a Christian also involves being chaste and walking by the light of Christ, which they received at Baptism, and being full of the Holy Spirit.

5. *Christian family life* (5:22—6:9). The Apostle explores what being Christian means in the context of husband–wife relations (5:22–23), parent–children relations (6:1–4), and master–servant relations (6:5–9). He exhorts all to love, obey and respect others in a way which reflects the relationship between Christ and the Church.

6. *Weapons in the spiritual struggle* (6:10–20). The Apostle invites all to equip themselves with the armour of God so as to be able to fend off the evil one; and he exhorts them to persevere in prayer and also to pray for himself and his ministry.

7. *Conclusion and farewell* (6:21–24). After mentioning the bearer of the letter, who can give them further news about himself and what he is doing (6:21–22), he ends with two farewell messages (6:23–24).

## DOCTRINAL CONTENT

The general content of the letter is the same as that of Colossians; but it is less polemical and more serene and its style is closer to that of a doctrinal letter.

In view of the dangers posed by certain pre-Gnostic religious Judaizing trends, St Paul is writing to help the Christians of Asia to delve deeper into the mystery of Christ. The particular problem arose from an improper cult rendered to the angels which undermined doctrinally the role of Christ in creation and redemption, a role which is absolutely primary and exclusive. In order to clarify this point of doctrine the letter approaches the matter from the point of view of Christ's supremacy, as in Colossians, and links it with his headship of the Church, and it has a great deal to say about the nature of the Church. Here is a summary of its teaching:

1. *Jesus Christ is Lord of all.* Christ's supremacy consists, firstly, in his lordship over all creation. The psalmist is referring to Christ when he says that God has "put all things under his feet" (Ps 8:6). God's power was displayed in full when he raised Christ from the dead and exalted him in glory, placing him at the right hand of the Father in heaven. That is why he is "far above all rule and authority and power and dominion, and above every name that is named, not only in this age but also in that which is to come" (Eph 1:20–21). However, because the Son of God became man and came down to earth, some people may be inclined to see that man, Jesus of Nazareth, as being like any other man and therefore on a lower level than the angels. To counter this error, which comes from judging by appearances, St Paul asserts that "he who descended is he who also ascended far above all the heavens, that he might fill all things" (Eph 4:10).

Christ's total supremacy is also to be seen in his role as head of the Church, which he founded and gives life to and loves. Christ, in other words, did not simply "gather together" the "scattered people of Israel", the "remnant of Yahweh" spoken of by the prophets; he also gathers-in the outsiders, the Gentiles. These two peoples, the Jews and the Gentiles, had even been physically separated in the temple, by a wall dividing the courtyards; but they are destined by God's will to form a single people, the people of God (this richly biblical image is explored at length in the Second Vatican Council's Dogmatic Constitution on the Church, *Lumen gentium*, in its second chapter, nos. 9–17).

Jesus Christ it is who builds up this new people, making it one body with himself, a body which he nourishes with all the graces it needs for its "upbuilding in love" (cf. Eph 4:16). Later in the letter St Paul will again refer to Christ as the head, as the "Saviour" of the Church which is his body (Eph 5:23): he is head not only in the sense of being the primary and most perfect member of the Church; he also has a soteriological—salvific—role with respect to the Church: its life flows from the head (Christ) to his body (the Church). The Second Vatican Council recalls this teaching when it says of Jesus Christ that "by the greatness of his power he rules heaven and earth, and with his all-surpassing perfection and activity he fills the whole body with the riches of his glory."[2]

2. *The Church.* This letter also has much to teach about the Church as the body of Christ, a perspective from which St Paul also views it in other letters.[3] The fact that Christ is the head also means that the Church, which comprises all Christians, forms a single body with Christ (cf. Eph 4:4), through whom God distributes his gifts and charisms to the faithful: "His gifts were that some should be apostles, some prophets, some evangelists, some pastors and teachers, for the equipment of the saints, for the work of the ministry, for building up the body of Christ" (Eph 4:11–12).

He later underlines this teaching when he says that Christ loves the Church as something that belongs to him, that he cherishes (cf. Eph 5:29) and nourishes with abundance of grace.

The Church is also considered in this letter as the temple of God, a dwelling place of God built on the foundation of the apostles and prophets, with Christ himself as the cornerstone, "in whom the whole structure is joined together and grows into a holy temple of the Lord" (Eph 2:21). The Christians are seen as living stones, harmoniously "built into it for a dwelling place of God in the Spirit" (Eph 2:22). Those who are part of this building are no longer strangers to one another but "fellow citizens with the saints and members of the household of God" (Eph 2:19).

Enlightened by the Holy Spirit, St Paul delves further into the mystery of the Church, showing it to be a supernatural institution with divine, transcendental dimensions which make it different from any merely human institution: the Church is Christ's spouse (cf. Eph 5:21–23). This image was often used in the Old Testament, and later in the New, to describe God's relationship with

**2.** *Lumen gentium,* 7; cf. Eph 1:18–23. **3.** Cf. Rom 12:5; 1 Cor 10:16; 12:13, 27; Col 1:18, 24; 2:19; 3:15; etc.

his people; of course the prophets and sacred writers also used many other similes to describe God's great love and mercy towards men.[4] St Paul uses the simile of husband and wife to explain that "Christ loved the church and gave himself up for her, that he might sanctify her, having cleansed her by the washing of water with the word, that he might present the church to himself in splendour, without spot or wrinkle or any such thing, that she might be holy and without blemish" (Eph 5:25–27). God's mystical betrothal with his people has reached its perfect form in Christ's union with his Church, which he unites to himself "by an unbreakable alliance [...] and whom he filled with heavenly gifts for all eternity, in order that we may know the love of God and of Christ for us, a love which surpasses all understanding."[5]

Comparing Christian marriage with the union between Christ and his Church, St Paul calls it a *sacramentum magnum*, a "great mystery" (Eph 5:23). This term, "sacrament", is applied in the strict sense to the seven sacraments instituted by Christ for the justification and sanctification of men, but it can also be applied in a broader sense to the Church, as the Second Vatican Council frequently does.[6] For the Church has the salvific role of presenting Christ to mankind as its Saviour: through the Church man arrives at knowledge of the Mystery of Redemption which God had kept hidden from eternity (cf. Eph 1:9). Redemption, which is brought about and set forth in Christ (cf. Eph 3:3, 9), is put within man's reach by the Church. "Since the Church, in Christ, is in the nature of a sacrament—a sign and instrument, that is, of communion with God and of unity among men—she [...] purposes, for the benefit of the faithful and of the whole world, to set forth, as clearly as possible [...] her own nature and universal mission."[7]

**4.** Cf. Is 1:21; 49:18; Jer 2:2; Ezek 16; Hos 2:16–18; Mt 19:15; Jn 3:24; Rev 19:7–9; 20:2, 17; etc. **5.** *Lumen gentium*, 6. **6.** Cf *Lumen gentium*, 1, 9, 48; *Sacrosanctum Concilium*, 5; etc. **7.** *Lumen gentium*, 1.

# THE LETTER OF PAUL TO THE EPHESIANS

*The Revised Standard Version, with notes*

# 1. INTRODUCTION

## Greeting

1 [1]Paul, an apostle of Christ Jesus by the will of God, To the saints who are* also faithful[a] in Christ Jesus: Rom 1:7 1 Cor 1:1

**1:1.** As usual St Paul begins with a greeting which identifies who he is, his authority to write this letter—he is an "apostle of Christ Jesus"—and the dignity of the people he is addressing—"saints" and "faithful in Christ Jesus". He presents himself as an "apostle", that is, an envoy, of Christ Jesus. A calling to the apostolate is something that comes from God: it is a grace, a sign of God's special love. In St Paul's case this calling was revealed to him by Christ on the road to Damascus (cf. Acts 9:3–18); the Holy Spirit then sent him out to preach (cf. Acts 13:2f), and the message which he received from the Lord he passed on orally and in writing (cf. 1 Cor 11:23), so that in every way it is right for him to say that he is an "apostle" (cf. note on Rom 1:1).

St Paul often refers to the Christians as "saints" (cf. Rom 1:7; 1 Cor 1:2; Phil 1:1; etc.) and "faithful" (cf. Col 1:2); these titles describe what Baptism does for a person (cf. Eph 5:26).

All the baptized are called to live a holy life: being "saints", being "believers", commits them to do so. Holiness is, therefore, a gift of God which at the same time implies an obligation to further its development, as the Second Vatican Council explains: "It is therefore quite clear that all Christians in any state or walk of life are called to the fullness of Christian life and to the perfection of love, and by this holiness a more human manner of life is fostered also in earthly society. In order to reach this perfection the faithful should use the strength dealt out to them by Christ's gift, so that, following in his footsteps and conformed to his image, doing the will of God in everything, they may wholeheartedly devote themselves to the glory of God and to the service of their neighbour. Thus the holiness of the people of God will grow in fruitful abundance, as is clearly shown in the history of the Church through the life of so many saints" (*Lumen gentium*, 40).

By describing the Christians as "faithful" St Paul is not only saying that they are people who have received the gift of faith (cf. Eph 2:8); he is also calling on them to stay true to the faith despite all the wiles of the devil (cf. Eph 6:10–13).

In the Church it has always been customary to refer to those who have received Baptism as "faithful": "Christ's faithful are those who, since they are incorporated into Christ through baptism, are constituted the people of God. For this reason they participate in their own way in the priestly, prophetic and kingly office of Christ. They are called, each according to his or her particular condition, to exercise the mission which God entrusted to the Church to fulfil in the world" (*Code of Canon Law*, can. 204, 1).

**1:2.** "Shalom!"—"Peace!"—is the usual way Jews greet one another. According to the prophets, peace was one of the gifts the Messiah would bring. After the incarnation of the Son of God, now that the "prince of peace" has come among us

**a.** Other ancient authorities read *who are at Ephesus and faithful*

Col 1:2 [2]Grace to you and peace from God our Father and the Lord Jesus Christ.

---

(cf. Is 9:6), when the apostles use this greeting they are joyfully proclaiming the advent of messianic peace: all good things, heavenly and earthly, are attainable because by his death and resurrection Jesus, the Messiah, has removed, once and for all, the enmity between God and men: "since we are justified by faith, we have peace with God through our Lord Jesus Christ" (Rom 5:1).

The same expression—"Grace to you and peace from God our Father and the Lord Jesus Christ"—is frequently to be found in St Paul's letters. For its meaning, see the notes on Rom 1:7 and 1 Cor 1:3.

**1:3–14.** Verses 3–14 are a hymn of praise to God for the plan of salvation he has devised and brought to fulfilment in benefit of men and all creation. It is written in a liturgical style of rhythmic prose, similar to that in Colossians 1:15–20. In the Greek it is one long complex sentence full of relative pronouns and clauses which give it a designed unity; we can, however, distinguish two main sections.

The first (v. 3–10), divided into four stanzas, describes the blessings contained in God's salvific plan; St Paul terms this plan the "mystery" of God's will. The section begins by praising God for his eternal design, a plan, pre-dating creation, to call us to the Church, to form a community of saints (first stanza: vv. 3f) and receive the grace of being children of God through Jesus Christ (second stanza: vv. 5f). It then reflects on Christ's work of redemption which brings this eternal plan of God to fulfilment (third stanza: vv. 7f). This section reaches its climax in the fourth stanza (vv. 9f) which proclaims Christ as Lord of all creation, thereby revealing the full development of God's salvific plan.

The second section, which divides into two stanzas, deals with the application of this plan—first to the Jews (fifth stanza: vv. 11f) and then to the Gentiles, who are also called to share what God has promised: Jews and Gentiles join to form a single people, the Church (sixth stanza: vv. 13f).

Hymns in praise of God, or "eulogies", occur in many parts of Scripture (cf. Ps 8; Ps 19; Dan 2:20–23; Lk 1:46–54, 68–78; etc.); they praise the Lord for the wonders of creation or for spectacular interventions on behalf of his people. Inspired by the Holy Spirit, St Paul here praises God the Father for all Christ's saving work, which extends from God's original plan which he made before he created the world, right up to the very end of time and the recapitulation of all things in Christ.

We too should always have this same attitude of praise of the Lord. "Our entire life on earth should take the form of praise of God, for the never-ending joy of our future life consists in praising God, and no one can become fit for that future life unless he train himself to render that praise now" (St Augustine, *Enarrationes in Psalmos*, 148).

Praise is in fact the most appropriate attitude for man to have towards God: "How can you dare use that spark of divine intelligence—your mind—in anything but in giving glory to your Lord?" (St Josemaría Escrivá, *The Way*, 782).

**Christ, head of the Church and source of unity**

3Blessed be the God and Father of our Lord Jesus Christ, who has
blessed us in Christ with every spiritual blessing in the heavenly
places, 4even as he chose us in him before the foundation of the Jn 17:24

---

**1:3.** St Paul blesses God as Father of our Lord Jesus Christ because it is through Christ that all God's blessings and gifts reach us. God's actions in favour of man are actions of all three divine Persons; the divine plan which the Apostle considers here has its origin in the Blessed Trinity; it is eternal. "These three Persons are not to be considered separable," the Eleventh Council of Toledo teaches, "since we believe that not one of them existed or at any time effected anything before the other, after the other, or without the other. For in existence and operation they are found to be inseparable" (*De Trinitate* Creed, *Dz-Sch*, 531).

In the implementation of this divine plan of salvation, the work of Redemption is attributed to the Son and that of sanctification to the Holy Spirit. "To help us grasp in some measure this unfathomable mystery, we might imagine the Blessed Trinity taking counsel together in their uninterrupted intimate relationship of infinite love. As a result of their eternal decision, the only-begotten Son of God the Father takes on our human condition and bears the burden of our wretchedness and sorrows, to end up sewn with nails to a piece of wood" (St Josemaría Escrivá, *Christ Is Passing By*, 95).

St Paul describes as "spiritual blessings" all the gifts which the implementation of God's plan implies, gifts which are distributed by the Holy Spirit. When he speaks of them as being "in the heavenly places" and "in Christ", he is saying that through Christ who has risen from the dead and ascended on high we too have been inserted into the world of God (cf. 1:20; 2:6).

When man describes God as "blessed" it means he recognizes God's greatness and goodness, and rejoices over the divine gifts he has received (cf. Lk 1:46, 68). Here is what St Thomas Aquinas has to say about the meaning of this passage: "The Apostle says, 'Benedictus' [Blessed be the God ...], that is, May I, and you, and everyone bless him, with our heart, our mouth, our actions—praising him as God and as Father, for he is God because of his essence and Father because of his power to generate" (*Commentary on Eph*, 1, 6).

Holy Scripture very often invites us to praise God our Lord (cf. Ps 8:19; 33; 46–48; etc.); this is not a matter only of verbal praise: our actions should prove that we mean what we say: "He who does good with his hands praises the Lord, and he who confesses the Lord with his mouth praises the Lord. Praise him by your actions" (St Augustine, *Enarrationes in Psalmos*, 91, 2).

**1:4.** As the hymn develops, the Apostle details each of the blessings contained in God's eternal plan. The first of these is his choice, before the foundation of the world, of those who would become part of the Church. The word he uses, translated here as "chose", is the same one as used in the Greek translation of the Old Testament to refer to God's election of Israel. The Church, the new people of God, is constituted by assembling in and around Christ those who have been chosen and called to holiness. This implies that although the Church was founded by Christ at a particular point in history, its origin goes right back to the eternal divine

Jn 1:12
Rom 8:29
1 Jn 3:1

world, that we should be holy and blameless before him. 5He
destined us in love[b] to be his sons through Jesus Christ, according

---

plan. "The eternal Father, in accordance with the utterly gratuitous and mysterious design of his wisdom and goodness, … 'predestined (the elect) to be conformed to the image of his Son in order that he might be the first-born among many brethren' (Rom 8:29). He determined to call together in a holy Church those who believe in Christ. Already present in figure at the beginning of the world, this Church was prepared in marvellous fashion in the history of the people of Israel and in the Old Alliance. Established in this last age of the world, and made manifest in the outpouring of the Spirit, it will be brought to glorious completion at the end of time" (Vatican II, *Lumen gentium*, 2).

God's choice seeks to have us become "holy and blameless before him". In the same way as in the Old Testament a victim offered to God had to be unblemished, blameless (cf. Gen 17:1), the blameless holiness to which God has destined us admits of no imperfection. By the very fact of being baptized we are made holy (cf. note on 1:1), and during our lifetime we try to grow holier with the help of God; however, complete holiness is something we shall attain only in heaven.

The holiness with which we have been endowed is an undeserved gift from God: it is not a reward for any merit on our part: even before we were created God chose us to be his: "'He chose us in him before the foundation of the world, that we should be holy.' I know that such thoughts don't fill you with pride or lead you to think yourself better than others. That choice, the root of your vocation, should be the basis of your humility. Do we build monuments to an artist's paintbrush? Granted the brush had a part in creating masterpieces, but we give credit only to the painter. We Christians are nothing more than instruments in the hands of the Creator of the world, the Redeemer of all men" (St Josemaría Escrivá, *Christ Is Passing By*, 1).

"He destined us in love": the loving initiative is God's. "If God has honoured us with countless gifts it is thanks to his love, not to our merits. Our fervour, our strength, our faith and our unity are the fruit of God's benevolence and our response to his goodness" (St John Chrysostom, *Hom. on Eph,* ad loc.).

God's election of Christians and their vocation to holiness, as also the gift of divine filiation, reveals that God is Love (cf. 1 Jn 4:8); we have become partakers of God's very nature (cf. 2 Pet 1:4), sharers, that is, in the love of God.

"He destined us in love", therefore, also includes the Christian's love of God and of others: charity is a sharing in God's own love; it is the essence of holiness, the Christian's law; nothing has any value if it is not inspired by charity (cf. 1 Cor 13:1–3).

**1:5.** The Apostle goes on to explore the further implications of God's eternal plan: those chosen to form part of the Church have been given a second blessing, as it were, by being predestined to be adoptive children of God. "The state of this people is that of the dignity and freedom of the sons of God, in whose

**b.** Or *before him in love, having destined us*

to the purpose of his will, [6]to the praise of his glorious grace
which he freely bestowed on us in the Beloved. [7]In him we have

Rom 3:24f
Col 1:14

hearts the Holy Spirit dwells as in a temple" (Vatican II, *Lumen gentium*, 9).

This predestination to which the Apostle refers means that God determined from all eternity that the members of the new people of God should attain holiness through his gift of adoptive sonship. It is God's desire that all be saved (cf. 1 Tim 2:4) and he gives each person the means necessary for obtaining eternal life. Therefore, no one is predestined to damnation (cf. Third Council of Valence, *De praedestinatione*, can. 3).

The source of the Christian's divine sonship is Jesus Christ. God's only Son, one in substance with the Father, took on human nature in order to make us sons and daughters of God by adoption (cf. Rom 8:15, 29; 9:4; Gal 4:5). This is why every member of the Church can say: "See what love the Father has given us, that we should be called children of God; and so we are" (1 Jn 3:1).

What is involved here is not simply formal adoption, which is something external and does not affect the very person of the child. Divine adoption affects man's entire being, it inserts him into God's own life; for Baptism makes us truly his children, partakers of the divine nature (cf. 2 Pet 1:4). Divine sonship is therefore the greatest of the gifts God bestows on man during his life on earth. It is indeed right to exclaim "Blessed be God" (v. 3) when one reflects on this great gift: it is right for children openly to acknowledge their father and show their love for him.

Divine filiation has many rich effects as far as the spiritual life is concerned. "A child of God treats the Lord as his Father. He is not obsequious and servile; he is not merely formal and well-mannered: he is completely sincere and trusting. God is not shocked by what we do. Our infidelities do not wear him out. Our Father in heaven pardons any offence when his child returns to him, when he repents and asks for pardon. The Lord is such a good father that he anticipates our desire to be pardoned and comes forward to us, opening his arms laden with grace" (St Josemaría Escrivá, *Christ Is Passing By*, 64). See the notes on Jn 1:12, 13.

**1:6.** The gift of divine filiation is the greatest expression of the glory of God (cf. note on 1:17 below), because it reveals the full extent of God's love for man. St Paul stresses what the purpose of this eternal divine plan is—to promote "the praise of his glorious grace". God's glory has been made manifest through his merciful love, which has led him to make us his children in accordance with the eternal purpose of his will. This eternal design "flows from 'fountain-like love', the love of God the Father [...]. God in his great and merciful kindness freely creates us and, moreover, graciously calls us to share in his life and glory. He generously pours out, and never ceases to pour out, his divine goodness, so that he who is Creator of all things might at last become 'everything to everyone' (1 Cor 15:28), thus simultaneously assuring his own glory and our happiness" (Vatican II, *Ad gentes*, 2).

The grace which St Paul speaks of here and which manifests the glory of God refers first to the fact that God's blessings are totally unmerited by us and include the grace-conferring gifts of holiness and divine filiation.

redemption through his blood, the forgiveness of our trespasses,
Col 1:9 according to the riches of his grace [8]which he lavished upon us.

---

"In the Beloved": the Old Testament stresses again and again that God loves his people and that Israel is that cherished people (cf. Deut 33:12; Is 5:1, 7; 1 Mac 6:11; etc.). In the New Testament Christians are called "beloved by God" (1 Thess 1:4; cf. Col 3:12). However, there is only one "Beloved", strictly speaking, Jesus Christ our Lord—as God revealed from the bright cloud at the Transfiguration: "This is my beloved Son, with whom I am well pleased" (Mt 17:5). The Son of his love has obtained man's redemption and brought forgiveness of sins (cf. Col 1:13f), and it is through his grace that we become pleasing to God, lovable by him with the same love with which he loves his Son. At the Last Supper, Jesus asked his Father for this very thing—"so that the world may know that thou hast sent me and hast loved them even as thou hast loved me" (Jn 17:23). "Notice", St John Chrysostom points out, "that Paul does not say that this grace has been given us for no purpose but that it has been given us to make us pleasing and lovable in his eyes, now that we are purified of our sins" (*Hom. on Eph,* ad loc.).

**1:7–8.** St Paul now centres his attention on the redemptive work of Christ— the third blessing—which has implemented the eternal divine plan described in the preceding verses.

Redemption means "setting free". God's redemptive action began in the Old Testament, when he set the people of Israel free from their enslavement in Egypt (cf. Ex 11:7ff): by smearing the lintels of their doors with the blood of the lamb, their first-born were protected from death. In memory of this salvation God ordained the celebration of the rite of the passover lamb (cf. Ex 12:47). However, this redemption from Egyptian slavery was but a prefigurement of the Redemption Christ would bring about. "Christ our Lord achieved this task [of redeeming mankind and giving perfect glory to God] principally by the paschal mystery of his blessed passion, resurrection from the dead, and glorious ascension" (Vatican II, *Sacrosanctum Concilium*, 5). By shedding his blood on the cross, Christ has redeemed us from the slavery of sin, from the power of the devil, and from death (cf. note on Rom 3:24–25). He is the true passover Lamb (cf. Jn 1:29). "When we reflect that we have been ransomed 'not with perishable things such as silver or gold but with the precious blood of Christ, like that of a lamb without blemish or spot' (1 Pet 1:18f), we are naturally led to conclude that we could have received no gift more salutary than this power [given to the Church] of forgiving sins, which proclaims the ineffable providence of God and the excess of his love towards us" (*St Pius V Catechism*, 1, 11, 10).

The Redemption wrought by Christ frees us from the worst of all slaveries—that of sin. As the Second Vatican Council puts it, "Man finds that he is unable of himself to overcome the assaults of evil successfully, so that everyone feels as though bound by chains. But the Lord himself came to free and strengthen man, renewing him inwardly and casting out the 'ruler of this world' (Jn 12:31), who held him in the bondage of sin. For sin

[9]For he has made known to us in all wisdom and insight the mystery of his will, according to his purpose which he set forth in Rom 16:25

brought man to a lower state, forcing him away from the completeness that is his to attain" (*Gaudium et spes*, 13).

In carrying out this Redemption, our Lord was motivated by his infinite love for man. This love, which far exceeds anything man could hope for, or could merit, is to be seen above all in the universal generosity of God's forgiveness, for though "sin increased, grace abounded all the more" (Rom 5:20); this forgiveness, achieved by Christ's death on the cross, is the supreme sign of God's love for us, for "greater love has no man than this, that a man lay down his life for his friends" (Jn 15:13). If God the Father gave up his Son to death for the remission of men's sins, "it was to reveal the love that is always greater than the whole of creation, the love that is he himself, since 'God is love' (1 Jn 4:8, 16)", John Paul II reminds us. "Above all, love is greater than sin, than weakness, than 'the futility of creation' (cf. Rom 8:20); it is stronger than death" (*Redemptor hominis*, 9).

By enabling our sins to be forgiven, the Redemption brought about by Christ has restored man's dignity. "Increasingly contemplating the whole of Christ's mystery, the Church knows with all the certainty of faith that the Redemption that took place through the Cross has definitely restored his dignity to man and given back meaning to his life in the world, a meaning that was lost to a considerable extent because of sin" (*Redemptor hominis*, 10). This action on God's part reveals his wisdom and prudence.

**1:9.** Through Christ's redemptive action, God has not only pardoned sin: he has also shown that his salvific plan embraces all history and all creation. This plan, which was revealed in Jesus Christ, St Paul calls "the mystery" of God's will; its revelation is a further divine blessing. The entire mystery embraces the establishment of the Church and the gift of divine filiation (vv. 4–7), the recapitulation of all things in Christ (v. 10), and the convoking of Jews and Gentiles to form part of the Church (vv. 11–14; cf. 3:4–7). All this has been revealed in Christ, in whom, therefore, God's revelation reaches its climax. Christ "did this by the total fact of his presence and self-manifestation—by words and works, signs and miracles, but above all by his death and glorious resurrection from the dead, and finally by sending the Spirit of truth. He revealed that God is with us, to deliver us from the darkness of sin and death, and to raise us up to eternal life" (Vatican II, *Dei Verbum*, 4).

The fact that God reveals his plans of salvation is a further proof of his love and mercy, for it enables man to recognize God's infinite wisdom and goodness and to hear his invitation to take part in these plans. As the Second Vatican Council puts it, "It pleased God, in his goodness and wisdom, to reveal himself and to make known the mystery of his will (cf. Eph 1:9). His will was that man should have access to the Father through Christ, the Word made flesh, in the Holy Spirit, and thus become sharers in the divine nature (cf. Eph 2:18; 2 Pet 1:4). By this revelation, then, the invisible God (cf. Col 1:15; 1 Tim 1:17), from the fullness of his love, addresses men as his friends (cf. Ex 33:11; Jn 15:14f), and moves among them (cf. Bar 3:38), in order to invite and receive them into his own company" (*Dei Verbum*, 2).

On the meaning of the word "mystery" in St Paul, see the notes on 1:26, 28; 2:9.

Gal 4:4
Col 1:16

Christ [10]as a plan for the fullness of time, to unite* all things in him, things in heaven and things on earth.

---

**1:10.** The "mystery" revealed by God in his love takes shape in a harmonious way, in different stages or moments (*kairoi*) as history progresses. The fullness of time came with the Incarnation (cf. Gal 4:4) and it will last until the End. Through the Redemption, Christ has rechannelled history towards God; he rules over all human history in a supernatural way. Not only have God's mysterious plans begun to take effect: they have been revealed to the Church, which God uses to implement these plans. "Already the final age of the world is with us (cf. 1 Cor 10:11) and the renewal of the world is irrevocably under way; it is even now anticipated in a certain real way, for the Church on earth is endowed already with a sanctity that is real though imperfect. However, until there be realized new heavens and a new earth in which justice dwells (cf. 2 Pet 3:13) the pilgrim Church, in its sacraments and institutions, which belong to this present age, carries the mark of this world which will pass, and she herself takes her place among the creatures which groan and travail yet and await the revelation of the sons of God (cf. Rom 8:19–22)" (Vatican II, *Lumen gentium*, 48).

The climax of God's pre-creation plan involves "uniting" ("recapitulating") all things in Christ: Christ is to be the cornerstone and head of all creation. This means that, through his redemptive activity, Christ unites and leads the created world back to God. Its unity had been destroyed as a result of sin, but now Christ binds it together, uniting heavenly things as well as mankind and other earthly things. St John Chrysostom teaches that "since heavenly things and earthly things were torn apart from each other, they had no head [...]. (God) made Christ according to the flesh the sole head of all things, of angels and of men; that is, he provided one single principle for angels and for men [...]; for all things will be perfectly united as they ought to be when they are gathered together under one head, linked by a bond which must come from on high" (*Hom. on Eph*, ad loc.).

Christ's being head of all things—as will be made manifest at the end of time—stems from the fact that he is true God and true man, the head and first-born of all creation. By rising from the dead, he has overcome the power of sin and death, and has become Lord of all creation (cf. Acts 2:36; Rom 1:4; Eph 1:19–23); all other things, invisible as well as visible, come under his sway.

The motto taken by Pius X when he became Pope echoes this idea of Christ's Lordship: "If someone were to ask us for a motto which conveys our purpose, we would always reply, 'Reinstating all things in Christ' [...], trying to bring all men to return to divine obedience" (*E supremi apostolatus*).

"Uniting all things in Christ": this includes putting Christ at the summit of human activities, as the founder of Opus Dei points out: "St Paul gave a motto to the Christians at Ephesus: '*Instaurare omnia in Christo*' (Eph 1:10), to fill everything with the spirit of Jesus, placing Christ at the centre of everything. 'And I, when I am lifted up from the earth, will draw all things to myself' (Jn 12:32). Through his incarnation, through his work at Nazareth and his preaching and miracles in the land of Judea and Galilee, through his death on the cross, and through his resurrection, Christ is the centre of the universe, the first-born and Lord of all creation.

[11]In him, according to the purpose of him who accomplishes all things according to the counsel of his will, [12]we who first hoped in

Deut 7:6
Rom 8:28

---

"Our task as Christians is to proclaim this kingship of Christ, announcing it through what we say and do. Our Lord wants men and women of his own in all walks of life. Some he calls away from society, asking them to give up involvement in the world, so that they remind the rest of us by their example that God exists. To others he entrusts the priestly ministry. But he wants the vast majority to stay right where they are, in all earthly occupations in which they work—in the factory, the laboratory, the farm, the trades, the streets of the big cities and the trails of the mountains" (*Christ Is Passing By*, 105).

**1:11–14.** The Apostle now contemplates a further divine blessing—the implementation of the "mystery" through the Redemption wrought by Christ: God calls the Jews (vv. 11f) and the Gentiles (v. 13) together, to form a single people (v. 14). Paul first refers to the Jewish people, of which he himself is a member, which is why he uses the term "we" (v. 12). He then speaks of the Gentile Christians and refers to them as "you" (v. 13).

**1:11–12.** The Jewish people's expectations have been fulfilled in Christ: he has brought the Kingdom of God and the messianic gifts, designed in the first instance for Israel as its inheritance (cf. Mt 4:17; 12:28; Lk 4:16–22). God's intention in selecting Israel was to form a people of his own (cf. Ex 19:5) that would glorify him and proclaim to the nations its hope in a coming Messiah. "God, with loving concern contemplating, and making preparation for, the salvation of the whole human race, in a singular undertaking chose for himself a people to whom he would entrust his promises. By his covenant with Abraham (cf. Gen 15:18) and, through Moses, with the race of Israel (cf. Ex 24:8), he did acquire a people for himself, and to them he revealed himself in words and deeds as the one, true, living God, so that Israel might experience the ways of God with men. Moreover, by listening to the voice of God speaking to them through the prophets, they had steadily to understand his ways more fully and more clearly, and make them more widely known among the nations (cf. Ps 21:28–9; 95:1–3; Is 2:1–4; Jer 3:17)" (Vatican II, *Dei Verbum*, 14).

St Paul emphasizes that even before the coming of our Lord Jesus Christ, the just of the Old Testament acted in line with their belief in the promised Messiah (cf. Gal 3:11; Rom 1:17); not only did they look forward to his coming but their hope was nourished by faith in Christ as a result of their acceptance of God's promise. As later examples of this same faith we might mention Zechariah and Elizabeth; Simeon and Anna; and, above all, St Joseph. St Joseph's faith was "full, confident, complete", St Josemaría Escrivá comments. "It expressed itself in an effective dedication to the will of God and an intelligent obedience. With faith went love. His faith nurtured his love of God, who was fulfilling the promises made to Abraham, Jacob and Moses, and his affection for Mary his wife and his fatherly affection for Jesus. This faith, hope and love would further the great mission which God was beginning in the world through, among others, a carpenter in Galilee—the redemption of mankind" (*Christ Is Passing By*, 42).

Col 1:5
2 Cor 1:22

Christ have been destined and appointed to live for the praise of his
glory. [13]In him you also, who have heard the word of truth, the gospel
of your salvation, and have believed in him, were sealed with the
promised Holy Spirit, [14]who is the guarantee of our inheritance until
we acquire possession of it, to the praise of his glory.

---

**1:13–14.** If St Paul recognizes the magnificence of God's saving plan in the fulfilment, through Jesus, of the ancient promises to the Jews, he is even more awed by the fact that the Gentiles are being called to share in God's largesse. This call of the Gentiles is, as it were, a further blessing from God.

It is through the preaching of the Gospel that the Gentiles come to form part of the Church: faith coming initially through hearing the word of God (cf. Rom 10:17). Once a person has accepted that word, God seals the believer with the promised Holy Spirit (cf. Gal 3:14); this seal is the pledge or guarantee of divine inheritance and proves that we have been accepted by God, incorporated into his Church, and given access to that salvation which had previously been reserved to Israel. Here we can see a parallelism between the "seal" of circumcision which made the Old Covenant believer a member of the people of Israel, and the "seal" of the Holy Spirit in Baptism which, in the New Testament, makes people members of the Church (Rom 4:11–22; 2 Cor 1:22; Eph 4:30). The "efficient cause" of our justification is "the merciful God, who freely washes and sanctifies (cf. 1 Cor 6:11), sealing and anointing with the Holy Spirit of the promise, who is the pledge of our inheritance" (Council of Trent, *De justificatione*, chap. 7).

A seal or pledge was the mark used in business to betoken or guarantee future payment of the agreed price in full. In this case it represents a firm commitment on God's part, to grant the believer full and permanent possession of eternal blessedness, an anticipation of which is given at Baptism and thereafter (cf. 2 Cor 1:22; 5:5). Through Christ, St Basil comments, "Paradise is restored to us; we are enabled to ascend to the kingdom of heaven; we are given back our adoption as sons, our confidence to call God himself our Father; we become partakers of Christ's grace, and are called children of light; we are enabled to share in the glory of heaven, to be enveloped in a plenitude of blessings both in this world and in the world to come [...]. If this be the promise, what will the final outcome not be? If this, the beginning, is so wonderful, what will the final consummation not be?" (*De Spiritu Sancto*, 15, 36).

The gift of the Holy Spirit, who, through faith, dwells in the soul of the Christian in grace, represents, in this last stanza of the hymn, the high point in the implementation of God's salvific plan. The Holy Spirit, who gathered together the Church at Pentecost (cf. Acts 2:1–4), continues to guide and inspire the apostolate of the members of the new people of God down through the centuries. The Magisterium of the Church reminds us that "throughout the ages the Holy Spirit makes the entire Church 'one in communion and ministry; and provides her with different hierarchical and charismatic gifts' (*Lumen gentium*, 4), giving life to ecclesiastical structures, being as it were their soul, and inspiring in the hearts of the faithful that same spirit of mission which impelled Christ himself. He even at times visibly anticipates apostolic action, just as in various ways he unceasingly accompanies and directs it" (Vatican II, *Ad gentes*, 4).

### Thanksgiving and prayer

[15]For this reason, because I have heard of your faith in the Lord Col 1:3ff
Jesus and your love[c] toward all the saints, [16]I do not cease to give Rom 1:9
thanks for you, remembering you in my prayers, [17]that the God of Col 1:3

---

God has acquired his new people at the cost of his Son's blood. This people made up of believers in Christ has replaced the people of the Old Testament, regardless of background. As the Second Vatican Council puts it, "As Israel according to the flesh which wandered in the desert was already called the Church of God (cf. 2 Ezra 13:1; Num 20:4; Deut 23:1ff), so too, the new Israel, which advances in this present era in search of a future and permanent city (cf. Heb 13:14), is called also the Church of Christ (cf. Mt 16:18). It is Christ indeed who has purchased it with his own blood (cf. Acts 20:28); he has filled it with his spirit; he has provided means adapted to its visible and social union. All those who in faith look towards Jesus, the author of salvation and the principle of unity and peace, God has gathered together and established as the Church, that it may be for each and every one the visible sacrament of this saving unity" (*Lumen gentium*, 9).

**1:15–23.** The news the Apostle has received moves him to thanksgiving and prayer (vv. 15–16). But he immediately returns to contemplate how wonderful it is to know God's goodness, and he asks God to give this gift to the readers of his letter (vv. 17–19). His petition hinges on Jesus Christ, through whom God has revealed his power by giving him dominion (vv. 20–21) and establishing him as head of the Church (vv. 22–23).

**1:15–16.** St Paul's solicitude sets a wonderful example, especially for those whose responsibility it is to give Christian instruction to others. Like him, they should pray for those entrusted to their care; they should thank God for their spiritual progress and ask the Holy Spirit to give them the gift of wisdom and understanding. "Fulfil the task entrusted to you with all diligence of body and soul", St Ignatius of Antioch exhorts Polycarp. "Pay special attention to unity, for there is nothing more important than this. Make yourself the support of all and sundry, as the Lord is to you. Bear lovingly with them all, as you are doing at present. Pray constantly and beg for ever greater gifts of wisdom. Be watchful and always awake in spirit. Address yourself to people personally, as is the way of God himself" (*Letter to Polycarp*, 1, 2–3).

This "faith in the Lord Jesus" is not just a matter of believing in Jesus Christ full stop; it is a complete system of belief which is founded on Jesus Christ: those who have received the gift of faith live in Christ, and this life in Christ means that their faith is truly a living faith, one which expresses itself in "love towards all the saints". Faith makes us discover that every baptized person is a son or daughter of God, and thus Christians' fraternal love is a logical consequence of this insight.

**1:17.** The God whom St Paul addresses is "the God of our Lord Jesus Christ", that is, the God who has revealed himself through Christ and to whom Jesus himself, as man, prays and asks for help (cf. Lk 22:42). The same God as was

**c.** Other ancient authorities omit *your love*

our Lord Jesus Christ, the Father of glory, may give you a spirit
of wisdom and of revelation in the knowledge of him, 18 having the
Col 1:5 eyes of your hearts enlightened, that you may know what is the
hope to which he has called you, what are the riches of his
2 Cor 13:4 glorious inheritance in the saints, 19 and what is the immeasurable

---

described in the Old Testament as "the God of Abraham, of Isaac and of Jacob" is now defined as "the God of our Lord Jesus Christ". He is the personal God, recognized by his relationship with Christ, his Son, who as mediator of the New Covenant obtains from God the Father everything he asks for. This will be our own experience too if we are united to Christ, for he promised that "if you ask anything of the Father, he will give it to you in my name" (Jn 16:23; 15:16). The founder of Opus Dei reminds us that "Jesus is the way, the mediator. In him are all things; outside of him is nothing. In Christ, taught by him, we dare to call Almighty God 'our Father': he who created heaven and earth is a loving Father" (*Christ Is Passing By*, 91).

The Apostle also calls God "the Father of glory". The glory of God means his greatness, his power, the infinite richness of his personality, which when it is revealed inspires man with awe. Already, in the history of Israel, God revealed himself through his saving actions in favour of his people. Asking God to glorify his name is the same as asking him to show himself as our Saviour and to give us his gifts. But the greatest manifestation of God's glory, of his power, was the raising of Jesus from the dead, and the raising, with him, of the Christian (cf. Rom 6:4; 1 Cor 6:14). In this passage St Paul asks God "the Father of glory" to grant Christians supernatural wisdom to recognize the greatness of the blessings he has given them through his Son; that is, to acknowledge that he is their Father and the origin of glory. By asking for a "spirit of wisdom and revelation" the Apostle is seeking special gifts—on the one hand, wisdom, that gift of the Holy Spirit which enables one to penetrate the mystery of God: "Who has learned thy counsel, unless thou hast given wisdom and sent thy holy Spirit from on high?" (Wis 9:17). This wisdom which the Church has been given (cf. Eph 1:8) can be communicated to Christians in a special way, as a special gift or charism of the Holy Spirit. The Apostle also asks God to give them a spirit "of revelation", that is, the grace of personal revelations, such as he himself (cf. 1 Cor 14:6) and other Christians (cf. 1 Cor 14:26) received. It is not a matter of revelation or recognition of new truths, but rather of special light from the Holy Spirit so as to have a deeper appreciation of the truth of faith, or of the will of God in a particular situation.

**1:18–19.** Along with this deeper knowledge of God, St Paul asks that Christians be given a fuller and livelier hope, because God and hope are inseparable. He recognizes the faith and charity of the faithful to whom he is writing (cf. 1:15); now he wants hope to shine more brightly for them; he wants God to enlighten their minds and make them realize the consequences of their election, their calling, to be members of the holy people of God, the Church. Hope, therefore, is a gift from God. "Hope is a supernatural virtue, infused by God into our soul, by which we desire and expect eternal life, promised by God to his servants, and the means necessary to obtain it" (*St Pius X Catechism*, 893).

greatness of his power in us who believe, according to the
working of his great might [20]which he accomplished in Christ
when he raised him from the dead and made him sit at his right
hand in the heavenly places, [21]far above all rule and authority and Col 1:16; 2:10
power and dominion, and above every name that is named, not
only in this age but also in that which is to come; [22]and he has put 1 Cor 15:25
all things under his feet and has made him the head over all things
for the church, [23]which is his body, the fullness of him who fills Rom 12:5 Col 1:18
all in all.

---

The ground for hope lies in God's love and power which have been manifested in the resurrection of Christ. This same power is at work in the Christian. Because God's plan for our salvation is an eternal one, he who has called us will lead us to an immortal life in heaven. The fact that God's power is at work in us (cf. Rom 5:5) does not mean that we encounter no difficulties. St Josemaría Escrivá reminds us that "as we fight this battle, which will last until the day we die, we cannot exclude the possibility that enemies both within and without may attack with violent force. As if that were not enough, you may at times be assailed by the memory of your own past errors, which may have been very many. I tell you now, in God's name: do not despair. Should this happen (it need not happen; nor will it usually happen), then turn it into another motive for uniting yourself more closely to the Lord, for he has chosen you as his child and he will not abandon you. He has allowed this trial to befall you so as to have you love him the more and discover even more clearly his constant protection and Love" (*Friends of God*, 214).

**1:20–21.** The Apostle is in awe at the marvels which God's power has worked in Jesus Christ. He sees Christ as the source and model of our hope. "For, just as Christ's life is the model and exemplar of our holiness, so is the glory and exaltation of Christ the form and exemplar of our glory and exaltation" (St Thomas Aquinas, *Commentary on Eph*, ad. loc.).

As elsewhere in the New Testament (cf. Acts 7:56; Heb 1:3; 1 Pet 3:22), the fact that the risen Christ is seated "at the right hand" of the Father means that he shares in God's kingly authority. The Apostle is using a comparison with which people of his time were very familiar—that of the emperor seated on his throne. The throne has always been the symbol of supreme authority and power. Thus, the *St Pius V Catechism* explains that being seated at the right hand "does not imply position or posture of body, but expresses the firm and permanent possession of royal and supreme power and glory, which he received from the Father" (1, 7, 3).

Christ's pre-eminence is absolute: he is Lord of all creation, material as well as spiritual, earthly as well as heavenly. "All rule and authority and power and dominion": this refers to the angelic spirits (cf. note on Eph 3:10), whom the false preachers were presenting as superior to Christ. St Paul argues against them: Jesus Christ at his resurrection was raised by God above all created beings.

**1:22–23.** In previous letters St Paul described the Church as a body (cf. Rom 12:4f; 1 Cor 12:12ff). Here, and in

Colossians 1:18, he pursues this comparison and says that it is the body of Christ, and that Christ is its head. He returns to this teaching elsewhere in the Captivity Epistles (cf. Col 1:18; Eph 5:23f). The image of body and head highlights the life-giving and salvific influence of Christ on the Church, and at the same time emphasizes his supremacy over the Church (cf. St Thomas Aquinas, *Commentary on Eph*, ad loc., and also the note on Col 1:18). This fact fills Christians with joy: by joining the Church through Baptism, they have become truly members of our Lord's body. "No, it is not pride", Paul VI says, "nor arrogance nor obstinacy nor stupidity nor folly that makes us so sure of being living, genuine members of Christ's body, the authentic heirs of his Gospel" (*Ecclesiam suam*, 33).

This image also reveals Christ's close union with his Church and his deep love for her: "he loved her so much", St John of Avila observes, "that although what normally happens is that a person raises his arm to take a blow and protect his head, this blessed Lord, who is the head, put himself forward to receive the blow of divine justice, and died on the Cross to give life to his body, that is, us. And after giving us life, through penance and the sacraments, he endows us, defends and keeps us as something so very much his own, that he is not content with calling us his servants, friends, brethren or children: the better to show his love and render us honour, he gives us his name. For, by means of this ineffable union of Christ the head with the Church his body, he and we are together called 'Christ'" (*Audi, filia*, chap. 84).

The Apostle also describes the Church, the body of Christ (cf. 1 Cor 12:12) as his "fullness" (cf. note on Col 1:19). What he means is that, through the Church, Christ becomes present in and fills the entire universe and extends to it the fruits of his redemptive activity. By being the vehicle which Christ uses to distribute his grace to all, the Church is different from the Israel of the Old Testament: it is not confined to a particular geographical location.

Because the Church has limitless grace, its call is addressed to all mankind: all are invited to attain salvation in Christ. "For many centuries now, the Church has been spread throughout the world," St Josemaría Escrivá comments, "and it numbers persons of all races and walks of life. But the universality of the Church does not depend on its geographical extension, even though that is a visible sign and a motive of credibility. The Church was catholic already at Pentecost; it was born catholic from the wounded heart of Jesus, as a fire which the Holy Spirit enkindles [...]. 'We call it catholic', writes St Cyril, 'not only because it is spread throughout the whole world, from one extreme to the other, but because in a universal way and without defect it teaches all the dogmas which men ought to know, of both the visible and the invisible, the celestial and the earthly. Likewise, because it draws to true worship all types of men, those who govern and those who are ruled, the learned and the ignorant. And finally, because it cures and makes healthy all kinds of sins, whether of the soul or of the body, possessing in addition—by whatever name it may be called—all the forms of virtue, in deeds and in words and in every kind of spiritual gift' (*Catechesis*, 18, 23)" (*In Love with the Church*, 9).

All grace reaches the Church through Christ. The Second Vatican Council reminds us: "He continually endows his body, that is, the Church, with gifts of ministries through which, by his power,

## 2. SALVATION IN CHRIST

2 [1]And you he made alive, when you were dead through the Col 1:21; 2:13
trespasses and sins [2]in which you once walked, following the

---

we serve each other unto salvation so that, carrying out the truth in love, we may through all things grow into him who is our head" (*Lumen gentium*, 7). This is why St Paul calls the Church the "body" of Christ; and it is in this sense that it is the "fullness" (*plêrôma*) of Christ—not because it in any way fills out or completes Christ but because it is filled with Christ, full of Christ, forming a single body with him, a single spiritual organism, whose unifying and life-giving principle is Christ, its head. This demonstrates Christ's absolute supremacy; his unifying and life-giving influence extends from God to Christ, from Christ to the Church, and from the Church to all men. It is he in fact who fills all in all (cf. Eph 4:10; Col 1:17–19; 2:9f).

The fact that the Church is the body of Christ is a further reason why we should love it and serve it. As Pope Pius XII wrote: "To ensure that this genuine and whole-hearted love will reign in our hearts and grow every day, we must accustom ourselves to see Christ himself in the Church. For it is indeed Christ who lives in the Church, and through her teaches, governs and sanctifies; and it is also Christ who manifests himself in manifold disguise in the various members of his society" (*Mystici Corporis*, 43).

**2:1–10.** St Paul moves on to consider those who make up the Church—Jews and Gentiles. Despite the sinful situation in which both found themselves (vv. 2–3), God in his great mercy (vv. 4–5) has acted on them and made them to be like Christ, now victorious and seated in heaven (vv. 6–7); this he has done through the unmerited gift of faith (vv. 8–10).

**2:1–2.** "You": he is referring to Christians of Gentile origin, in contrast with "we" (v. 3), Christians of Jewish background.

Prior to his conversion to Christ a pagan was, as it were, en route to death, that is, liable to condemnation on account of sin—both original sin and sin caused by worldly behaviour, that is, actions opposed to God. That is what the Apostle means here by "this world"—a world which is under the power of the devil (cf. note on Jn 1:10).

The description of the devil as "prince of the power of the air" reflects the notion, widely held in ancient times, that demons dwelt in the earth's atmosphere, from where they exercised a baneful influence over mankind (cf. Mt 12:24; Jn 12:31). St Paul uses the language of his time without taking on board the cosmology it implies. He is teaching theology, and the devil he identifies as the one who is at work in the "sons of disobedience", "the rebels"—an apposite description, for Satan is characterized by his rebellion against God, and his influence on men leads them into rebellion to seek their fulfilment in created things or in things of their own fashioning, thereby refusing to give God his primary place. St Paul could see this happening in the pagan world around him (cf. Rom 1:18–23); and in fact it happens in all periods of history when man refuses to recognize God: "Although set by God in a state of rectitude, man, enticed by the evil one, abused his freedom at the very start of history. He lifted himself up against God, and sought to attain his goal apart from him. Although they had known God, they did not glorify him as God, but their senseless hearts were darkened, and they

Jn 12:31 Eph 6:12

course of this world, following the prince of the power of the air,
the spirit that is now at work in the sons of disobedience. 3Among
these we all once lived in the passions of our flesh, following the
desires of body and mind, and so we were by nature children of
wrath, like the rest of mankind. 4But God, who is rich in mercy,

---

served the creature rather than the Creator (cf. Rom 1:21–25) [...] Often refusing to acknowledge God as his source, man has also upset the relationship which should link him to his last end; and at the same time he has broken the right order that should reign within himself as well as between himself and other men and all the rest of creation" (Vatican II, *Gaudium et spes*, 13).

**2:3.** Before the coming of Christ, those who were Jews were likewise guilty of sin and merited denunciation. St Paul has already discussed this in his Letter to the Romans (cf. Rom 2:1–3:10); now he sketches out the same ideas, to emphasize that everyone, Jew and Gentile alike, obtains salvation through Christ (v. 5). The Jews know the true God and have the benefit of the Law; therefore, their sinfullness derives not so much from the seductions of the world and the devil as from human passion. The "desires of body and mind" does not refer simply to the weakness of human nature (cf. Jn 1:14) or lustful desires but to all the desires and appetites of human nature when it does not obey God—to man's tendency to do whatever he wants, even when he knows that it conflicts with God's law (cf. Rom 7:5; 2 Cor 7:1; Col 2:13). The Jews also were subject to this power of the flesh, for they were "children of wrath, like the rest of mankind".

"Children of wrath": this expression describes man's state of enmity towards God; it does not imply that God sees man as his enemy but that by sinning man incurs divine punishment. It has this effect for Jews and Gentiles alike.

In this verse the Apostle is referring to the behaviour of both Jews and Gentiles; thus, the words "by nature" do not exactly mean the weakness of human nature as such but rather refer to the fact that man, if left to his own devices, cannot avoid sin and therefore cannot escape God's wrath. St John Chrysostom, St Jerome and other Fathers read "by nature" as opposed to "by grace". This would mean that "by nature" refers to human existence considered on its own, that is, unaided by grace—life in a state of sin, which would mean it merited God's wrath. But the reason why this is so is that human nature has been debilitated by original sin; some Fathers in fact, including St Augustine, read this passage as a recognition of the fact of original sin. Certainly St Paul is at least implying that there is such a thing as original sin, as St Thomas Aquinas explains: "He says that we were (children of wrath) 'by nature', that is, by our natural origin, but not meaning nature as such, for (sheer) nature is good and comes from God: he is referring to nature in its vitiated form" (*Commentary on Eph,* ad loc.).

**2:4.** God's mercy is the greatest expression of his love because it shows the total gratuitousness of God's love towards the sinner, whereby instead of punishing him he forgives him and gives him life. The words "God, who is rich in mercy" have great theological and spiritual depth: they are a kind of summary of all St Paul's teaching about God's approach to people who are under the rule of sin, who are "by nature children of wrath".

out of the great love with which he loved us, [5]even when we were dead through our trespasses, made us alive together with Christ (by grace you have been saved), [6]and raised us up with him, and

Rom 6:13
Col 2:13
Rom 8:10
Phil 3:20

Pope John Paul II has chosen these words of Scripture—*dives in misericordia*—as the title of one of his encyclicals, an encyclical which explores the divine dimension of the mystery of Redemption. Here is how the Pope sums up biblical teaching on mercy: "The concept of 'mercy' in the Old Testament has a long and rich history [...]. It is significant that in their preaching the prophets link mercy, which they often refer to because of the people's sins, with the incisive image of love on God's part. The Lord loves Israel with the love of a special choosing, much like the love of a spouse (cf. e.g. Hos 2:21–25 and 15; Is 54:6–8) and for this reason he pardons its sins and even its infidelities and betrayals. When he finds repentance and true conversion, he brings his people back to grace (cf. Jer 31:20; Ezek 39:25–29). In the preaching of the prophets *mercy* signifies a *special power of love*, which *prevails over the sin and infidelity* of the chosen people [...] The Old Testament encourages people suffering from misfortune, especially those weighed down by sin—as also the whole of Israel, which had entered into the covenant with God—*to appeal for mercy*, and enables them to count upon it" (*Dives in misericordia*, 4).

In the New Testament also there are many references to God's mercy, sometimes very touching ones, like the parable of the prodigal son (cf. Lk 15:11–32); others take a more dramatic form, for example, Christ's sacrifice, the supreme expression of the love of God, which is stronger than death and sin. "The *Cross of Christ*, on which the Son, consubstantial with the Father, *renders full justice to God*, is also *a radical revelation of mercy*, or rather of the love that goes against what constitutes the very root of evil in the history of man: against sin and death" (ibid., 8).

**2:5–6.** The power of God works in the Christian in a way similar to that in which it worked in Christ. St Paul here uses almost the same language as he did earlier (cf. 1:20), to show how radical is the change produced in men by Christ's salvation.

Just as a dead person is unable to bring himself back to life, so those who are dead through sin cannot obtain grace, supernatural life, by their own effort. Only Christ, by means of the Redemption, offers us that new life which begins with justification and ends with resurrection and eternal happiness in heaven. The Apostle is speaking here of that life of grace, and therefore of our future resurrection and glorification with Christ in heaven; he refers to this as if it were an accomplished fact, and the reason he does so is this: Jesus Christ is our head and we form one body with him (cf. Gal 3:28), and therefore we share in the head's condition. Christ, after his resurrection, sits at the right hand of the Father. "The body of Christ, which the Church is", St Augustine comments, "must be at the right hand, that is, in the glory of heaven, as the Apostle says: 'we have been raised up with him and made to sit with him in heaven.' Even though our body is not yet there, our hope is already placed there" (*De agone christiano*, 26).

From the moment of our incorporation into Christ by Baptism, his resurrection and exaltation is something which is already present in us in an incomplete

made us sit with him in the heavenly places in Christ Jesus, 7that
in the coming ages he might show the immeasurable riches of his
grace in kindness toward us in Christ Jesus. 8For by grace you
Gal 2:16 have been saved through faith; and this is not your own doing, it
is the gift of God—9not because of works, lest any man should

---

way: "Thus by Baptism", Vatican II teaches, "men are grafted into the paschal mystery of Christ; they die with him, are buried with him, and rise with him (cf. Rom 6:4; Eph 2:6; Col 3:1; 2 Tim 2:11f). They receive the spirit of adoption as sons in which 'we cry, Abba, Father' (Rom 8:15) and thus become true adorers such as the Father seeks (cf. Jn 4:23)" (*Sacrosanctum Concilium*, 6). See the note on Rom 6:9–10.

The Redemption has already been accomplished, and man has available to him all the grace he needs for salvation: the gates of heaven are open wide; it is now the responsibility of every individual to make room for grace in his soul, to avail of grace to respond to our Lord's call. Through Christ, "we have been reborn spiritually, for through him we are crucified to the world," St Zozimus comments. "By his death that decree of death has been destroyed which Adam caused and which was passed on to every soul—that sentence which we incur through our descent, from which absolutely no one is free prior to being set free by Baptism" (*Epist. "tractoria"*, *Dz–Sch*, 231).

**2:8–9.** Salvation is the work of God, a gratuitous gift of God: it originates in God's mercy. It acts in man by means of faith, that is, by man's acceptance of the salvation offered him in Jesus Christ. But even faith, St Paul tells us, is a divine gift; man cannot merit it by his own efforts alone; it is not exclusively the outcome of human freedom; at all stages, from the very beginning, recognition and acceptance of Christ as Saviour means that God's grace is at work.

On the basis of this passage in Ephesians and other passages of Scripture, the Church has taught: "According to the passages of Sacred Scripture and the explanations of the Holy Fathers [specified], we, with God's help must believe and preach the following. The free will of man was made so weak and unsteady through the sin of the first man that, after the Fall, no one could love God as was required, or believe in God, or perform good works for God unless the grace of divine mercy anticipated him [...]. Even after the coming of Christ this grace of faith is not found in the free will of all who desire to be baptized, but is conferred through the generosity of Christ, according to what has already been said and according to what the Apostle Paul teaches: 'It has been granted to you that for the sake of Christ you should not only believe in him but also suffer for his sake' (Phil 1:29). And also: 'he who began a good work in you will bring it to completion at the day of Jesus Christ' (Phil 1:6). And again: 'By grace you have been saved through faith; and this is not your own doing, it is the gift of God' (Eph 2:8). And the Apostle says of himself: 'As one who by the Lord's mercy is trustworthy' (1 Cor 7:25; cf. 1 Tim 1:13) [...]. And Scripture says further: 'What have you that you did not receive?' (1 Cor 4:7). And again: 'Every good endowment and every perfect gift is from above, coming down from the Father of lights' (Jas 1:17). And again: 'No one can receive anything except what

boast. [10]For we are his workmanship, created in Christ Jesus for
good works, which God prepared beforehand, that we should walk
in them.

## 3. MEMBERSHIP OF THE CHURCH

[11]Therefore remember that at one time you Gentiles in the flesh, Col 1:21; 2:11, 13
called the uncircumcision by what is called the circumcision,

---

is given from heaven' (Jn 3:27)" (Second Council of Orange, *De gratia*, conclusion).

The Second Vatican Council provides the same teaching: "By faith man freely commits his entire self to God [...]; before this faith can be exercised, man must have the grace of God to move and assist him; he must have the interior help of the Holy Spirit, who moves the heart and converts it to God, who opens the eyes of the mind and 'makes it easy for all to accept and believe the truth' (*De gratia*, can. 7; *Dei Filius*)" (*Dei Verbum*, 5).

When St Paul says that faith does not come from works (v. 9), he is referring to things man can do on his own, without the help of grace. If faith did come from works, then man would have something to boast to God about, something which would bring salvation without dependence on Christ—which would be inadmissible, because then our Lord's death would make no sense, nor would even the Incarnation of the Word, whom "God has made our wisdom, our righteousness and sanctification and redemption; therefore, as it is written, 'Let him who boasts, boast of the Lord'" (1 Cor 1:30–31). See also the notes on Jas 2:14; Rom 3:20–31; 9:31.

**2:10.** The Christian became a new creation—"we are his workmanship"—when he was inserted into Christ at Baptism (cf. 2 Cor 5:17). Once justified by Baptism, he should live in a manner consistent with his faith, that is, with his new life. The life of grace in fact moves him to do those good works that God wishes to see performed (he had already laid down that this should be so) and which perfect the work of salvation. Deeds, works, prove the genuineness of faith: "faith by itself, if it has no works, is dead" (Jas 2:17). Without these works—the practice of the theological and moral virtues—not only would faith be dead; our love for God and neighbour would be false. But it is also true that to bring about this renewal in man God counts on man's readiness to respond to grace and on his carrying out "good works".

Christian Tradition has always taught that the fruits of faith are a proof of its vitality. For example, this is what St Polycarp has to say: "It does my heart good to see how the solid roots of your faith, which have such a reputation ever since early times, are still flourishing and bearing fruit in Jesus Christ [...]. Many desire to share in your joy, well knowing that it is by the will of God that you are saved through Jesus Christ" (*Letter to the Philippians*, chap. 1).

**2:11–22.** What is the significance of the calling of the Gentiles to the Church? Their previous situation, separated from Christ (vv. 11–12), has undergone radical change as a result of the Redemption Christ achieved on the Cross: that action has, on the one hand, brought the two peoples together (made peace between them: vv. 13–15) and, on the other, it has reconciled them with God, whose enemy

Rom 9:4 which is made in the flesh by hands—[12]remember that you were
1 Thess 4:13 at that time separated from Christ, alienated from the common-
wealth of Israel, and strangers to the covenants of promise, having
Is 57:19 no hope and without God in the world. [13]But now in Christ Jesus
Col 1:20 you who once were far off have been brought near in the blood of
Gal 3:28 Christ.[14]For he is our peace, who has made us both one, and has

---

each was (vv. 16–18). The Redemption has given rise to the Church, which St Paul here describes as a holy temple built on the foundation of the apostles and prophets (vv. 19–22).

**2:11–12.** Prior to the coming of the Messiah, the Gentiles bore the mark of paganism even on their bodies: they were uncircumcised; and on this account they were despised by the Jews. St Paul, however, goes much further: he says that the essential distinction between Jews and Gentiles was not circumcision but the grace of election, which previously was extended only to the Jewish people. To them "belong the sonship, the glory, the covenants, the giving of the law, the worship, and the promises; to them belong the patriarchs" (Rom 9:4–5). The Gentiles had been given no such grace; it had been reserved to the people to whom God had promised the Messiah. Despite their myriad gods, the Gentiles did not know the true God.

Thus, one of the great results of the Redemption wrought by Christ and by God's mercy is that the Gentiles have been admitted to the covenants God made with the patriarchs, covenants which contained the promise that a Messiah would bring salvation (cf. note on Rom 9:4–6). This fulfilled the promise made to Abraham that through him all the families of the earth should account themselves blessed (cf. Gen 12:3). The prophets proclaimed this many times (cf. Is 2:1–3; 56:6–8; 60:11–14; etc.), and Jesus Christ saw it as imminent when he said that many would come from east and west and sit at table with Abraham, Isaac and Jacob (cf. Mt 8:11).

**2:14–15.** "He is our peace": through his death on the cross Christ has abolished the division of mankind into Jews and Gentiles. The Gentiles, who had been far away from God, from his covenant and from his promises (cf. v. 12), are now on a par with the Jews: they share in the New Covenant that has been sealed with the blood of Christ. That is why he is "our peace". In him all men find that solidarity they yearned for, because, through his obedient self-sacrifice unto death, Christ has made up for the disobedience of Adam, which had been the cause of human strife and division (cf. Gen 3–4). "Christ, the Word made flesh, the prince of peace, reconciled all men to God by the cross, and, restoring the unity of all in one people and one body, he abolished hatred in his own flesh (cf. Eph 2:16; Col 1:20–22) and, having been lifted up through his resurrection, he poured forth the Spirit of love into the hearts of men" (Vatican II, *Gaudium et spes*, 78).

God's plan to attract mankind to himself and to re-establish peace included the election of the Jewish people, from whom the Messiah would be born; and in that Messiah all the nations of the world would be blessed (cf. Gen 11:3). He is in fact called "prince of peace" (Is 9:6; cf. Mic 5:4). However, many Jews had come to regard their election in such a narrow-minded way that they saw it as creating a permanent barrier between themselves and the Gentiles. Some rabbis of our

broken down the dividing wall* of hostility, 15by abolishing in his Col 2:14
flesh the law of commandments and ordinances, that he might 2 Cor 5:17

---

Lord's time despised and even hated the Gentiles. The separation between the two peoples was reflected in the temple wall which divided the court of the Gentiles from the rest of the sacred precincts (cf. Acts 21:28). The real roots of the separation lay in Jewish pride at being the only ones to have the Law of God and keep it by scrupulous attention to countless legal niceties.

By his death on the cross Jesus Christ has broken down the barriers dividing Jews from Gentiles and also those which kept man and God apart. St Paul says this metaphorically when he says that Christ "has broken down the dividing wall", referring to the wall in the temple. But he is not resorting to metaphor when he says that Christ abolished "in his flesh the law of commandments and ordinances". Christ, through his obedience to the Father unto death (cf. Phil 2:8), has brought the Law to fulfilment (cf. Mt 5:17 and note on Mt 5:17–19); he has become, for all mankind, the way to the Father. The Law of the Old Testament, although it was something good and holy, also created an unbridgeable gap between God and man, because man, on his own, was incapable of keeping the Law (cf. notes on Gal 3:19–20; 3:21–25; and Acts 15:7–11). Christ, through grace, has created a new man who *can* keep the very essence of the Law—obedience and love.

The "new man" of whom St Paul speaks here is Jesus Christ himself, who stands for both Jews and Gentiles, because he is the new Adam, the head of a new mankind: the "new man", St Thomas Aquinas explains, "refers to Christ himself, who is called 'new man' because of the new form his conception took, ... the newness of the grace which he extends ..., and the new commandment which he brings" (*Commentary on Eph,* ad loc.).

By taking human nature and bringing about our redemption, the Son of God has become the cause of salvation for all, without any distinction between Jew and Greek, slave and free, male and female (cf. Gal 3:28): only through Christ's grace can peace be achieved and all differences overcome. Pope John XXIII explains this in his encyclical *Pacem in terris*: peace is "such a noble and elevated task that human resources, even though inspired by the most praiseworthy goodwill, cannot bring it to realization alone. In order that human society may reflect as faithfully as possible the Kingdom of God, help from on high is necessary. For this reason, during these sacred days Our supplication is raised with greater fervour towards him who by his painful passion and death overcame sin—the root of discord and the source of sorrows and inequalities—and by his blood reconciled mankind to the Eternal Father: 'For he is our peace, who has made us both one'."

**2:16.** Through his death on the cross, Jesus Christ re-establishes man's friendship with God, which sin had destroyed. Pope John Paul suggests that "With our eyes fixed on the mystery of Golgotha we should be reminded always of that *'vertical' dimension* of division and reconciliation concerning the relationship between man and God, a dimension which in the eyes of faith always prevails over the *'horizontal' dimension*, that is to say, over the reality of division between people and the need for reconciliation between them. For we know that reconciliation between people is and can only

create in himself one new man in place of the two, so making
Col 1:20, 22 peace, [16]and might reconcile us both to God in one body through
Is 57:19 the cross, thereby bringing the hostility to an end. [17]And he came
Zech 9:10 and preached peace to you who were far off and peace to those
who were near; [18]for through him we both have access in one

---

be the fruit of the redemptive act of Christ, who died and rose again to conquer the kingdom of sin, to re-establish the covenant with God and thus break down the dividing wall which sin had raised up between people" (*Reconciliatio et paenitentia*, 7). Redemption therefore brings about our reconciliation with God (cf. Rom 5:10; 2 Cor 5:18) and it affects everyone, Gentiles as well as Jews, and all creation (cf. Col 1:20). This reconciliation is achieved in the physical body of Christ sacrificed on the cross (cf. Col 1:22) and also in his mystical body, in which Christ convokes and assembles all whom he has reconciled with God by his redemptive sacrifice (cf. 1 Cor 12:13ff). The words "in one body" can be taken in two senses—as referring to Christ's physical body on the cross and to his mystical body, the Church.

The sacrifice of the body and blood of Christ, "the memorial of the death and resurrection of the Lord, in which the Sacrifice of the cross is forever perpetuated, is the summit and the source of all worship and Christian life. By means of it the unity of the body of Christ is signified and brought about, and the building up of the body of Christ is perfected" (*Code of Canon Law*, can. 897).

**2:18.** Prior to Christ's coming, man was excluded from the Father's house, living like a slave rather than a son (cf. Gal 4:1–5). But in the fullness of time God sent his Son to give us the spirit of sonship that enables us to call God our Father (cf. note on Rom 8:15–17).

"The way that leads to the throne of grace would be closed to sinners had Christ not opened the gate. That is what he does: he opens the gate, leads us to the Father, and by the merits of his passion obtains from the Father forgiveness of our sins and all those graces God bestows on us" (St Alphonsus, *Thoughts on the Passion*, 10, 4).

Here we see the part played by the Holy Spirit in the work of salvation decreed by the Father and carried out by the Son. The words "in one Spirit", as well as identifying the access route to the Father, also imply two basic facts: on the one hand, that the mysterious union which binds Christians together is caused by the action of the Holy Spirit who acts in them; on the other, that this same Holy Spirit, inseparable from the Son (and from the Father) because they constitute the same divine nature, is always present and continually active in the Church, the mystical body of Christ. "When the work which the Father gave the Son to do on earth (cf. Jn 17:4) was accomplished, the Holy Spirit was sent on the day of Pentecost in order that he might continually sanctify the Church, and that, consequently, those who believe might have access through Christ in one Spirit to the Father (cf. Eph 2:18). [...] Hence the universal Church is seen to be 'a people brought into unity from the unity of the Father, the Son and the Holy Spirit' (cf. St Cyprian, *De oratione dominica*, 23)" (Vatican II, *Lumen gentium*, 4).

Christ has brought about salvation, and, to enable all to appropriate that salvation, he calls them to form part of his body, which is the Church. The Holy Spirit is, as it were, the soul of this

Spirit to the Father. [19]So then you are no longer strangers and sojourners, but you are fellow citizens with the saints and members of the household of God, [20]built upon the foundation of the

Heb 12:22
Is 28:16
Rev 21:14

---

mystical body; it is he who gives it life and unites all its members. "If Christ is the head of the Church, the Holy Spirit is its soul: 'As the soul is in our body, so the Holy Spirit is in the body of Christ, that is, the Church' (St Augustine, *Sermon*, 187)" (Leo XIII, *Divinum illud munus*, 8). The Holy Spirit is inseparably united to the Church, for St Irenaeus says, "where the Church is, there is the Spirit of God; and where the Spirit of God is, there is the Church and the fullness of grace" (*Against Heresies*, 3, 24).

**2:19.** After describing the Redemption wrought by Christ and applied in the Church by the Holy Spirit, St Paul arrives at this conclusion: the Gentiles are no longer strangers; they belong to Christ's Church.

In the new Israel (the Church) privileges based on race, culture or nationality cease to apply. No baptized person, be he Jew or Greek, slave or free man, can be regarded as an outsider or stranger in the new people of God. All have proper citizenship papers. The Apostle explains this by using two images: The Church is the city of saints, and God's family or household (cf. 1 Tim 3:15). The two images are complementary: everyone has a family, and everyone is a citizen. In the family context, the members are united by paternal, filial and fraternal links, and love presides; family life has a special privacy. But as a citizen one is acting in a public capacity; public affairs and business must be conducted in a manner that is in keeping with laws designed to ensure that justice is respected. The Church has some of the characteristics of a family, and some of those of a polity (cf. St Thomas Aquinas, *Commentary on Eph*, ad loc.).

The head of the Church is Christ himself, and in his Church are assembled the children of God, who are to live as brothers and sisters, united by love. Grace, faith, hope, charity and the action of the Holy Spirit are *invisible* realities which forge the links bringing together all the members of the Church, which is moreover something very *visible*, ruled by the successor of Peter and by the other bishops (cf. Vatican II, *Lumen gentium*, 8), and governed by laws—divine and ecclesiastical—which are to be obeyed.

**2:20–22.** To better explain the Church, the Apostle links the image of "the household of God" to that of God's temple and "building" (cf. 1 Cor 3:9). Up to this he has spoken of the Church mainly as the body of Christ (v. 16). This image and that of a building are connected: our Lord said, "Destroy this temple, and in three days I will raise it up" (Jn 2:19), and St John goes on to explain that he was speaking "of the temple of his body" (Jn 2:21). If the physical body of Christ is the true temple of God because Christ is the Son of God, the Church can also be seen as God's true temple, because it is the mystical body of Christ.

The Church is the temple of God. "Jesus Christ is, then, the foundation stone of the new temple of God. Rejected, discarded, left to one side, and done to death—then as now—the Father made him and continues to make him the firm, immovable basis of the new work of building. This he does through his glorious resurrection [...].

"The new temple, Christ's body, which is spiritual and invisible, is con-

apostles and prophets, Christ Jesus himself being the cornerstone,
21 in whom the whole structure is joined together and grows into
1 Pet 2:5 a holy temple in the Lord; 22 in whom you also are built into it for
a dwelling place of God in the Spirit.

## 4. PAUL'S MISSION

### Revelation of the mystery of Christ

Phil 1:13 3 1 For this reason I, Paul, a prisoner for Christ Jesus on behalf of
Col 1:24 you Gentiles—2 assuming that you have heard of the steward-

---

structed by each and every baptized person on the living cornerstone, Christ, to the degree that they adhere to him and 'grow' in him towards 'the fullness of Christ'. In this temple and by means of it, the 'dwelling place of God in the Spirit', he is glorified, by virtue of the 'holy priesthood' which offers spiritual sacrifices (1 Pet 2:5), and his kingdom is established in the world.

"The apex of the new temple reaches into heaven, while, on earth, Christ, the cornerstone, sustains it by means of the foundation he himself has chosen and laid down—'the apostles and prophets' (Eph 2:20) and their successors, that is, in the first place, the college of bishops and the 'rock', Peter (Mt 16:18)" (John Paul II, *Homily at Orcasitas, Madrid*, 3 November 1981).

Christ Jesus is the stone: this indicates his strength; and he is the cornerstone, because in him the two peoples, Jews and Gentiles, are joined together (cf. St Thomas Aquinas, *Commentary on Eph,* ad loc.). The Church is founded on this strong, stable bedrock; this cornerstone is what gives it its solidity. St Augustine expresses his faith in the perennial endurance of the Church in these words: "The Church will shake if its foundation shakes, but can Christ shake? As long as Christ does not shake, so shall the Church never weaken until the end of time" (*Enarrationes in Psalmos*, 103).

Every faithful Christian, every living stone of this temple of God, must stay fixed on the solid cornerstone of Christ by cooperating in his or her own sanctification. The Church grows "when Christ is, after a manner, built into the souls of men and grows in them, and when souls also are built into Christ and grow in him; so that on this earth of our exile a great temple is daily in course of building, in which the divine majesty receives due and acceptable worship" (Pius XII, *Mediator Dei*, 6).

**3:1–21.** Christ's saving work on behalf of the Gentiles, calling them to be, with the Jews, living stones in the edifice of the Church, leads the Apostle once again to overflow in prayer (vv. 14–21). But first he considers his own position and what Christ has done in him by making him a minister or servant of the Mystery of Christ (vv. 2–13). He witnesses to the revelation he himself has received, which made this Mystery known to him (vv. 2–5); and he goes on to give a summary of the Mystery, emphasizing the call of the Gentiles to the Church through the

ship of God's grace that was given to me for you, [3]how the Eph 1:9–10
mystery* was made known to me by revelation, as I have written Col 1:26
briefly. [4]When you read this you can perceive my insight into the
mystery of Christ, [5]which was not made known to the sons of men Col 1:26

---

preaching of the Gospel (v. 6); he then explains that his mission is precisely to preach the Mystery of Christ to the Gentiles (vv. 7–13).

**3:1–4.** What led to St Paul's imprisonment was Jewish charges that he had preached against the Law and had brought Gentiles into the temple (they thought Trophimus, a citizen of Ephesus, was a Gentile: cf. Acts 21:28f). He did not mind so much the chains or the imprisonment or the Romans being his judges and jailers: what he wanted to make clear was that he was imprisoned for preaching to the Gentiles the salvation won by Jesus Christ.

He is very conscious of being an instrument specially chosen by God: he has been given the grace to reveal the "mystery" (cf. Rom 1:15; 2 Cor 12:2f). He is clearly referring to the vision he had on the road to Damascus (cf. Acts 9:2) and possibly to later revelations as well. His encounter with the risen Christ, who identifies himself with his Church (cf. Acts 9:5), is the origin and basis of his grasp of God's eternal plan, the "mystery", which is one of the central teachings in this letter. The fact that Christ revealed himself to Paul and chose him to be the preacher of the Gospel to the Gentiles is something which Paul sees as part of the systematic implementation—the *oikonomia*—of God's plan.

**3:5.** In the Old Testament the promise made to Abraham revealed that in his offspring all the nations of the earth would be blessed (cf. Gen 12:3; Sir 44:21); but how this would happen was not revealed. The Jews always thought that it would come about through their exaltation over other nations. Through the revelation Jesus made to him, St Paul has discovered that God has chosen another way—that of bringing the Gentiles into the Church, the body of Christ, on equal terms with the Jews. This is the "mystery", the plan of God as revealed by the mission Christ gave his apostles or envoys (cf. Mt 28:19), of whom St Paul is one (cf. 3:8). Once again, as in 2:20, prophets are mentioned together with apostles; this may mean either the Old Testament prophets who announced the coming Messiah, or the New Testament prophets, that is, the Apostles themselves and other Christians who had insight, through revelation, into God's saving plans for the Gentiles and who proclaimed them under the inspiration of the Spirit. The context and other passages in Ephesians and elsewhere in the New Testament (cf. Eph 4:11; 1 Cor 12:28f; Acts 11:27; etc.) would suggest that he is referring to New Testament prophets. The Holy Spirit has revealed the Mystery to them "that they might preach the Gospel, stir up faith in Jesus the Messiah and Lord, and bring together the Church" (Vatican II, *Dei Verbum*, 17). St Paul does not see himself as the only person to whom it has been given to know the Mystery revealed in Jesus Christ. All that he is saying is that, by the grace of God, it has been made known to him and that its preaching has been entrusted to him in a special way, just as it was given to St Peter to preach it to the Jews (cf. Gal 2:7).

St Paul attributes to the Holy Spirit the revelation of the Mystery, recalling,

in other generations as it has now been revealed to his holy
apostles and prophets by the Spirit; 6that is, how the Gentiles are
fellow heirs, members of the same body, and partakers of the
promise in Christ Jesus through the gospel.
2 Cor 3:6 Col 1:25, 29 7Of this gospel I was made a minister according to the gift of
God's grace which was given me by the working of his power.

---

no doubt, how he himself came to know it after his meeting with Jesus on the road to Damascus (cf. Acts 9:17). It is the Spirit also who acts in the apostles and prophets (cf. Acts 2:17), and it is he who on an on-going basis vivifies the Church, enabling it to proclaim the Gospel. "The Holy Spirit is the soul of the Church. It is he who explains to the faithful the deep meaning of the teaching of Jesus and of his mystery. It is the Holy Spirit who, today just as at the beginning of the Church, acts in every evangelizer who allows himself to be possessed and led by him. The Holy Spirit places on his lips the words which he could not find himself, and at the same time the Holy Spirit predisposes the soul of the hearer to be open and receptive to the Good News and to the Kingdom being proclaimed" (Paul VI, *Evangelii nuntiandi*, 75).

**3:7.** The preacher of the Gospel carries out a ministry, a service to the people of God and to the Gospel itself. St Paul stresses that he has been made a "minister" of the Gospel; he seems to be saying, "I am not carrying out this task as if it were an initiative of my own; I am performing it as a service which comes from God" (St Thomas Aquinas, *Commentary on Eph,* ad loc.). Those who teach Christian doctrine are not passing on their personal opinions, but a divine message. "That is how one should regard us, as servants of Christ and stewards of the mysteries of God" (1 Cor 4:1).

In all generations, God, in his mercy and by his power, calls people to the ministry of the Word, to ensure that the Gospel is forever proclaimed and made known to all mankind. This ministry belongs, in the first place, to bishops. As successors to the apostles, "the bishops are heralds of the faith, who draw new disciples to Christ; they are authentic teachers, that is, teachers endowed with the authority of Christ, who preach the faith to the people assigned to them, the faith which is destined to inform their thinking and direct their conduct; and under the light of the Holy Spirit they make that faith shine forth, drawing from the storehouse of revelation new things and old (cf. Mt 13:52)" (*Lumen gentium*, 25). Alongside the bishops and acting as their helpers, priests and deacons also carry out the ministry of the Word: "it is the first task of priests as co-workers of the bishops to preach the Gospel of God to all men. In this way they carry out the Lord's command 'Go into all the world and preach the gospel to the whole creation' (Mk 16:15) and thus set up and increase the people of God" (Vatican II, *Presbyterorum ordinis*, 4).

The Christian faithful have the basic right, recognized by the Church, to have the word of God preached to them. "The people of God are first united through the word of the living God, and are fully entitled to seek this word from their priests. For this reason sacred ministers are to consider the office of preaching as of great importance, since proclaiming the Gospel of God to all is among their principal duties" (*Code of Canon Law*, can. 762).

[8]To me, though I am the very least of all the saints, this grace was 1 Cor 15:8f
given, to preach to the Gentiles the unsearchable riches of Christ, Rom 16:25
[9]and to make all men see what is the plan of the mystery hidden Col 1:26

---

"When carrying out the ministry of the word", Benedict XV comments, "preachers should have this purpose in mind, as clearly indicated by St Paul: 'we are ambassadors for Christ' (2 Cor 5:20). Every preacher should make these words his own. But if they are ambassadors for Christ, when exercising their mission they have a duty to keep strictly to Christ's purpose when he gave them this charge; they must not have any other aims than those which Christ himself had when he lived on this earth [...]. Therefore, preachers must have these two goals—to spread the truth taught by God; and to awaken and nurture supernatural life in those who are listening to them. To sum up: they must seek the salvation of souls, promote the glory of God" (*Humani generis redemptionem*).

**3:8.** Humble abandonment to the action of God in his soul leads St Paul to regard himself as the very lowest of Christians (cf. 1 Cor 15:9); his only credit is the grace God has given him. This grace includes the revelation of "the mystery" and also the mission to proclaim it (cf. note on Phil 1:7).

He sees the gifts which Christ extends to all, the Gentiles included, as an inexhaustible source of riches (cf. 1:18; 2:7; 3:16). In this present life no one can fully grasp the marvels God has done (cf. Job 5:9) or plumb the depths of God's mercy as manifested in Jesus Christ (cf. note on Col 2:2–3).

Every generation can and should discover in the mystery of Christ "full awareness of (man's) dignity, of the heights to which he is raised, of the surpassing worth of his own humanity, and of the meaning of his existence" (John Paul II, *Redemptor hominis*, 11). The Church's mission is precisely this: "the revealing of Christ to the world, helping each person to find himself in Christ, and helping the contemporary generations of our brothers and sisters, the peoples, nations, states, mankind, developing countries and countries of opulence—in short, helping everyone to get to know 'the unsearchable riches of Christ', since these riches are for every individual and are everybody's property" (ibid.).

**3:9.** The Apostle establishes a close parallel between God's plan of Redemption and the very act of creation (cf. 1 Cor 2:7; Eph 1:4). This saving design, hidden until now, is what has been revealed by Christ; it enables us to grasp God's infinite love for men, for it shows that creation itself is part of God's plan of salvation. For if "all things were created" (Col 1:16) in and for and with Christ, the "mystery" of which he is speaking was already latent in the very creation of the world. Hence God's eternal plan, which envisages man's salvation, affects the very act of creation and includes the incarnation of the Son of God.

Pope John Paul II says this in *Redemptor hominis*, 8: "The Redeemer of the world! In him has been revealed in a new and more wonderful way the fundamental truth concerning creation to which the Book of Genesis gives witness when it repeats several times, 'God saw that it was good' (cf. Gen 1 *passim*). The good has its source in Wisdom and Love. In Jesus Christ the visible world which God created for man (cf. Gen 1:26–30)—the world which, when sin entered, 'was

1 Pet 1:12 for ages in[d] God who created all things; [10]that through the church
the manifold wisdom of God might now be made known to the
principalities and powers in the heavenly places. [11]This was
according to the eternal purpose which he has realized in Christ
Jn 14:6 Heb 4:16 Jesus our Lord, [12]in whom we have boldness and confidence of
access through our faith in him. [13]So I ask you not to[e] lose heart
over what I am suffering for you, which is your glory.

---

subjected to futility' (Rom 8:19–22)—recovers again its original link with the divine source of Wisdom and Love."

**3:10–12.** This text shows that the apostolic ministry of preaching has a universal, cosmic, impact. Thanks to the Church's preaching of the "mystery", it is made known not only to mankind but also to the principalities and powers of the heavens. This preaching reveals the hidden, eternal plans of salvation whereby Jews and Gentiles, by being converted to Christ, come to have an equal place in the Church, and this fact in turn reveals the "mystery" of salvation even to the angels (cf. 1 Pet 1:12), who come to realize the harmony that lies in God's various interventions in the course of history, from the Creation to the Redemption, including the history of the people of Israel.

The "principalities" and "powers" refer to the angelic powers which, according to Jewish belief, were the promulgators and guardians of the Law and whose mission included the government of men. But these "powers" did not know what God's plans were until they were carried out by Christ and his Church. In this passage St Paul does not say anything about whether these powers are good or evil (cf. note on 1:21). What he does re-assert, very clearly, is Christ's supremacy over all these powers, and the Church's role in bringing all creation to recognize that Christ is Lord of all. Therefore, the powers in the heavenly places no longer have any mastery over the Christian: through faith in Christ he acquires the freedom of a son of God and is able to address God confidently.

St Jerome, St Thomas and others interpret "the principalities and powers" as being good angels, like the "thrones" and "dominions" (cf. Col 1:16) and *virtutes* ("powers": cf. Eph 1:21). If we add to these titles appearing in St Paul's letters those to be found in other books of Holy Scripture—cherubim, seraphim, archangels and angels—we get the nine angelic hierarchies known to tradition. The names simply reflect the qualities with which angels are endowed: they are spiritual beings, personal and free; they are incorporeal; and because they are pure spirits, they have intellect, will and power far in excess of man's.

**3:13.** For a Christian, suffering is a privileged opportunity to embrace Christ's cross, a true source of joy and supernatural effectiveness, as Scripture tells us: "if we are afflicted, it is for your comfort and salvation" (2 Cor 1:6). And suffering also strengthens our links of love with God: "Who shall separate us from the love of Christ? Shall tribulation, or distress, or persecution, or famine, or nakedness, or peril, or sword? [...] For I am sure that neither death, nor life, nor angels, nor principalities, nor things present, nor things to come, nor powers,

**d.** Or *by* **e.** Or *I ask that I may not*

**Prayer for the faithful**

[14]For this reason I bow my knees before the Father, [15]from whom
every family in heaven and on earth is named, [16]that according to the Col 1:11
riches of his glory he may grant you to be strengthened with might
through his Spirit in the inner man, [17]and that Christ may dwell in Jn 12:33 Col. 1:23; 2:7
your hearts through faith; that you, being rooted and grounded in

---

nor height, nor depth, nor anything else in all creation, will be able to separate us from the love of God in Christ Jesus our Lord" (Rom 8:35, 38–39).

**3:14.** St Paul now continues the prayer which he interrupted in v. 1, to entreat the Father to let Christians understand as deeply as possible the divine plan for salvation implemented in Christ (vv. 16–19).

"I bow my knees": the Jews generally prayed standing up. Only at moments of special solemnity did they kneel or prostrate themselves in adoration. The Apostle, by introducing this almost liturgical reference, is expressing the intensity of his prayer, and the humility which inspires it.

Bodily gestures—genuflexions, bowing of the head, beating the breast, etc.—which accompany prayer should be sincere expressions of devotion. They allow the entire person, body and soul, to express his love for God. "Those who love acquire a refinement, a sensitivity of soul, that makes them notice details which are sometimes very small but which are important because they express the love of a passionate heart" (St Josemaría Escrivá, *Christ Is Passing By*, 92).

**3:15.** To "take a name" from something means to derive one's being or existence from it, and the word translated here as "family" (*patría* in Greek) means a grouping of individuals who are descended from a common father; it could be translated as "paternity", as the New Vulgate does.

The Apostle is saying that every grouping which is regarded as a family, whether it be on earth (like the Church or the family), or in heaven (like the Church triumphant and the choirs of angels), takes its name and origin from God, the only Father in the full meaning of the word. Thus, the word "Father" can be correctly used to designate not only physical but also spiritual fatherhood. It is quite correct, for example, to describe the Pope as the "father of all Christians".

The parenthood of married people is an outstanding example of the love of God the Creator. They are cooperators in that love, and, in a certain sense, its interpreters (cf. Vatican II, *Gaudium et spes*, 50). Hence, "when they become parents, spouses receive from God the gift of a new responsibility. Their parental love is called to become for the children the visible sign of the very love of God, 'from whom every family in heaven and on earth is named'" (John Paul II, *Familiaris consortio*, 14).

**3:16–17.** The strengthening of the inner man through the Spirit means growth in faith, charity and hope, which is what the Apostle prays for here (cf. vv. 16–19).

"Faith is the assurance of things hoped for, the conviction of things not seen" (Heb 11:1); it is, then, a virtue whereby the Christian in this life anticipates, imperfectly, the object of his hope—that perfect union with God which will take place in heaven.

Love follows from knowledge: one cannot love someone one does not know. And so, when goodness is known, it comes to be loved. Thus, the knowledge

Col 2:2 love, [18]may have power to comprehend with all the saints what is the
Eph 1:23 breadth and length and height and depth, [19]and to know the love of
Col 2:3 Christ which surpasses knowledge, that you may be filled with all
the fullness of God.

---

of God, which faith provides, is followed by the love of God, which stems from charity. Charity, for its part, is the basis of the Christian's spiritual life. "The spiritual edifice cannot stay standing—the same is true of a tree without roots, or a house without a foundation, which can easily be toppled—unless it be rooted and grounded in love" (St Thomas Aquinas, *Commentary on Eph*, ad loc.).

**3:18.** St Paul asks God to give Christians understanding of the "mystery of Christ", which essentially is the outcome of his love. In referring to the vast dimensions of this mystery he uses an enigmatic phrase—"the breadth and length and height and depth". These and similar terms were used by Stoic philosophy to designate the cosmos as a whole. Here they express the immense scale of the "mystery" which embraces the entire plan of salvation, the actions of Christ and the activity of the Church. St Augustine interpreted these words as referring to the cross, the instrument of salvation which Christ used to show the full extent of his love (cf. *De doctrina christiana*, 2, 41).

St Paul may indeed be trying to sum up all the richness of the "mystery" of Christ in a graphic way—in terms of a cross whose extremities reach out in all four directions seeking to embrace the whole world. The blood which our Lord shed on the cross brought about the Redemption, the forgiveness of sins (cf. Eph 1:7). It did away with hostility, reconciling all men and assembling them into one body (cf. Eph 2:15–16), the Church. Therefore the cross is an inexhaustible source of grace, the mark of the true Christian, the instrument of salvation for all. When, through the action of Christians, the cross of Christ is made present at all the crossroads of the world, then is that "mystery" implemented whose purpose it is to "unite all things in Christ" (cf. Eph 1:10).

**3:19.** Christ's love for us is infinite; it is beyond our grasp, because it is of divine dimensions (cf. Jn 15:9 and note on Jn 15:9–11).

Knowledge of the history of salvation and of the "mystery" of Christ is ultimately what gives us a notion of the scale of God's love. Therefore, it is the basis of the Christian life: "We know and believe the love which God has for us. God is love, and he who abides in love abides in God" (1 Jn 4:16). Eternal life will consist in enjoying the love of God without any type of distraction. During his life on earth, the believer receives a foretaste of this joy to the degree that he abides in the love of Christ (cf. Jn 15:9), that is, is rooted and grounded in love (v. 17). However, this knowledge of Christ is always very imperfect compared with that in heaven.

It is worth pointing out that the "knowledge" (*gnosis*) which St Paul is speaking about is not simply intellectual cognition but rather a kind of knowledge which permeates one's whole life. It does not consist so much in knowing that God is love as in realizing that we are personally the object, the focus, of God's love: he loves us one by one, as good parents love their children.

**Doxology** Eph 1:19

20Now to him who by the power at work within us is able to do far Col 1:29
more abundantly than all that we ask or think, 21to him be glory
in the church and in Christ Jesus to all generations, for ever and
ever. Amen.

## 5. UNITY IN THE CHURCH

**Bases of unity**

4 1I therefore, a prisoner for the Lord, beg you to lead a life Phil 1:27
worthy of the calling to which you have been called, 2with all Col 1:10

---

**3:20–21.** The dogmatic section of the letter concludes at this point, and St Paul breaks into a short hymn of praise or doxology, in awe at the divine plan of salvation revealed in Christ. He speaks his praise "in the church and in Christ Jesus".

God knows more than we do; and, since he is a Father who loves us unreservedly, he is always providing us with those things we stand in real need of; moreover, he anticipates our requests, "for he responds to the inner, hidden desires of the needy, not waiting for them to make explicit requests" (*St Pius V Catechism*, 4, 2, 5).

St Thomas Aquinas points out that "neither the mind nor the will of man could have thought or conceived or asked God that he might become man and that man might become God, a sharer in the divine nature; yet the latter has been wrought in us by his power, and the former has been effected by the incarnation of his Son" (*Commentary on Eph*, ad loc.).

In its liturgy the Church is forever giving God the honour which is his due and praising him for the gifts which it receives in Jesus Christ: in the Mass, for example, at the end of the Eucharistic Prayer it proclaims, "Through him [Christ], with him, in him, in the unity of the Holy Spirit, all glory and honour is yours, almighty Father, for ever and ever. Amen."

**4:1–16.** The second part of the letter points out certain practical consequences of the teaching given earlier. The underlying theme of the previous chapters was the revelation of the "mystery" of Christ —the calling of all men, Gentiles and Jews, to form a single people, the Church. The second part of the letter begins with an appeal to maintain the unity of the Church in the face of factors making for division—internal discord (vv. 1–3), misuse of the different gifts or charisms with which Christ endows individuals (v. 7), and the danger of being led astray by heretical ideas (v. 14). Against this, St Paul teaches that the Church's unity is grounded on the oneness of God (vv. 4–6), and that Christ acts with full authority in the building up of his body, through its various ministries (vv. 8–13) and through its members' solidarity (vv. 14–16).

**4:1.** The exhortation begins by stating a general principle: a Christian's conduct should be consistent with the calling he has received from God.

Col 3:12 lowliness and meekness, with patience, forbearing one another in
Col 3:14 love, 3eager to maintain the unity of the Spirit in the bond of

---

Enormous consequences flow from the fact of being called to form part of the Church through Baptism: "Being members of a holy nation," St Josemaría Escrivá says, "all the faithful have received a call to holiness, and they must strive to respond to grace and to be personally holy [...]. Our Lord Jesus Christ, who founds the holy Church, expects the members of this people to strive continually to acquire holiness. Not all respond loyally to his call. And in the spouse of Christ there are seen, at one and the same time, both the marvel of the way of salvation and the shortcomings of those who take up that way" (*In Love with the Church*, 5–6).

Speaking about incorporation into the Church, which is the way of salvation, Vatican II exhorts Catholics to "remember that their exalted condition results, not from their own merits, but from the grace of Christ. If they fail to respond in thought, word and deed to that grace, not only shall they not be saved, but they shall be the more severely judged (see Lk 12:48: 'everyone to whom much is given, of him will much be required'; cf. Mt 5:19–20; 7:21–22; 25:41–46; Jas 2:14)" (*Lumen gentium*, 14).

**4:2–3.** The virtues which the Apostle lists here are all different aspects of charity which "binds everything together in perfect harmony" (Col 3:14) and is the mark of the true disciple of Christ (cf. Jn 13:35). Charity originates not in man but in God: "it is a supernatural virtue infused by God into our soul by which we love God above everything else for his own sake, and our neighbour as ourselves for love of God" (*St Pius X Catechism*, 898). In its decree on ecumenism the Second Vatican Council shows the perennial relevance of these words of St Paul: "There can be no ecumenism worthy of the name without interior conversion. For it is from interior renewal of mind (cf. Eph 4:23), from self-denial and unstinted love, that desires of unity take their rise and develop in a mature way. We should therefore pray to the Holy Spirit for the grace to be genuinely self-denying, humble, gentle in the service of others and to have an attitude of brotherly generosity toward them" (*Unitatis redintegratio*, 7).

Charity is basic to the building up of a peaceful human society. "The consciousness of being trespassers against each other goes hand in hand with the call to fraternal solidarity, which St Paul expressed in his concise exhortation to 'forbear one another in love'. What a lesson of humility is to be found here with regard to man, with regard both to one's neighbour and to oneself! What a school of good will for daily living, in the various conditions of our existence!" (John Paul II, *Dives in misericordia*, 14).

The peace which unites Christians is the peace which Christ brings, or rather it is Christ himself (cf. 2:14). By having the same faith and the same Spirit, "all find themselves", says St John Chrysostom, "brought together in the Church—old and young, poor and rich, adult and child, husband and wife: people of either sex and of every condition become one and the same, more closely united than the parts of a single body, for the unity of souls is more intimate and more perfect than that of any natural substance.

peace. [4]There is one body and one Spirit, just as you were called Rom 12:5 Col 3:14f
to the one hope that belongs to your call, [5]one Lord, one faith, one
baptism, [6]one God and Father of us all, who is above all and 1 Cor 1:13; 8:6

---

However, this unity is maintained only by 'the bond of peace'. It could not exist in the midst of disorder and enmity. [...] This is a bond which does not restrict us, which unites us closely to one another and does not overwhelm us: it expands our heart and gives us greater joy than we could ever have if we were unattached. He who is strong is linked to the weaker one to carry him and prevent him from falling and collapsing. Does the weak person feel weak?: the stronger person tries to build up his strength. 'A brother helped is like a strong city', says the wise man (Prov 18:19)" (*Hom. on Eph*, 9, ad loc.).

Union of hearts, affections and intentions is the result of the action of the Holy Spirit in souls, and it makes for effectiveness and strength in apostolate.

"Do you see? One strand of wire entwined with another, many woven tightly together, form that cable strong enough to lift huge weights.

"You and your brothers, with wills united to carry out God's will, can overcome all obstacles" (St Josemaría Escrivá, *The Way*, 480).

**4:4–6.** To show the importance of unity in the Church, and the theological basis of that unity, St Paul quotes an acclamation which may well have been taken from early Christian baptismal liturgy. It implies that the unity of the Church derives from the unicity of the divine essence. The text also reflects the three persons of the Blessed Trinity who are at work in the Church and who keep it together—one Spirit, one Lord, one God and Father.

There is *only one* Holy Spirit, who brings about and maintains the unity of Christ's mystical body; and there is *only one* such body, the Church: "After being lifted up on the cross and glorified, the Lord Jesus pours forth the Spirit whom he had promised, and through whom he has called and gathered together the people of the New Covenant, which is the Church, into a unity of faith, hope and charity, as the Apostle teaches us (Eph 4:4–5; Gal 3:27–28). [...] It is the Holy Spirit, dwelling in believers and pervading and ruling over the entire Church, who brings about that wonderful communion of the faithful and joins them together so intimately in Christ, for he [the Spirit] is the principle of the Church's unity" (Vatican II, *Unitatis redintegratio*, 2). All—Gentiles as well as Jews—are called to join this Church; all, therefore, share the one single hope—that of being saints which is implied in the vocation they have received.

Recognition of there being *only one* Lord, who is head of the mystical body, underlines the unity that should obtain among all the many members of this single body. All its members are solidly built on Christ when they confess *only one* faith—the faith that he taught and which the apostles and the Church have expressed in clear statements of doctrine and dogma. "There can be only one faith; and so, if a person refuses to listen to the Church, he should be considered, so the Lord commands, as a heathen and a publican (cf. Mt 18:17)" (Pius XII, *Mystici Corporis*, 10). All Christians have also received *only one* Baptism, that is, a Baptism by means of which, after making a profession of faith, they join the other members of the Church as their equals. Since there is only "one Lord, one faith, one baptism," "there is a

Rom 12:3, 6
1 Cor 12:11
through all and in all. 7But grace was given to each of us according to the measure of Christ's gift. 8Therefore it is said,

Ps 68:18
"When he ascended on high he led a host of captives,
and he gave gifts to men."

---

common dignity of members deriving from their rebirth in Christ, a common grace as sons, a common vocation to perfection, one salvation, one hope and undivided charity. In Christ and in the Church there is, then, no inequality arising from race or nationality, social condition or sex, for 'there is neither Jew nor Greek; there is neither slave nor free; there is neither male nor female; for you are all one in Christ Jesus' (Gal 3:28; cf. Col 3:11)" (Vatican II, *Lumen gentium*, 32).

God, the Father of all, is, in the last analysis, the basis of the natural unity of mankind. Pope Pius XII, after recalling that the sacred books tell us that all the rest of mankind originated from the first man and woman, and how all the various tribes and peoples grew up which are scattered throughout the world, exclaimed, "This is a wonderful vision which allows us to reflect on the unity of mankind: all mankind has a common origin in the Creator, as we are told, 'one God and father of us all' (Eph 4:6); moreover, all men and women share one and the same nature: all have a material body and an immortal and spiritual soul" (*Summi Pontificatus*, 18). God is "above all": his lordship and control over things means that he is the author and maintainer of their unity. Throughout history he has acted "through all" his children, that is, believers, whom he has used to bring about unity among men and over all created things. And he dwells "in all" the faithful, for they belong to him; even the deepest recesses of their hearts are his.

**4:7.** The diversity of graces or charisms that accompany the various kinds of vocation given to members of the Church do not undermine its unity; rather, they enhance it, because it is Christ himself who bestows these gifts (vv. 8–10). Christ also provides the Church with ministers who devote themselves to building up his body (vv. 11–12).

So just as there is a great variety of personality and situation, the Church evidences many kinds of "charisms" or different ways of actually living out the calling to holiness which God addresses to all. "In the Church", John Paul II points out, "as the community of the people of God under the guidance of the Holy Spirit's working, each member has 'his own special gift', as St Paul teaches (1 Cor 7:7). Although this 'gift' is a personal vocation and a form of participation in the Church's saving work, it also serves others, builds the Church and the fraternal communities in the various spheres of human life on earth" (*Redemptor hominis*, 21).

**4:8–9.** The quotation in v. 8 comes from Psalm 68:18. In it we see God entering Zion in triumph, where his people receive him, pay him homage and offer him gifts. Jewish tradition applied these words of the psalm to Moses, by changing the meaning somewhat: Moses ascended on high, that is, went up Mount Sinai, and brought down gifts for men, that is, the Law of God. St Paul teaches that this psalm finds its fulfilment in Jesus Christ, for it is through him that God's gifts reach us. He sees Jesus, as it were, from the glory of heaven, which he has already entered, distributing to all men the gifts he won through the Redemption.

[9](In saying, "He ascended," what does it mean but that he had also Jn 3:13
descended into the lower parts of the earth? [10]He who descended
is he who also ascended far above all the heavens, that he might fill
all things.)

**Building up Christ's body**

[11]And his gifts were that some should be apostles, some prophets, 1 Cor 12:28

---

When he says "he ascended on high" he is speaking figuratively. According to the cosmology of the ancient world, which the Jews tended to follow, heaven, where God dwelt, was thought of as being in the highest firmament. The "lower parts of the earth" can be understood as simply the earth, or else, *sheol*, the dwelling-place of the dead, according to Jewish notions (cf. Gen 37:25; Deut 32:22; Job 10:21; etc.); thus, the passage may refer to Christ's life on earth, or else to his death. Whichever is the correct interpretation, it underlines the fact that Christ was truly man, and that he was humiliated and then raised up after his life on earth, and is recognized to have the same lordship over all creation as the Father. Christ exercises his lordship by raising all things to find total fulfilment in him: he is the head of all creation for the glory of the Father: "The Word of God, through whom all things were made, was made flesh, so that as a perfect man he could save all men and sum up all things in himself. The Lord is the goal of human history, the focal point of the desires of history and civilization, the centre of mankind, the joy of all hearts, and the fulfilment of all aspirations (cf. Paul VI, *Address*, 3 February 1965). It is he whom the Father raised from the dead, exalted and placed at his right hand, constituting him judge of the living and the dead. Animated and drawn together in his Spirit we press onwards on our journey towards the consummation of history which fully corresponds to the plan of his love—'to unite all things in him, things in heaven and things on earth' (Eph 1:10)" (Vatican II, *Gaudium et spes*, 45).

Previously we were subject to the slavery of sin (cf. Rom 6:20; 7:14). Christ's redeeming action has freed us from that tyranny, thereby fulfilling the words of the psalm: "he led captivity captive", "he led a host of captives".

**4:11–12.** The Apostle here refers to certain ministries or offices in the Church, which are performed not only in a charismatic way, under the influence of the Holy Spirit, but as an assignment or ministry entrusted to the particular individual by the glorified Lord.

These ministries have to do with preaching (teaching) and government. In 1 Corinthians 12:27–30 and Romans 12:6–8, mention is made, alongside ministries, of other charisms which complete the array of the gifts to be found in the mystical body of Christ. St Paul here presents them as gifts given by Christ, the head of his body, gifts which make for the strengthening of its unity and love. In this connexion, see the quotation from *Lumen gentium*, 7, in the note on 1:22–23 above. These graces are provided by the Holy Spirit who, "distributing various kinds of spiritual gifts and ministries (cf. 1 Cor 12:4–11), enriches the Church of Jesus Christ with different functions in order to equip the saints for the works of service" (*Unitatis redintegratio*, 2).

2 Tim 3:17 some evangelists, some pastors and teachers, [12]to equip the saints
1 Pet 2:5 for the work of ministry, for building up the body of Christ, [13]until
Col 1:28 we all attain to the unity of the faith and of the knowledge of

---

In the list which St Paul gives the first to appear are apostles. These may be the first apostles (including Paul himself) or a wider group (cf. 1 Cor 15:7; Rom 16:7) which includes others sent as missionaries to establish new Christian communities. Alongside them (as in Eph 2:20; 3:5) come prophets, who are also the bedrock of the Church, trustees of revelation. Essentially a prophet was not someone "sent" but rather one whose role was to "upbuild, encourage and console" (cf. 1 Cor 14:3; Acts 13:1) and who normally stayed within a particular community. The "evangelists" were others, who had not received a direct revelation but who devoted themselves to preaching the Gospel which the apostles had passed on to them (cf. Acts 21:8; 2 Tim 4:5). It may be that St Paul mentions them here, along with apostles and prophets, because it was evangelists who first preached the Gospel in Ephesus. The last to be mentioned are pastors and teachers, whose role was that of ruling and giving ongoing instruction to particular communities.

There is no necessary reason why the terminology used in apostolic times for ministries in the Church should be the same as that used nowadays; however, the ministries themselves do not change: "Guiding the Church in the way of all truth (cf. Jn 16:13) and unifying her in communion and in the works of ministry, the Holy Spirit bestows upon her varied hierarchic and charismatic gifts, and in this way directs her; and he adorns her with his fruits (cf. Eph 4:11–12; 1 Cor 12:4; Gal 5:22)" (Vatican II, *Lumen gentium*, 4).

And, of course, all Christians have a responsibility to spread Christ's teaching, to cooperate in the Church's work of catechesis. "Catechesis always has been and always will be", John Paul II teaches, "a work for which the whole Church must feel responsible and must wish to be responsible. But the Church's members have different responsibilities, derived from each one's mission. Because of their charge, pastors have, at differing levels, the chief responsibility for fostering, guiding and coordinating catechesis [...]. Priests and religious have in catechesis a pre-eminent field for their apostolate. On another level, parents have a unique responsibility. Teachers, the various ministers of the Church, catechists, and also organizers of social communications, all have in various degrees very precise responsibilities in this education of the believing conscience, an education that is important for the life of the Church and affects the life of society as such" (*Catechesi tradendae*, 16).

**4:13.** The building up of the body of Christ occurs to the extent that its members strive to hold on to the truths of faith and to practise charity. The "knowledge of the Son of God" refers not only to the object of faith—which is basically the acceptance of Christ as true God and true man—but also to a vital and loving relationship with him. A conscientious approach to the personal obligations that faith implies is the mark of maturity, whereas an undeveloped, childish personality is marked by a certain instability.

As Christians develop in faith and love, they become more firmly inserted into the body of Christ and make a greater

the Son of God, to mature manhood, to the measure of the stature
of the fullness of Christ; 14so that we may no longer be children, 1 Cor 14:20
tossed to and fro and carried about with every wind of doctrine, by
the cunning of men, by their craftiness in deceitful wiles. 15Rather,

---

contribution to its development. In this way "mature manhood" is reached: this seems to refer not to the individual Christian but rather to the "total Christ" or "whole Christ" in St Augustine's phrase, that is, all the members in union with the head, Christ. "It is due to this communication of the Spirit of Christ that all the gifts, virtues, and miraculous powers which are found eminently, most abundantly, and fontally in the head, stream into all the members of the Church and in them are perfected daily according to the place of each in the mystical body of Jesus Christ; and that, consequently, the Church becomes as it were the fullness and completion of the Redeemer, Christ in the Church being in some sense brought to complete achievement" (Pius XII, *Mystici Corporis*, 34).

"The fullness of Christ" must mean the Church itself or Christians incorporated into Christ; the "fullness" (*plêrôma*) of a boat is the sum total of the gear, crew and cargo which "fill" the boat, and mean it is ready to weigh anchor. "As members of the living Christ, incorporated into him and made like him by Baptism, Confirmation and the Eucharist, all the faithful have an obligation to collaborate in the spreading and growth of his body, so that they might bring it to fullness as soon as possible" (Vatican II, *Ad gentes*, 36).

**4:14.** "It is natural for a child not to stay fixed in (his ideas) but to be influenced by everything he is told. But if we wish to show that we are mature people we need to get rid of changeable, that is, unstable, thoughts" (St Thomas Aquinas, *Commentary on Eph*, ad loc.). Serenity of mind and clearness of thought are characteristics of human maturity. In the presentation of Christian doctrine, firmness in the faith, and prudence, as distinct from a penchant for new ideas, are a sign of supernatural maturity. This maturity guarantees that a person will not wander from the truth, will not be led astray—even involuntarily—by erroneous ideas. Pius XII warns us that "to neglect, or to reject, or to devalue so many and such great resources which have been conceived, expressed and perfected so often by the age-old work of men endowed with no common talent and holiness, working under the vigilant supervision of the holy Magisterium and with the light and leadership of the Holy Spirit in order to state the truths of the faith ever more accurately, to do this so that these things may be replaced by conjectural notions and by some formless and unstable tenets of a new philosophy, tenets which, like the flowers of the field, are in existence today and die tomorrow; this is supreme imprudence and something that would make dogma itself a reed shaken by the wind" (*Humani generis*).

**4:15.** Truthfulness and charity should be very much in evidence in a Christian's public and private life. When one meets people who think differently from oneself —in matters of opinion—one should respect their point of view, respect their God-given freedom, and remember that in matters of this kind no one can be

speaking the truth in love, we are to grow up in every way into
Col 2:19 him who is the head, into Christ, [16]from whom the whole body,
joined and knit together by every joint with which it is supplied,
when each part is working properly, makes bodily growth and
upbuilds itself in love.

---

said to be absolutely right or absolutely wrong.

However, situations will arise where a Christian is dealing with people who regard the truth as merely a matter of opinion—or who in fact regard as true something which is quite the opposite. In these situations too one should practise "the truth with charity", by being very understanding towards the person(s) involved, yet refusing to accept the error proposed. "A disciple of Christ", St J. Escrivá writes, "will never treat anyone badly. Error he will call error, but the person in error he will correct with kindliness. Otherwise he will not be able to help him, to sanctify him. We must learn to live together, to understand one another, to make allowances, to be brotherly and, at all times, in the words of St John of the Cross, 'where there is no love, put love and you will find love' " (*Friends of God*, 9).

Truth, then, should always be presented in a friendly, gentle way, never imposed by any type of coercion. Otherwise, it would be impossible to bring about peace between individuals or groups; on the contrary, it would lead to endless strife: "Peace on earth, which flows from love of one's neighbour, symbolizes and derives from the peace of Christ who proceeds from God the Father. Christ, the Word made flesh, the prince of peace, reconciled all men to God by the cross, and, restoring the unity of all in one people and one body, he abolished hatred in his own flesh, having been lifted up through his resurrection he poured forth the Spirit of love into the hearts of men. Therefore, all Christians are earnestly to speak the truth in love (cf. Eph 4:15) and join with all peace-loving men in pleading for peace and trying to bring it about. In the same spirit we cannot but express our admiration for all who forego the use of violence to vindicate their rights and resort to those other means of defence which are available to weaker parties, provided it can be done without harm to the rights and duties of others and of the community" (Vatican II, *Gaudium et spes*, 78).

**4:16.** In the same sort of way as happens in the human body, the Church, as Christ's body, receives from him, its head, the grace it needs for its full development. The head rules the various members to get them to perform particular functions: "In the organism of a living body no member plays a purely passive part; sharing in the life of the body it shares at the same time in its activity. The same is true for the mystical body of Christ, the Church: 'the whole body ..., when each part is working properly, makes full growth' (Eph 4:16)" (Vatican II, *Apostolicam actuositatem*, 2).

Christ is the head, and therefore from him comes the life and supernatural impulse that inspires each of his members. "As the nerves extend from the head to all the members of our body, giving them the power to feel and move, so our Saviour pours forth into the Church his power and virtue, giving to the faithful a clearer understanding and a more ardent desire of the things of God. From him flows into the body of the Church all the

## 6. NEW LIFE IN CHRIST AND IN THE CHURCH

**Corruption, a thing of the past**

17Now this I affirm and testify in the Lord, that you must no longer Rom 1:21
live as the Gentiles do, in the futility of their minds; 18they are Col 2:6
darkened in their understanding, alienated from the life of God Col 1:21
because of the ignorance that is in them, due to their hardness of
heart; 19they have become callous and have given themselves up to
licentiousness, greedy to practise every kind of uncleanness. 20You
did not so learn Christ!—21assuming that you have heard about him
and were taught in him, as the truth is in Jesus. 22Put off your old Rom 8:13
nature which belongs to your former manner of life and is corrupt Col 3:9

---

light which divinely illumines those who believe, and all the grace which makes them holy as he himself is holy [...]. Christ is the author and efficient cause of holiness; for there can be no salutary act which does not proceed from him as from its supernatural source: 'Without me,' he said, 'you can do nothing' (Jn 15:5). If we are moved to sorrow and repentance for the sins we have committed, if we turn to God with filial fear and hope, it is always his power that leads us on. His inexhaustible fullness is the fount of grace and glory. Especially the more eminent members of his body are constantly enriched by our Saviour with the gifts of counsel, fortitude, fear and piety, so that the whole body may daily increase in holiness and integrity of life" (Pius XII, *Mystici Corporis*, 22–23).

**4:17–19.** The Christian, who has been configured to Christ by Baptism, is called to holiness and therefore should not lead a dissolute life alienated from God, as the Gentiles do. The "futility of their minds" has led them away from God, the source of all truth (cf. Rom 1:18–32). Hence it is that when man is put in the place of God the mind operates in a vacuum and the resulting knowledge produces nothing but mere illusion and total deceit.

As St Paul tells the Romans, people who act in that way are those "who by their wickedness suppress the truth" (Rom 1:18). The human mind is capable of recognizing God as the creator of all things; but when people give their passions full rein, their will becomes weakened; they thus suppress the truth and their minds easily tend to adopt wrong ideas. All this is a result of arrogance and pride which makes man unwilling to accept God and acknowledge his own limitations as a creature: this eventually leads to the "ignorance that is in them, due to their hardness of heart" (v. 18).

Impurity opens the way to a whole series of vices and disorders connected with greed (cf. notes on Rom 1:29–31 and Rom 1:32). The term "callous" is used to indicate that these people lost their desire to try to lead a good life and even lose their very sense of morality.

**4:22–24.** The sacred text emphasizes two basic points—one's duty to put off one's "old nature" (the "old man") and, in parallel with that, the urgent need to put on the "new nature" (the "new man"). These two expressions refer directly to the symbolism of Christian Baptism, which effects the transition from the life

Rom 12:2 through deceitful lusts, 23and be renewed in the spirit of your minds,
Gen 1:26 24and put on the new nature, created after the likeness of God in true
righteousness and holiness.
Zech 8:16 25Therefore, putting away falsehood, let every one speak the
Col 3:8f truth with his neighbour, for we are members one of another.

---

of sin to the life of grace, thanks to the merits of Christ (cf. Rom 6:3–11).

In Baptism we have "put on Christ" (Gal 3:27) and become "partakers of the divine nature" (2 Pet 1:4). From that moment onwards a Christian's life is so radically different that to revert to one's previous—pagan—conduct is the greatest insult we could offer the body of Christ. St Paul, therefore, is not just exhorting people to root out this or that defect, but to strip themselves of the "old nature" entirely.

The "old nature" is the carnal man, vitiated from conception by original sin and become the slave of his own passions; whereas, the "new man" has been born again through the Holy Spirit at Baptism: he is no longer ruled by sin, although he is still subject to passions which have been made unruly by sin. That is why the Apostle urges us to put off the "old nature" by fighting against disordered desires and their evil effects (cf. Rom 6:12–14; 8:5–8) and by being conscious that the renewal brought about by the Holy Spirit helps the baptized person to see each and every event in his life from a new, supernatural perspective, as befits the "new man".

The change from the old to the new nature St Paul describes in terms of creation (v. 24). It does not involve any external change, as when someone changes his clothes, but rather an inner renewal, whereby the Christian, by becoming a new creature in Jesus Christ, is enabled to practise righteousness and holiness in a manner that exceeds his natural human capacity. It is not enough, then, for one to have simply a veneer of piety. "Entering the church and venerating sacred images and crosses is not sufficient for pleasing God, just as washing one's hands does not make one clean all over. What truly pleases God is that a person flees from sin and gets rid of his stains by means of confession and penance. Let him break the chains of his faults by being humble of heart" (St Anastasius of Sinai, *Sermon on the Holy Synaxis*).

This inner renewal of the person is something which takes a lifetime. "The power of God is made manifest in our weakness and it spurs us on to fight, to battle against our defects, although we know that we will never achieve total victory during our pilgrimage on earth. The Christian life is a continuous beginning again each day. It renews itself over and over" (St Josemaría Escrivá, *Christ Is Passing By*, 114).

**4:25.** Truthfulness is a virtue to which our Lord gives much importance—as we can see, for example, from his public praise of Nathaniel, in whom there was no guile (cf. Jn 1:47), and from his condemnation of the hypocrisy of the Pharisees (cf. Lk 11:39ff). It leads one always to tell the truth and to present oneself exactly as one really is. It is a virtue essential for the proper functioning of society and of the Church, because it fosters a climate of trust and makes for loyal solidarity. As St Thomas Aquinas explains: "Since man is by nature a social being, there is a natural indebtedness of the individual to his fellow man in regard to those things

[26]Be angry but do not sin; do not let the sun go down on your anger, [27]and give no opportunity to the devil. [28]Let the thief no

Ps 4:5
Jas 4:7
1 Thess 4:11

without which society could not be maintained. For example, men could not live together if they were unable to trust one another to speak the truth in everyday affairs" (*Summa theologiae*, 2–2, 109, 3, ad. 1).

Christ said of himself "I am the truth" (Jn 14:6), and he taught his disciples to be sincere in everyday conversation: "Let what you say be simply 'Yes' or 'No'" (Mt 5:37). A Christian has a further reason to practise this virtue: he realizes that others are members, like him, of Christ's mystical body.

**4:26.** Holy Scripture sometimes speaks of a holy "anger" which derives from an upright intention and from the pain caused by the infringement of moral precepts, especially those referring directly to God. Our Lord shows this kind of anger, for example, when he drives the money-changers out of the temple (cf. Jn 2:13–17).

However, anger as a capital sin usually comes from pride, which clouds a person's mind and inclines his will towards evil. To avoid committing these sins one needs to practise the virtue of prudence; prudence avoids precipitous action. "Always remain silent when you feel the upsurge of indignation within you. And do so, even when you have good reason to be angry. For, in spite of your discretion, in such moments you always say more than you wish" (St Josemaría Escrivá, *The Way*, 656).

"Do not let the sun go down on your anger": this can be taken as meaning one should avoid harbouring thoughts of revenge: if a person does become irate, he should try to control his temper quickly (cf. St Thomas Aquinas, *Commentary on Eph*, ad loc.). It can also be interpreted as a call to vigilance and self-control.

**4:27.** The devil "was a murderer from the beginning, and has nothing to do with the truth [...]. When he lies, he speaks according to his nature, for he is a liar and the father of lies" (Jn 8:44). Insincerity often leads one to sin against justice, and, indeed, against charity as well—which is exactly what the devil has in mind when he tempts us, since as the father of lies he is the declared enemy of God and of those who stay true to God's word.

**4:28.** God created man to work (cf. Gen 2:15). Work, therefore, is not a punishment but something essential to human nature. As John Paul II teaches, "Man is made to be in the visible universe an image and likeness of God himself (cf. Gen 1:26), and he is placed in it in order to subdue the earth (cf. Gen 1:28). From the beginning therefore he is *called to work. Work is one of the characteristics that distinguish* man from other creatures [...]. Only man has the capacity to work; he alone can carry it out, filling with it as he does his whole existence on earth. Thus work bears in itself a particular mark of man and of humanity [...]. And this mark decides its interior characteristics; in a sense it constitutes its very nature" (*Laborem exercens*, introduction).

Work, in its turn, is normally the means man uses to meet his material needs. Although economic resources are not an end in themselves, they are essential to us—in moderation—if we are to enjoy a certain level of comfort which makes the search for holiness easier and more pleasant. This means that work

longer steal, but rather let him labour, doing honest work with his hands, so that he may be able to give to those in need. [29]Let no evil talk come out of your mouths, but only such as is good for edifying, as fits the occasion, that it may impart grace to those who hear. [30]And do not grieve the Holy Spirit of God, in whom

---

helps one "obtain, on the one hand, sufficient for one's needs and not to suffer by being unable to meet them; on the other hand, it enables us to help those we ought. For, if no one had anything, how could there be any mutual sharing of things among men [...], how could one give food to the hungry, drink to the thirsty, clothe the naked or assist the needy, [...] if everyone found himself in the same needy circumstances to start with?" (Clement of Alexandria, *Quis dives salvetur*, 18).

"We must be convinced that work is something wonderful, and that it has been imposed on us as an inexorable law which one way or another binds everyone, even though some may try to seek exemption from it. Make no mistake about it: our obligation to work is not a consequence of original sin, nor is it a modern phenomenon. Work is an indispensable resource which God has entrusted to us here on this earth. It is meant to fill our days and make us sharers in God's creative power. It enables us to earn our living and, at the same time, to reap 'the fruits of eternal life' (Jn 4:36)" (St Josemaría Escrivá, *Friends of God*, 57).

**4:29.** "Scandal is any word, act or omission which to another is the occasion of committing sin. Scandal is a grave sin because it tends to destroy the greatest work of God, namely the Redemption, by the loss of souls; it brings death to the soul of another by taking from it the life of grace, which is more precious than the life of the body; and it is the source of a multitude of sins" (*St Pius X Catechism*, 417–418). Hence the need to be always watchful that in everyday conversation one does not even accidentally say something which might harm someone else.

On the other hand, prudent and well-timed remarks, flavoured with the grace of God, are helpful to the listener: "Those well-timed words, whispered in the ear of your wavering friend; the helpful conversation you managed to start at the right moment; the ready professional advice that improves his university work; the discreet indiscretion by which you open up unexpected horizons for his zeal. This all forms part of the 'apostolate of friendship'" (St Josemaría Escrivá, *The Way*, 973).

**4:30.** The Holy Spirit, who is the bond of unity in Christ's mystical body (cf. Eph 4:3–4), is "grieved" by anything which might cause disunity among the faithful. The Holy Spirit dwells in the souls of believers from Baptism onwards, and his presence is reinforced when they receive Confirmation and the other sacraments. As the Council of Florence teaches, in Confirmation "we are given the Holy Spirit to strengthen us, as happened to the Apostles on the day of Pentecost, enabling the Christian boldly to confess the name of Christ" (*Pro Armeniis*, *Dz–Sch*, 1319). St Ambrose, commenting on the effects of Confirmation, says that the soul receives from the Holy Spirit "the spiritual seal, the Spirit of wisdom and understanding, the Spirit of counsel and fortitude, the Spirit of knowledge and piety, the Spirit of holy fear. God the Father has sealed you, Christ the Lord

you were sealed for the day of redemption. 31Let all bitterness and Cor 3:8
wrath and anger and clamour and slander be put away from you,
with all malice, 32and be kind to one another, tenderhearted, Col 3:12
forgiving one another, as God in Christ forgave you.

**The purity of life of God's children**

5 1Therefore be imitators of God, as beloved children. 2And Mt 5:48
walk in love, as Christ loved us and gave himself up for us, a Gal 2:20
fragrant offering and sacrifice to God.

---

has strengthened you, the mark of the Spirit has been impressed on your heart" (*De mysteriis*, 7, 42). Since Confirmation is one of the three sacraments which imprints a character on the soul, this seal remains forever.

When the time came for Israel's redemption from slavery in Egypt, the blood of the passover lamb, which had been smeared on the doors of the Israelites' houses, acted as the mark which identified those to be saved. In a parallel way, the seal of the Holy Spirit which is given at Baptism is the permanent sign engraved on the souls of those who are called to salvation by virtue of the Redemption worked by Christ.

"The Apostle is speaking here of the configuration by virtue of which an individual is deputed to future glory, and this takes place through grace. Now grace is attributed to the Holy Spirit inasmuch as it is from love that God freely imparts something to us, and this belongs to the meaning of grace. And it is the Holy Spirit that is love" (*Summa theologiae*, 3, 63, 3, ad 1).

**4:32.** Forgiveness is one of the virtues which characterize the "new nature", for it leads a person to treat his neighbour as Jesus taught: "If you are offering your gift at the altar, and there remember that your brother has something against you, leave your gift there before the altar and go; first be reconciled to your brother" (Mt 5:23–24). Our Lord has shown by his own example what really forgiving one's neighbour involves. Even in the midst of his suffering on the cross he asked his father to forgive those who condemned him and those who nailed him to the wood so violently and sadistically.

"Force yourself, if necessary, always to forgive those who offend you, from the very first moment. For the greatest injury or offence that you can suffer from them is as nothing compared with what God has pardoned you" (St Josemaría Escrivá, *The Way*, 452).

**5:1.** A good child tries to please his parents and to follow their good example. Christians are adopted children of God and therefore should be guided in their behaviour by the way God treats people (cf. Mt 6:12; etc.); we have in fact a very accessible way to follow—that given us by Jesus.

If we wish our actions to be very pleasing to God our Father, we should learn from his Son made man. However, it "is not enough to have a general idea of Jesus; we have to learn the details of his

Rom 1:28 / Col 3:5 — [3]But fornication and all impurity or covetousness must not even
be named among you, as is fitting among saints. [4]Let there be no
Col 3:8 — filthiness, nor silly talk, nor levity, which are not fitting; but instead

---

life and, through them, his attitudes. And, especially, we must contemplate his life, to derive from it strength, light, serenity, peace.

"When you love someone, you want to know all about his life and character, so as to become like him. That is why we have to meditate on the life of Jesus, from his birth in a stable right up to his death and resurrection" (St Josemaría Escrivá, *Christ Is Passing By, 107).*

**5:2.** Christ gave himself up to death of his own free will, out of love for man. The words "a fragrant offering and sacrifice", recalling the sacrifices of the Old Law, underline the sacrificial character of Christ's death and emphasize that his obedience was pleasing to God the Father.

Jesus Christ "came to show us the immense love of his heart, and he gave himself to us entirely," St Alphonsus teaches, "submitting himself first to all the hardships of this life, then to the scourging, the crowning with thorns and all the pain and ignominy of his passion; finally he ended his life forsaken by all on the infamous wood of the cross" (*Shorter Sermons*, 37, 1, 1).

The founder of Opus Dei says in this connexion: "Reflect on the example that Christ gave us, from the crib in Bethlehem to his throne on Calvary. Think of his self-denial and of all he went through—hunger, thirst, weariness, heat, tiredness, ill-treatment, misunderstandings, tears [...]. But at the same time think of his joy at being able to save all mankind. And now I would like you to engrave deeply on your mind and on your heart—so that you can meditate on it often and draw your own practical conclusions—the summary St Paul made for the Ephesians when he invited them to follow resolutely in our Lord's footsteps: [Eph 5:1–2 follows]" (*Friends of God,* 128).

**5:3.** Like the early Christians in Asia Minor, many Christians today find themselves in a somewhat paganized society marked by immoral practices (cf. Rom 1:24–27), including fornication and impurity in general (cf. Col 3:5). However, no matter how corrupt public morality may be, it should be vigorously resisted, especially by means of that upright living which befits those who aspire to holiness because they are temples of the Holy Spirit (cf. 1 Cor 6:19) and members of Christ's body (cf. 1 Cor 6:15).

That is why the Apostle warns that "immorality and all impurity or covetousness must not even be named among you." The last part of the sentence could also be translated as "should not be mentioned in connexion with you"; that is, Christians should be so refined in the practice of chastity and its associate virtues that non-Christians have no grounds whatever for accusing them of impurity. However, the main reason for practising this virtue is not fear of what others may say but rather love of God, who is our Father, and respect for one's own body, which is the dwelling-place of the Blessed Trinity. "Tell me," asks St Anastasius of Sinai, "if your hands were stained with manure, would you dare to use them to touch the king's garments? You would not even touch your own clothes with dirty hands; you would clean

let there be thanksgiving. [5]Be sure of this, that no fornicator or impure man, or one who is covetous (that is, an idolater), has any inheritance in the kingdom of Christ and of God. [6]Let no one deceive you with empty words, for it is because of these things that the wrath of God comes upon the sons of disobedience. [7]Therefore do not associate with them,

1 Cor 6:9f
Col 3:5
Col 2:4–8

---

them first and then dry them carefully, and then touch things. Well then, why do you not give God the same honour as you show miserable clothes?" (*Sermon on the Holy Synaxis*).

"Take special care of chastity and also of the other virtues which go with it—modesty and refinement. They are as it were the safeguard of chastity. Don't take lightly those norms of conduct which help so much to keep us worthy in the sight of God: a watchful guard over our senses and our heart; the courage—the courage to be a 'coward'—to flee from occasions of sin; going to the sacraments frequently, particularly to the sacrament of Confession; complete sincerity in personal spiritual direction; sorrow, contrition and reparation after one's falls. And all this imbued with a tender devotion to our Lady to have her obtain for us from God the gift of a clean and holy life" (St Josemaría Escrivá, *Friends of God*, 185).

**5:5–7.** The Christian also has to fight against covetousness and greed, vices which make one a slave to power and money, which can become a kind of idol (cf. Mt 6:24). When using the things of this world, the Christian must avoid growing attached to them: "The Lord does not command us to demolish our house and have no truck with money. What he does desire is that we remove from our soul the priority given to possessions, uncontrolled greed and desire for riches, the cares, the thorns of this life, which smother the seed of the true life" (Clement of Alexandria, *Quis dives salvetur*, 11). Economic affairs are in fact a channel whereby the spirit of the Gospel can exert an influence on private and public life. "Christians engaged actively in modern economic and social progress and in the struggle for justice and charity must be convinced that they have much to contribute to the prosperity of mankind and to world peace. Let them, as individuals and as members of groups, give a shining example to others. Endowed with the skill and experience so absolutely necessary for them, let them preserve a proper sense of values in their earthly activity in loyalty to Christ and his Gospel, in order that their lives, individual as well as social, may be inspired by the spirit of the Beatitudes, and in particular by the spirit of poverty.

"Anyone who in obedience to Christ seeks first the Kingdom of God will derive from it a stronger and purer love for helping all his brethren and for accomplishing the task of justice under the inspiration of charity. (For the right use of goods according to the teaching of the New Testament cf. Lk 3:11; 10:30ff; 11:41; Mk 8:36; 12:29–31; 1 Pet 5:3; Jas 5:1–6; 1 Tim 6:8; Eph 4:28; 2 Cor 8:13; 1 Jn 3:17–18.)" (Vatican II, *Gaudium et spes*, 72).

### Walking in the light

Jn 12:36
1 Pet 2:9

8for once you were darkness, but now you are light in the Lord;
walk as children of light 9(for the fruit of light is found in all that
is good and right and true), 10and try to learn what is pleasing to
the Lord. 11Take no part in the unfruitful works of darkness, but

---

**5:8–9.** In contrast to the Christian's previous situation, which St Paul describes as "darkness", he now goes on to speak about the proper course for a believer, for someone enlightened by faith. The Christian is in a different position from that of a pagan; he knows our Lord Jesus Christ and he has a new way of thinking: he is a "child of light", because Christ has given him insight into the criteria which should govern his behaviour. In his new life, he should be light; he has been reborn to be the "light of the world" (cf. Mt 5:14–16; Jn 1:5; 8:12), a pursuer of all that is good and right and true; this means that he has a new way of being and thinking and acting, and is an example and a help to those around him. There is no room for excuses when what is at stake is the salvation of souls to whom we could be giving a helping hand: "Do not say, I cannot help others," St John Chrysostom preached; "if you are truly a Christian, it is impossible for you not to be able to do so [...]. If we act properly, every thing else will follow as a natural consequence. Christians' light cannot be hidden, a lamp so brilliant cannot fail to be seen" (*Hom. on Acts*, 20).

**5:10.** Created in the image and likeness of God, man is guided by reason, which can lead him to recognize his Creator and shape his life in line with the moral law God has impressed upon creation itself. He should always be trying to grow in wisdom and knowledge: that is an essential feature of the human spirit. The Second Vatican Council explained this in these terms: "The intellectual nature of man finds at last its perfection, as it should, in wisdom, which gently draws the human mind to look for and to love what is true and good. Filled with wisdom man is led through visible realities to those which cannot be seen" (*Gaudium et spes*, 15). If a person uses his natural intellect properly, it will bring him closer to God; moreover, the light of faith gives one a supernatural capacity to obtain better insight into the nature of God and his plans, and greater discernment as to what to do to please God.

A person who is in love tries to discover what the loved one likes, in order to do what pleases the loved one. The love of God should also lead one to prove that love with deeds, and not leave it at the level of words. If one is to offer God actions which are pleasing to him, one needs to have a good grasp of his commandments, of Christian doctrine and moral teaching. A first sign of the sincerity of a person's love of God is the effort he makes to obtain good spiritual and doctrinal training; that shows that he is at least making an effort in the right direction.

**5:11–13.** By his word and example, a Christian sheds light on all human realities, and thereby helps others to distinguish right from wrong. Anything that becomes visible is "light": that is, when things are properly identified—when good is shown to be good, and evil exposed for what it is (charitably but unambiguously)—the result is to dispel the confusion and moral relativism which does such harm to society. Hence the

instead expose them. [12]For it is a shame even to speak of the Rom 1:24
things that they do in secret; [13]but when anything is exposed by Jn 3:20f
the light it becomes visible, for anything that becomes visible is
light. [14]Therefore it is said, Is 26:19; 60:1

> "Awake, O sleeper, and arise from the dead, Rom 13:11
> and Christ shall give you light."*

[15]Look carefully then how you walk, not as unwise men but as Col 4:5
wise, [16]making the most of the time, because the days are evil.
[17]Therefore do not be foolish, but understand what the will of the Rom 12:2

---

Second Vatican Council's exhortation to all Christians, especially lay people: "At a time when new questions are being put and when grave errors aiming at undermining religion, the moral order and human society itself are rampant, the Council earnestly exhorts the laity to take a more active part, each according to his or her talents and knowledge and in fidelity to the mind of the Church, in the explanation and defence of Christian principles and in the correct application of them to the problems of our times" (*Apostolicam actuositatem*, 6).

**5:14.** St Paul seems to be quoting from an early liturgical hymn, which depicts Baptism as true enlightenment (cf. Heb 6:4; 10:32). By their good works—the light of the world—Christians can help "the dead", that is, those separated from God by sin, to move out of darkness into the light, where they will attain through Baptism that new life which membership of Christ brings. The Apostle is comparing this situation to the luminous clarity a person obtains when he awakens from a deep sleep, in contrast to the profound darkness experienced by one who remains asleep. A sinner's conversion is the equivalent of rising up out of the sleep of death into a new existence, life in a new world illuminated by Christ, who possesses and radiates the glorious light of God (cf. Heb 1:3).

**5:15–17.** The new life received in Baptism is characterized by a wisdom which contrasts with the foolishness of those who are bent on turning their backs on God (cf. 1 Cor 1:18). This wisdom, this sanity, stems from one's knowledge of the will of God and full identification with his plans. When a person's life is coherent with his faith, true wisdom is the result; and this immediately leads him to "make the most of the time" ("redeeming the time", in the famous words of the King James version). In fact, we have to make up for lost time. "Redeeming the time", St Augustine explains, "means sacrificing, when the need arises, present interests in favour of eternal ones, thereby purchasing eternity with the coin of time" (*Sermon* 16, 2).

The word *kairós*, translated as "time", has a more specific meaning in Greek. It refers to the content of the point in time in which we find ourselves, the situation which it creates, and the opportunities which that very moment offers as regards the ultimate purpose of this life. Hence, "making the most of the time" is saying much more than "not wasting a minute": it means "using every situation and every moment" to give glory to God. For,

Prov 23:30f Lk 21:34

Lord is. 18And do not get drunk with wine, for that is debauchery;
but be filled with the Spirit, 19addressing one another in psalms

---

"time is a treasure that melts away," St Josemaría Escrivá reminds us. "It escapes from us, slipping through our fingers like water through the mountain rocks. Tomorrow will soon be another yesterday. Our lives are so very short. Yesterday has gone and today is passing by. But what a great deal can be done for the love of God in this short space of time!" (*Friends of God*, 52).

This is a particularly pressing matter, "because the days are evil", as the Apostle puts it. St Peter makes the same point: "Be sober, be watchful. Your adversary the devil prowls around like a roaring lion, seeking someone to devour. Resist him, firm in your faith, knowing that the same experience of suffering is required of your brotherhood throughout the world" (1 Pet 5:8–9).

**5:18.** This verse is an invitation to temperance. In a pagan environment, so easily to be found then and now, one often meets people who think that happiness and joy can be attained simply through material things. Nothing could be further from the truth. St Paul identifies the source of true happiness—docility to the action of the Holy Spirit in one's soul. This docility gives a peace and a joy which the world is incapable of providing.

Temperance is "the virtue which holds our passions and desires in check, especially the sensual ones, and which brings us to moderation in using temporal goods" (*St Pius X Catechism*, 917). This virtue expresses man's lordship over everything that God has made, and its practice is essential if one is to see life from the correct, supernatural, perspective. "Any food excessive to the body's needs eventually stimulates impurity. A soul in this position, sated with food, cannot wear the bridle of temperance. So, it is not just wine that intoxicates the mind. Any kind of excessive eating renders it dull and easily influenced and completely undermines its purity and integrity" (Cassian, *Institutions*, 5, 6).

Temperance is a sign of the genuineness of the Christian life of the "children of light", and it is something that attracts and wins over all naturally noble people. "Temperance makes the soul sober, modest, understanding. It fosters a natural sense of reserve which everyone finds attractive because it denotes intelligent self-control. Temperance implies not narrowness but greatness of soul" (St Josemaría Escrivá, *Friends of God*, 84).

**5:19.** From the very beginning of the Church, Christian liturgy has expressed its appreciation to God through psalms, hymns and spiritual canticles. Because man is made up of body and soul, proper worship of God needs to have a certain external expression. "God has disposed that 'while recognizing God in visible form we may through him be wrapt to the love of things invisible' (Christmas preface). Moreover it is natural that the outpourings of the soul should be expressed by the senses" (Pius XII, *Mediator Dei*, 8). In the Church's liturgical ceremonies, canticles are a form of celebration of the greatness of God, and an expression of gratitude for blessings received. For their part, "in the psalms there is an opportunity for the people to bless and praise God; the psalms express the admiration that people feel and what the people want to say; in them the Church speaks, the faith is professed in a

and hymns and spiritual songs, singing and making melody to the
Lord with all your heart, 20always and for everything giving Col 3:17f
thanks in the name of our Lord Jesus Christ to God the Father.

**Marriage compared to Christ's union with the Church**

21Be subject to one another out of reverence for Christ. 22Wives, 1 Pet 5:5 Col 3:18
be subject to your husbands, as to the Lord. 23For the husband is 1 Cor 11:3 1 Pet 3:1–7

---

melodious way, and authority finds a ready acceptance; there too is heard the joyful call of freedom, the cry of pleasure and the sound of happiness" (St Ambrose, *Enarratio in Psalmos* 1, 9).

Dignified recital and chant of liturgical prayers makes for active participation of the faithful in liturgical ceremonies, allowing everyone to share what St Augustine tells us was his experience: "I wept at the beauty of your hymns and canticles, and was powerfully moved by the sweet sound of your Church's singing. Those sounds flowed into my ears, and the truth streamed into my heart—so that my feeling of devotion overflowed, and the tears poured from my eyes, and I was happy in them" (*Confessions*, 9, 6).

Liturgical prayer in this way becomes a source of genuine fervour and piety, while at the same time promoting solidarity with other members of the Church, not only those who praise God while still on their earthly pilgrimage, but also those who unceasingly glorify him in heaven. "What a wonderful thing it is to imitate on earth the choir of the angels!", St Basil explains; "preparing oneself for prayer at the first hour of the day and glorifying the Creator with hymns and praise. And later, when the sun is at its height, full of splendour and light, doing one's work to the accompaniment of prayer on all sides, seasoning one's actions, so to speak, with the salt of ejaculatory prayers" (*Epistle*, 2, 3).

**5:20.** We need to be continually thanking God, "for everything works for good with those who love (God)" (Rom 8:28) or, in another version, "everything helps to secure the good of those who love God" (Knox). Everything that happens in life falls within the providence of God. He permits us to experience sorrows and joys, successes and failures. Therefore, for a Christian who acts in line with his faith, everything is success, even things which in human terms he may find negative and painful; for, if he views disagreeable things in a supernatural way and approaches them with love for Christ's cross, they bring him joy and peace and merit. That is why we should always be grateful to God: "Get used to lifting your heart to God, in acts of thanksgiving, many times a day. Because he gives you this and that. Because you have been despised. Because you haven't what you need or because you have [...]. Thank him for everything, because everything is good" (St Josemaría Escrivá, *The Way*, 268).

**5:21.** St Paul here provides a general principle which should govern relationships among members of the Church: they should submit to one another, knowing that Christ is their true judge. At the same time, the Apostle uses this principle to say something about relationships in society, specifically family relationships; in

the head of the wife as Christ is the head of the church, his body,
and is himself its Saviour. 24As the church is subject to Christ, so

---

these there is an element of natural dependence—of wife on husband (5:22–24), of children on parents (6:1–4), and of servants on masters (6:5–9). However, although there is an inbuilt natural element of authority in these situations, the Apostle sees it as having a new dimension in the Christian context, for he is acutely conscious of the dignity that belongs to each, and of Christ's lordship over all.

**5:22–24.** The basis of the supernatural grandeur and dignity of Christian marriage lies in the fact that it is an extension of the union between Christ and his Church. To exhort Christian married couples to live in accordance with their membership of the Church, the Apostle establishes an analogy whereby the husband represents Christ and the wife the Church. This teaching has its roots in the Old Testament, where the relationships between Yahweh and his people are expressed, in the preaching of the prophets, in terms of the relationships between husband and wife. The husband loves his wife truly, he is completely faithful to her (Hos 1:3; Jer 2:20; Ezek 16:1–34). God is forever faithful to the love he has shown Israel, and he is ever ready to pardon her (cf. Is 54:5–8; 62:4–5; Jer 31:21–22) and to re-establish his Covenant with the people (cf. Is 16:5–63). Jesus also describes himself as the bridegroom (cf. Mt 9:15; Jn 3:29) and he uses the image of the wedding banquet to explain the significance of his coming (cf. Mt 22:1–14; 25:1–13). He brings into being the New Covenant, which gives rise to the new people of God, the Church (cf. Mt 26:26–29 and par.); and so the relationship between Christ and the Church appears in the New Testament in terms of husband-wife; as the Second Vatican Council put it, "The Church is also [...] described as the spotless spouse of the spotless Lamb (Rev 19:7; 21:2, 9; 22:17). It is she whom Christ 'loved and for whom he delivered himself up that he might sanctify her' (Eph 5:26). It is she whom he unites to himself by an unbreakable alliance, and whom he constantly 'nourishes and cherishes' (Eph 5:29). It is she whom, once purified, he willed to be joined to himself, subject in love and fidelity (cf. Eph 5:24)" (*Lumen gentium*, 6).

St Paul is not just using Christian marriage as a comparison to explain Christ's relationship with the Church: he is saying that that relationship is actually symbolized and verified between Christian husband and wife. This means that marriage between baptized people is a true sacrament, as the Church has always taught and as Vatican II has repeated: "Christ our Lord has abundantly blessed this love, which is rich in its various features, coming as it does from the spring of divine love and modelled on Christ's own union with the Church. Just as of old God encountered his people with a covenant of love and fidelity, so our Saviour, the spouse of the Church, now encounters Christian spouses through the sacrament of marriage. He abides with them in order that by their mutual self-giving spouses will love each other with enduring fidelity, as he loved the Church and delivered himself for it. Authentic married love is caught up into divine love and is directed and enriched by the redemptive power of Christ and the salvific action of the Church, with the result that the spouses are effectively led to God and are helped and strengthened in their lofty role as fathers and mothers" (*Gaudium et spes*, 48).

When St Paul exhorts wives to be "subject" to their husbands, he is not only taking into account the social position of women at the time but also the fact that a Christian wife, by the way she relates to her husband, should reflect the Church itself, in its obedience to Christ. The husband, for his part, is asked to be similarly submissive to his wife, for he is a reflection of Jesus Christ, who gave himself up even to death out of love for the Church (cf. v. 25). In 1930 Pope Pius XI taught that "the submission of the wife neither ignores nor suppresses the liberty to which her dignity as a human person and her noble functions as wife, mother, and companion give her the full right. It does not oblige her to yield indiscriminately to all the desires of her husband, which may be unreasonable or incompatible with her wifely dignity. Nor does it mean that she is on a level with persons who in law are called minors, and who are ordinarily denied the unrestricted exercise of their rights on the ground of their immature judgment and inexperience. But it does forbid such abuse of freedom as would neglect the welfare of the family; it refuses, in this body which is the family, to allow the heart to be separated from the head, with great detriment to the body itself and even with risk of disaster. If the husband is the head of the domestic body, then the wife is its heart; and as the first holds the primacy of authority, so the second can and ought to claim the primacy of love" (*Casti connubii*, 10).

Thus, in contrast with the low regard in which women were held in the East in ancient times (when they were in general seen as lesser mortals), Christian teaching recognizes the essential equality of man and woman: "Above all it is important to underline the equal dignity and responsibility of women with men. This equality is realized in a unique manner in that reciprocal self-giving by each one to the other and by both to the children which is proper to marriage and the family. What human reason intuitively perceives and acknowledges is fully revealed by the word of God: the history of salvation, in fact, is a continuous and luminous testimony to the dignity of women.

"In creating the human race 'male and female' (Gen 1:27), God gives man and woman an equal personal dignity, endowing them with the inalienable rights and responsibilities proper to the human person. God then manifests the dignity of women in the highest form possible, by assuming human flesh from the Virgin Mary, whom the Church honours as the Mother of God, calling her the new Eve and presenting her as the model of redeemed woman. The sensitive respect of Jesus towards the women whom he called to his following and his friendship, his appearing on Easter morning to a woman before the other disciples, the mission entrusted to women to carry the good news of the Resurrection to the Apostles—these are all signs that confirm the special esteem of the Lord Jesus for women" (John Paul II, *Familiaris consortio*, 22).

St Josemaría Escrivá provides another summary of this teaching: "Women, like men, possess the dignity of being persons and children of God. Nevertheless, on this basis of fundamental equality, each must achieve what is appropriate to him or her [...]. Women are called to bring to the family, to society and to the Church characteristics which are their own and which they alone can give—their gentle warmth and untiring generosity, their love for detail, their quick-wittedness and intuition, their simple and deep piety, their constancy ..." (*Conversations*, 87).

let wives also be subject in everything to their husbands.
Col 3:19 [25]Husbands, love your wives, as Christ loved the church and gave
1 Pet 3:7 himself up for her, [26]that he might sanctify her, having cleansed
Ps 45:14 her by the washing of water with the word, [27]that he might present
2 Cor 11:2 the church to himself in splendour, without spot or wrinkle or any
Rev 19:7f such thing, that she might be holy and without blemish. [28]Even so

---

**5:25–27.** Love between husband and wife is also founded on Christ's love for his Church. New Testament revelation fixes this high standard for a husband's love for his wife because the model for this life is nothing less than Christ's love for the Church. St Paul, in fact, expresses this in terms of a betrothed couple, with the bride all dressed up to be presented to the groom: Christ similarly sanctifies and purifies, through Baptism, those who are going to become members of his Church. The sacrament of Baptism, reflected in the words "by the washing of water with the word", applies that redemption which Jesus has brought about through his sacrifice on the cross.

**5:27.** "The Church", Vatican II teaches, "[...] is held, as a matter of faith, to be unfailingly holy. This is because Christ, the Son of God, who with the Father and the Spirit is hailed as 'alone holy,' loved the Church as his Bride, giving himself up for her so as to sanctify her (cf. Eph 5:25–26); he joined her to himself as his body and endowed her with the gift of the Holy Spirit for the glory of God. Therefore all in the Church, whether they belong to the hierarchy or are cared for by it, are called to holiness, according to the Apostle's saying: 'For this is the will of God, your sanctification' (1 Thess 4:3; cf. Eph 1:4). This holiness of the Church is constantly shown forth in the fruits of grace which the Spirit produces in the faithful and so it must be; it is expressed in many ways by the individuals who, each in his own state of life, tend to the perfection of love, thus sanctifying others" (*Lumen gentium*, 39).

**5:28–32.** St Paul alludes to the text of Genesis 2:24 which has to do with marriage as an institution and applies it to Christ and the Church. He thereby teaches that marriage, as established by God from the beginning, is already in some way saved, because it is a kind of reflection and symbol of God's love for mankind.

"Receiving and meditating faithfully on the word of God, the Church has solemnly taught and continues to teach that the marriage of the baptized is one of the seven sacraments of the New Covenant [...].

"By virtue of the sacramentality of their marriage, spouses are bound to one another in the most profoundly indissoluble manner. Their belonging to each other is the real representation, by means of the sacramental sign, of the very relationship of Christ with the Church.

"Spouses are therefore the permanent reminder to the Church of what happened on the Cross; they are for one another and for the children witnesses to the salvation in which the sacrament makes them sharers" (John Paul II, *Familiaris consortio*, 13).

The vocation of marriage is, then, a true way of holiness. The founder of Opus Dei was always very emphatic about this: "For a Christian, marriage is not just a social institution, much less a mere remedy for human weakness. It is a genuine supernatural calling. A great sacrament, in Christ and in the Church, says St Paul (Eph 5:32). At the same

husbands should love their wives as their own bodies. He who
loves his wife loves himself. [29]For no man ever hates his own
flesh, but nourishes and cherishes it, as Christ does the church,
[30]because we are members of his body. [31]"For this reason a man 1 Cor 6:15f
shall leave his father and mother and be joined to his wife, and the Gen 2:24
two shall become one flesh." [32]This mystery is a profound one, Mt 19:5
and I mean in reference to Christ and the church; [33]however, let Rom 16:23ff
each one of you love his wife as himself, and let the wife see that
she respects her husband.

**Advice to children and parents**

6 [1]Children, obey your parents in the Lord, for this is right. Col 3:20f
[2]"Honour your father and mother" (this is the first command- Ex 20:12

---

time, it is a permanent contract between a man and a woman. Whether we like it or not, marriage instituted by Christ cannot be dissolved. It is a sacred sign that sanctifies an action of Jesus whereby he helps the souls of those who marry and invites them to follow him transforming their whole married life into an occasion for God's presence on earth" (*Christ Is Passing By*, 23).

The holiness of their family and of those connected with it is very much a function of the holiness of the married couple: "But they must not forget that the secret of married happiness lies in everyday things, not in daydreams. It lies in discovering the hidden joy of coming home in the evening; in affectionate relations with their children; in everyday work in which the whole family cooperates; in good humour in the face of difficulties that should be met with a sporting spirit; in making the best use of all the advances that civilization offers to help us bring up children, to make the house pleasant and life more simple" (St Josemaría Escrivá, *Conversations*, 91). See the note on Col 3:18–19.

**5:31.** On the indissolubility of marriage see the notes on Mt 5:31–32; Mk 10:1–12; 10:5–9; Lk 16:18; 1 Cor 7:10–11.

**6:1–4.** St Paul now goes on to deal with parent-children relationships. He recalls the fourth commandment (the first of the commandments to do with our neighbour) to which a promise of blessing is attached for those who keep it (cf. Ex 20:12; Deut 5:16). Honouring one's parents means loving and obeying them, as is right, and caring for them spiritually and materially when their age or circumstances so require. To those who keep this commandment, the Lord promises happiness and a long life on earth.

"In the Lord": although these words are missing from some early codexes, there is no doubt about their authenticity. They locate parent-children relationships on a supernatural plane. In the last analysis, obedience of children to parents is a divine commandment, which justice demands be kept. Parents, for their part, are called to be understanding with their children, and to educate them in a truly Christian way: discipline and instruction should always be motivated by a desire for their good.

"As it is the parents who have given life to their children, on them lies the gravest obligation of educating their family. They must therefore be recognized as being primarily and principally

Deut 5:16 ment with a promise), 3"that it may be well with you and that you
Col 3:21 may live long on the earth." 4Fathers, do not provoke your
children to anger, but bring them up in the discipline and
instruction of the Lord.

---

responsible for their education. The role of parents in education is of such importance that it is almost impossible to provide an adequate substitute. It is therefore the duty of parents to create a family atmosphere inspired by love and devotion to God and their fellow-men which will promote an integrated, personal and social education of their children [...] which are necessary to every society. It is therefore above all in the Christian family, enriched by the grace and the responsibility of the sacrament of matrimony, that children should be taught to know and worship God and to love their neighbour, in accordance with the faith which they have received in earliest infancy in the sacrament of Baptism [...]. Finally it is through the family that they are gradually initiated into association with their fellow-men in civil life and as members of the people of God" (Vatican II, *Gravissimum educationis*, 3).

"Therefore the responsibility and consequently also the right of educating children comes to the family direct from the Creator. It is a right which cannot be surrendered, because it is combined with a very serious responsibility; it is therefore prior to any right of the civil society or the State and for that reason may not be infringed by any power on earth.

"The sacred character of this right is thus shown by St Thomas Aquinas: 'The son is by nature something of the father ... : and so the law of nature requires that until it reaches the use of reason the child shall be under the father's care. It would therefore be against natural justice if before reaching the use of reason the child were removed from the parents' charge or if any disposition were made concerning it against the parents' will' (*Summa theologiae* 2–2, 10, 12). And since the parents' obligation to exercise this care persists until the offspring is capable of looking after itself, it is evident that their inviolable right to educate their offspring continues until that time. 'For nature', says St Thomas, 'intends not only the generation of offspring but also its development and progress to the state of man as man, that is, to the state of virtue' (ibid., Supplement, 41, 1)" (Pius XI, *Divini illius magistri*).

Parents must not abuse their authority nor should their children obey them if asked to do anything that is against the moral law. Therefore, parents may not make unreasonable demands. The Apostle warns about this when he says, "do not provoke your children to anger" (v. 4). Christian education, therefore, must be based on charity, on affection and on parents' sensitive respect of their children's freedom. "The parents are the main persons responsible for the education of their children, in human as well as in spiritual matters. They should be conscious of the extent of their responsibility. To fulfil it, they need prudence, understanding, a capacity for teaching and loving and a concern for giving good example. Imposing things by force, in an authoritarian manner, is not the right way to teach. The ideal attitude of parents lies more in becoming their children's friends—friends who will be willing to share their anxieties, who will listen to their problems, who will help them in an effec-

**Advice to servants and masters**

[5]Slaves, be obedient to those who are your earthly masters, with Col 3:22
fear and trembling, in singleness of heart, as to Christ; [6]not in the Tit 2:9
way of eye-service, as men-pleasers, but as servants[f] of Christ, 1 Pet 2:18

---

tive and agreeable way" (St Josemaría Escrivá, *Christ Is Passing By*, 27). See the note on Col 3:20–21.

**6:5–9.** In St Paul's time labour relations were largely based on slavery. He does not directly denounce slavery, but he uses this letter to establish the correct basis for the master–servant relationship. By emphasizing the dignity of the human person, the Apostle is clearly teaching that human relationships are to be raised to a supernatural level, that is, made to involve Christ. Hence masters must be just towards servants, not coercing them by threats, for all—masters as well as servants—have one and the same Lord on high, "with whom there is no partiality" (v. 9). On the other hand, slaves should work not merely because they expect a human reward or, as it were, are resigned to their fate: they should render "service with a good will as to the Lord and not to men" (v. 7). This teaching established conditions which, centuries later, would lead to the abolition of slavery when the spirit of Christianity imbued the whole gamut of human relationships, including those to do with work.

The Church's social teaching has projected the light of faith and charity onto the world of work, thereby fulfilling an essential role in the building of a more human and more Christian society. Thus, for example, the Magisterium teaches that "even though a state of things be pictured in which everyone will receive at last all that is his due, a wide field will always remain open for charity. For justice alone, however faithfully observed, though it can indeed remove the cause of social strife, can never bring about a union of hearts and minds [...]. Only when all sectors of society have the intimate conviction that they are members of one great family, and children of the same heavenly Father [...] will it be possible to unite all in harmonious striving for the common good [...]. Then the rich and others in power will change their former neglect of their poorer brethren into solicitious and effective love, will listen readily to their just demands, and will willingly forgive them the faults and mistakes they may possibly make. The workers too will lay aside all feelings of hatred or envy, which the instigators of social strife exploit so skilfully. Not only will they cease to feel discontent at the position assigned them by divine providence in human society; they will become proud of it, well aware that they are working usefully and honourably for the common good, each according to his office and function and following more closely in the footsteps of him who, being God, chose to become a tradesman among men, and to be known as 'the son of the tradesman'" (Pius XI, *Quadragesimo anno*, 56).

More recently, John Paul II has reminded us that "work is *a key*, probably *the essential key*, to the whole social question, if we try to see that question really from the point of view of man's good" (*Laborem exercens*, 3). In this connexion he makes it clear that "work is a good thing for man—a good thing for

**f.** Or *slaves*

doing the will of God from the heart, 7rendering service with a
good will as to the Lord and not to men, 8knowing that whatever
good any one does, he will receive the same again from the Lord,
Acts 10:34 whether he is a slave or free. 9Masters, do the same to them, and
Col 4:1 forbear threatening, knowing that he who is both their Master and
yours is in heaven, and that there is no partiality with him.

**Weapons for spiritual combat**

1 Cor 16:13 1 Jn 2:14 10Finally, be strong in the Lord and in the strength of his might.
11Put on the whole armour of God, that you may be able to stand
2 Cor 10:14 against the wiles of the devil. 12For we are not contending against
1 Pet 5:8 flesh and blood, but against the principalities, against the powers,
against the world rulers of this present darkness, against the
spiritual hosts of wickedness in the heavenly places. 13Therefore

---

his humanity—because through work man *not only transforms nature*, adapting it to his own needs, but he also *achieves fulfilment* as a human being and indeed, in a sense, becomes 'more a human being'" (ibid., 9).

"It is time for us Christians to shout from the rooftops that work is a gift from God and that it makes no sense to classify people differently, according to their occupation, as if some jobs were nobler than others. Work, all work, bears witness to the dignity of man, to his dominion over creation. It is an opportunity to develop one's personality. It is a bond of solidarity with others ..." (St Josemaría Escrivá, *Christ Is Passing By*, 47).

**6:10–20.** After these counsels to parents and children, servants and masters, the Apostle says something very important: all need to be prepared to struggle "against the principalities" of this world (v. 12). He is referring to those angels who rebelled against God and whom Christ has already overcome (1 Cor 15:24; Col 1:13–14; 2:15), but against whom we still have to contend. This is a struggle which must be pursued to the end: Paul uses language to do with the armour and weapons of Roman soldiers to describe the form this combat must take. First he recommends that they put on the "armour of God" (v. 13), for the "world rulers" who have to be striven against can be defeated only with spiritual weapons, which God supplies to those who love him—truth, righteousness, peace, faith (vv. 14–16), not forgetting the need for constant prayer moved by the Spirit (v. 18) and a strong sense of brotherhood.

These weapons, since they are supernatural, are a guarantee of victory and therefore they enable one to engage in the struggle cheerfully and confidently. "Let us be filled with confidence", St John Chrysostom exhorts, "and let us discard everything so as to be able to meet this onslaught. Christ has equipped us with weapons more splendid than gold, more resistant than steel, weapons more fiery than any flame and lighter than the slightest breeze [...]. These are weapons of a totally new kind, for they have been forged for a previously unheard-of type of combat. I, who am a mere man, find myself called upon to deal blows to demons; I, who am clothed in flesh, find myself at war with incorporeal powers. God has designed for me also an armour

take the whole armour of God, that you may be able to withstand
in the evil day, and having done all, to stand. [14]Stand therefore, Is 11:5 Lk 12:35
having girded your loins with truth, and having put on the 1 Thess 5:8
breastplate of righteousness, [15]and having shod your feet with the Is 40:3–9; 52:7
equipment of the gospel of peace; [16]besides all these, taking the
shield of faith, with which you can quench all the flaming darts of 1 Jn 5:4
the evil one. [17]And take the helmet of salvation, and the sword of Rom 8:26f
the Spirit, which is the word of God. [18]Pray at all times in the Col 4:2
Spirit, with all prayer and supplication. To that end keep alert with
all perseverance, making supplication for all the saints, [19]and also Rom 15:30
for me, that utterance may be given me in opening my mouth 2 Thess 3:1
boldly to proclaim the mystery of the gospel, [20]for which I am an
ambassador in chains; that I may declare it boldly, as I ought to 2 Cor 5:20
speak.

---

made, not of metal, but of justice; he has designed for me a shield not of bronze but of faith. I hold in my hand a keen sword, the word of the Spirit [...]. Your victory must be that of a man who rests content" (*Baptismal Catechesis*, 3, 11–12).

St Paul, who is here writing from prison, in chains (v. 20) and in need of the help of God and of all his brethren in the faith, asks them to pray for him (v. 19), so that he may freely and effectively preach the Gospel.

**6:16.** The devil never ceases to try to find ways to bring about man's eternal damnation. But once overcome by Christ on the cross he has no longer any real power over us provided we use in our struggle against him the weapons provided by faith and complete trust in God. St John of Avila argues in this way: "Since this enemy is stronger than we are, we must avail of the 'shield of faith', which is something supernatural, whether it be by using a word of God, or receiving the sacraments or (countering the devil with) a doctrine of the Church. We need to believe firmly with our mind that all our strength comes from God" (*Audi, filia*, 30).

**6:18.** Prayer is our outstanding supernatural resource for fighting the wiles of the enemy, "Prayer is, beyond doubt, the most powerful weapon the Lord gives us to conquer evil passions and temptations of the devil; but we must really put ourselves into our prayer: it is not enough just to say the words, it must come from the heart. And also prayer needs to be continuous, we must pray no matter what kind of situation we find ourselves in: the warfare we are engaged in is on-going, so our prayer must be on-going also [...]. The Apostle adds 'for all the saints', because we should not only pray for ourselves but for the perseverance of all the faithful in the grace of God" (St Alphonsus, *Thoughts on the Passion*, 9, 3).

The Apostle also identifies, as a supernatural resource in this struggle, a solicitous care for the holiness of others. It is quite likely that this concern will lead us to notice defects as well as virtues in our neighbour. This should not cause us to look down on him or criticize him, but rather to pray for him and help him improve. "If you notice some defect in your friend," St Ambrose recommends, "correct him privately; if he fails to listen to you, take him to task openly. For

**Conclusion and blessing**

Acts 20:4 [21]Now that you also may know how I am and what I am doing,
Col 4:7 Tychicus the beloved brother and faithful minister in the Lord will
2 Tim 4:12 tell you everything. [22]I have sent him to you for this very purpose,
that you may know how we are, and that he may encourage your
hearts.
[23]Peace be to the brethren, and love with faith, from God the
1 Pet 1:8 Father and the Lord Jesus Christ. [24]Grace be with all who love
our Lord Jesus Christ with love undying.

---

corrections are helpful and they are much more useful that a mute friendship. If your friend feels offended, you should still correct him; do not be afraid to insist on the point, even if the bitter taste of correction does not appeal to him. It is written in the Book of Proverbs: 'Faithful are the wounds of a friend, profuse the kisses of an enemy'" (*De officiis ministrorum*, 3, chap. 12, 127).

**6:21–22.** These verses are the only verses in the letter which contain personal references; on them—especially the expression "you also" in v. 21—is based the opinion of those who think that news of this letter had already been communicated to other churches. It is possible that there is a reference here to the letter sent to the Colossians, which was written prior to Ephesians and in which there is a noticeably close parallel to this passage (cf. Col 4:7–8).

**6:23–24.** This final blessing, which is very formal and in the third person, appears to be addressed to Christians in general. Peace and grace, which are usually joined in the same phrase in Pauline letters, are separated here. The word "undying" at the end may refer to Christians who love Christ and already enjoy here on earth an anticipation of the glory of heaven; or else to the faithful who already enjoy the vision of Christ in eternal glory.

# Introduction to the Letter to the Philippians

## THE CITY OF PHILIPPI

Philippi was quite an important city in St Paul's time, both commercially and from an historical point of view. It was in Macedonia, on the border with Thrace, on the Via Egnatia, the Roman road which ran east-west through those two regions, and anyone travelling from Asia Minor to Greece would have stopped there. It was built on a hill, very close to the sea, overlooking a delightful valley. There, in the fourth century BC, Philip of Macedon, the father of Alexander the Great, had built a fortified camp, which was called after him. In 168 BC it was overrun by the Romans, and in 42 BC Augustus established it as the Colonia Iulia Augusta Philippensium and endowed it with the *ius italicum*, which meant that its inhabitants enjoyed the same rights and privileges as those of an Italian city.

In the middle of the first century AD, as is borne out by inscriptions which have been unearthed, at least half of the city's population were people of Roman origin and culture and very proud of their Roman citizenship (cf. Acts 16:21). Many had served with the armies of Rome and had settled in Philippi after they retired. The Jewish colony, however, must have been very small because they did not even have a synagogue (unlike almost every other large city); this meant that they had to meet on the riverside for their religious services and ritual ablutions (cf. Acts 16:13).

The church of Philippi was the first to be founded by St Paul when he came into Europe—during his second missionary journey, around the year 50 or 51. The Acts of the Apostles give a fairly detailed account of his visit. On a sabbath, shortly after arriving in the city, Paul, Silas, Timothy and Luke went to the place where the Jews used to meet; they preached to them there, and a woman called Lydia, a dealer in purple, was converted, along with all her family (cf. Acts 16:12–14). One day they cured a girl possessed by a spirit of divination (cf. Acts 16:15–18). This did not please her masters, who dragged Paul and Silas before the authorities. After appearing in court, they were beaten with rods and imprisoned (cf. Acts 16:19–24); but then, miraculously, they were set free (cf. Acts 16:25–39). They called on Lydia again and, once they had seen the brethren (cf. Acts 16:40), they set out for Thessalonica. St Paul may have visited Philippi twice during his third journey (cf. Acts 20:1–2; 20:3), but he does not seem to have stayed very long.

Given the background of the people of Philippi, most of the Christians would have been of Gentile origin. All, whether of Jewish or Gentile background, had great affection for St Paul and were very generous towards him. For his part, St Paul had great confidence in them, for only from them did he accept material help (cf. Phil 4:15). His letter demonstrates very clearly his deep affection for them: "I hold you in my heart" (Phil 1:7), "my brethren, whom I love and long for, my joy and my crown" (Phil 4:1).

## PAUL'S AUTHORSHIP OF THE LETTER

Some very early evidence supports the authenticity of this letter. In the first third of the second century, St Polycarp refers to it in his *Letter to the Philippians*: "Paul [...] when living among you clearly and steadfastly taught the word of truth to his contemporaries. And when he was absent he wrote you letters: by reading these attentively you will be able to strengthen yourselves in the faith that has been given to you."[1]

Not until the nineteenth century do we find certain scholars, non-Catholics, arguing that it was not written by St Paul. Modern research, however, has supported its Pauline authorship. It is in fact one of the epistles which most clearly reflects St Paul's personality and his inner feelings and desires.

## AN AMALGAM OF LETTERS?

The structure of this letter is not as well defined as that of other letters of the Apostle. This has led some scholars to think that it was not originally composed in the form that has come down to us, and that it is really an amalgam of three separate letters sent to the Philippians from different places and at different times. The first of these would be included as Philippians 4:10–20; the second, and most extensive piece, would correspond to Philippians 1:1—3:1 and some verses of chapter 4; the third would be the denouncement of the Judaizers in Philippians 3:2—4:1 and some verses of the last chapter. The arguments in support of this theory, or similar theories, are not compelling. It is quite possible for the writer of a letter as familiar in tone as this one to allow himself the freedom to move rapidly from one subject to another, from prayer to personal news, from exhortation to treatment of doctrinal matters which occur to him in the course of writing (rather than leave them for later); quite possible for him to convey greetings and discuss plans all in the one breath. The arguments in favour of the letter being an original, single, letter are at least as strong as those in favour of its being a combination of originally independent letters.

1. Chap. 3.

## THE REASON FOR THE LETTER

When St Paul was in prison, the Philippians, ever ready to help the Apostle, decided to send Epaphroditus—with gifts (cf. Phil 4:18)—to minister to his needs (cf. Phil 2:25). Epaphroditus, however, took ill while he was with Paul, and almost died; once he recovered, Paul decided to send him home, for the consolation of the Philippians (cf. Phil 2:26–30). He used the opportunity to send this letter, thanking the Philippians for their kindness and exhorting them to be ever more faithful to the Christian way of life; and in it he warns them about the Judaizers, who were everywhere sowing discord and making it difficult for the Gospel to progress.

## PLACE AND DATE OF COMPOSITION

This letter has traditionally been seen as written during St Paul's first imprisonment in Rome (in the years 61–63). This can be deduced from the letter itself if one takes in its most obvious sense Paul's reference to the praetorian guard (cf. Phil 1:13) and the greetings he sends on behalf of "those of Caesar's household" (Phil 4:22).

However, more and more scholars are coming round to the view that the letter was written in Ephesus, at a time when the Apostle was imprisoned in that city during his third journey, before he moved on again into Macedonia (sometime in 54–57). The reason why they say this is the impression contained in the letter that the Apostle and the Philippians were in fairly frequent contact with each other, which would be difficult to explain if the Apostle had been in Rome, which was a long way from Philippi.[2] It is also strange that he should speak about the Philippians not having had an opportunity to show him their affection since the time they had come to his aid in Thessalonica (cf. Phil 4:16, 10) because prior to being imprisoned in Rome he had visited Philippi twice, in the course of his third apostolic journey (cf. Acts 20:1–3). Furthermore, they add that certain expressions used in this letter[3] are more akin to the language of his "Great Epistles" than to that of the other Captivity Letters. The "praetorium", they suggest, can refer also to the palace of a provincial governor, and "those of Caesar's household" could perhaps refer to imperial officials, who were to be found in every province, and who were particularly numerous in Ephesus.

Research into all this is not sufficiently advanced to establish with any certainty whether the letter was written in Rome, during Paul's first imprisonment, or in Ephesus, some few years earlier.

**2.** Cf. Phil 2:19–24: this passage give the impression that St Paul is writing from somewhere relatively near Philippi, quite possibly from Ephesus. **3.** Superiority of God's righteousness over that of the law (Phil 3:9); the description of the frequent mention of the "day of Christ" (Phil 1:6, 10; 2:16; etc.).

The dating depends on which of these two possibilities one chooses; if in fact it was a letter from Rome, then all would agree that it was written in the period 62–63; if it was written in Ephesus, then it would have to be dated 54–57.

## STRUCTURE

The Letter to the Philippians is written in a personal, intimate style. This explains why it does not have a well defined structure and why it is not possible clearly to distinguish a dogmatic part and a moral part.

1. *Introduction* (1:1–26). The initial greeting, very simple in style (1:1–2), is similar to that in other Pauline epistles, but its tone is more familiar. It is followed by very affectionate words in which the Apostle thanks God for the Philippians' faithfulness to the Gospel and prays that they persevere in this way and grow in charity, righteousness and discernment (1:3–11).

It changes tone when he describes his conditions in prison. At this point he dwells on the positive results of his imprisonment as far as the spread of the Gospel is concerned (1:12–26).

2. *Teachings* (1:27—2:18). St Paul stresses the need for ascetical struggle, and offers himself as an example (1:27–30).

He exhorts them to be humble and of one mind and heart (2:1–4), following the Lord's example: this passage is a hymn which extols the humiliation and later exaltation of Christ as man (2:5–11); it is among the most explicit and profound testimonies in the New Testament to Christ's divinity and humanity.

Christ's admirable example should make Christians conduct themselves in a manner worthy of the children of God (2:12–18).

3. *Plans and news* (2:19–30). Then there is a sudden change of subject, not an unusual thing in a family letter; St Paul tells them that soon he will send Timothy (2:19–23), and that he hopes to be able himself to visit them shortly (2:24). However, for the moment he is sending Epaphroditus, whom they will be very happy to find fully recovered from his illness (2:25–30).

4. *The Christian life* (3:1—4:9). He warns the Philippians about harm being done to the faith by Judaizers (3:1–3). These were teaching that circumcision and keeping the Law of Moses were necessary for salvation (3:4–6), whereas what is really necessary is knowing Christ Jesus (3:7–8), because justification, righteousness, comes only through faith in Jesus Christ, not through fulfilment of the Mosaic Law (3:9–12).

The Apostle himself is striving to win the prize (3:12) and he invites his readers to do the same, by pressing on, optimistically, the way athletes do (3:13–16). They should be living now like citizens of heaven, imitating the example given them by our Lord and not that of the enemies of his cross (3:17–21).

This is followed by a further exhortation to perseverance (4:1), a call to two members of the Philippi community to bury their differences (4:2–3), and an invitation to rejoice (4:4–7) and to imitate his (Paul's) example (4:8–9).

5. *Thanksgiving and farewell* (4:10–23). He repeats his thanks for the kindness and help they have shown him through Epaphroditus; God will more than reward them for their generosity (4:10–20).

And then there are a few words of farewell at the end (4:21–23).

## DOCTRINAL CONTENT

The general tone of the epistle is more exhortative than doctrinal. In tender, familiar language St Paul gives his readers news about the progress of the Gospel. From his prison he encourages them to put his teachings into practice and to foster the growth of Christian virtues. Despite its brevity the letter does deal with important points of doctrine—the eternal destiny of man; the Christian's attitude to earthly realities; the profound mystery of Christ and the example of his life on earth.

1. *What the Christian vocation involves.* Even in this life the Christian can properly be called a "saint" (Phil 1:1) because of the sanctifying grace that is in him. However, this does not mean that he can claim to have reached definitive holiness, to be already "perfect" (Phil 3:12). St Paul shows the way that leads to this perfection—sharing in Christ's suffering and becoming like him in his death (cf. Phil 3:10–11).

Being a Christian, therefore, means being identified with Christ, trying to have "this mind among yourselves, which was in Christ Jesus" (Phil 2:5), following the example he set. He is our true model, and he is a perfect one, for he became "obedient unto death, even death on a cross" (Phil 2:8). The Christian who strives to be one with Christ will, like him, be exalted (cf. Phil 2:9) in the glory of heaven. Thus, whatever sufferings he experiences in this life, even the shedding of his blood if necessary, are a cause of joy for him (cf. Phil 2:17); for he knows that life, and the death of the body, makes for the glory of God if one is united to Christ (cf. Phil 1:20).

The Christian also possesses the hope—never disappointed (ibid.)—that his mortal body will become like Christ's glorious body (cf. Phil 3:21). This is what the Apostle means when he says that for him "to die is gain" (Phil 1:21) and that he yearns "to depart and be with Christ" (Phil 1:23). This apparent eagerness for death is very significant, because it means that one can enjoy Christ immediately after death, and not have to wait until the General Judgment: one simply needs to die in grace and to have done enough penance for one's sins.

"For me to live is Christ" (Phil 1:21), St Paul says; for the life of the new man is supported and nourished by the grace which our Lord won for him on the cross; and this grace leads him, furthermore, to accept the moral demands of the Gospel. Hence the Christian should always be striving to act fully in harmony with the teachings Christ has left him.

2. *The Christian in the world.* For the most part, Christians live in the world, rubbing shoulders with other people. With God's grace they should always act honourably, motivated by high ideals; however, some allow ambition and greed to take hold of them (cf. Phil 2:15). Irrespective of the kind of environment a Christian finds himself in, he should remember that he is a citizen of heaven (cf. Phil 3:20) and should always act in a manner worthy of the Gospel (cf. Phil 1:27); that is, he should be humble; he should not be motivated by self-interest but rather by the good of others (cf. Phil 2:3–4); he should always be joyful (cf. Phil 4:4), blameless and innocent (cf. Phil 2:15), and understanding towards others (cf. Phil 4:5). The good lives of the children of God will shine out as "lights in the world" (Phil 2:15), showing everyone the way with the light of Christ.

Countering man's natural tendency to think only of his own interest and to be deceived by devilish temptation to "be like God" (Gen 3:5), this message of St Paul's identifies the right way to live in the world. It shows that all earthly things, and the human person, will obtain their true dignity and grandeur if they are united to Christ, who is the Lord of the universe. Christians have nothing to fear, therefore, provided they are always motivated by an upright purpose: "Whatever is true, whatever is honourable, whatever is just, whatever is pure, whatever is lovely, whatever is gracious, if there is any excellence, if there is anything worthy of praise, think about these things [hold them in high regard]. What you have learned and received and heard and seen in me, do; and the God of peace will be with you" (Phil 4:8–9).

3. *The mystery of Jesus Christ the Redeemer.* The Apostle sets before us as our model the life of Christ. In the hymn of Philippians 2:6–11 he provides a wonderful summary of the life and redeeming work of our Lord, praising the heavenly exaltation of the man Christ, a glory which he has attained after his life on earth, inspired as it was by a freely accepted obedience, whereby he humbled himself even unto death on a cross.

This hymn, which is very profound, proclaims the divine nature of Christ pre-existing before the Incarnation, and, therefore, his oneness in substance with God the Father, as also his self-emptying to become man—for, without ceasing to be God, he lowered himself, taking the form or nature of man; and then, after his sacrificial death, came his exaltation in glory: "God has highly exalted him and bestowed on him the name which is above every name, that at the name of Jesus every knee should bow, in heaven and on earth and under the earth, and every tongue confess that Jesus Christ is Lord, to the glory of God the Father" (Phil 2:9–11).

The hymn is, therefore, a great canticle in praise of Christ's divinity and his lordship over the entire universe—which is one of the central themes of the Captivity Letters. The exaltation of Christ is described here in terms reminiscent of the letters to the Ephesians and the Colossians. Christ raised on high is the Man-God who was born and died on a cross for our sake.

The language and content of what St Paul has to say here show that the Revelation made by God in the Old Testament reaches its fulfilment in Jesus Christ. By his redeeming death Jesus atones for the disorder caused by Adam, the first man. Adam's disobedience and self-seeking led to the reign of sin and death. Christ's humility and obedience even to death on a cross have won salvation for men. In Christ, the New Adam (cf. Rom 5:14) the salvation promised in the proto-Gospel comes about (cf. Gen 3:15). Jesus takes the form of a servant by freely accepting the way of obedience. As foretold of the Servant of Yahweh in the book of Isaiah, his humiliation and death are the cause of salvation for all (cf. Is 53:2–11). In Christ, in fact, all the prophecies find fulfilment. In the light of what St Paul says in vv. 9–11, Jesus Christ can be recognized as the expected Messiah, who was to come in the clouds of heaven, like the Son of man (cf. Dan 7:13–14); by using an image taken from prophetical literature the lordship of Christ is unequivocally proclaimed.

St Paul centres his attention on the Son of man—on his life on earth as well as his glorification in heaven. Christ is thus contemplated as being truly man according to the expressions used in vv. 7–8. His divine nature is, however, shrouded in mystery since although he reveals himself as man he does in fact possess an infinitely superior origin and dignity. And for the very reason that he is both God and man, his life on earth, as summarized in this text, is of singular importance and culminates in his exaltation in glory.

# THE LETTER OF PAUL TO THE PHILIPPIANS

*The Revised Standard Version, with notes*

# 1. INTRODUCTION

## Greeting

1 [1]Paul and Timothy, servants[a] of Christ Jesus, 1 Cor 1:2
To all the saints in Christ Jesus who are at Philippi, with the 2 Cor 1:1
bishops[b] and deacons:

**1:1–2.** The epistle begins with the normal words of greeting. St Paul calls the Philippians "saints", which was the usual way Christians referred to one another, because they had been consecrated or sanctified by Baptism (cf. note on Eph 1:1). This description underlines, for one thing, the fact that they have been chosen by God, an election which is signified by the ceremony of anointing or consecration that forms part of the baptismal rite whereby they become members of the holy people of God, the Church. The term "saints" also recalls the privilege their God-given vocation involves, and their consequent duty to respond faithfully to the personal call to holiness which each has received.

The entire epistle has the tone of a family letter with dogmatic and moral teachings alternating with personal news. The Apostle's deep affection for his readers makes his words especially convincing. When identifying himself at the start of the letter, he simply gives his name, without adding any reference to his authority—as Apostle of Jesus Christ (cf. Rom 1:1; 1 Cor 1:1; 2 Cor 1:1; Gal 1:1; Eph 1:1, Col 1:1); there is no need to do so, so obedient is the community at Philippi, so much at one with him.

Timothy, whose name appears alongside Paul's in the heading of the letter, had worked with the Apostle in the evangelization of the Philippians and accompanied him on one of his apostolic journeys (cf. Acts 16:1, 3, 10ff; 20:4) and acted as his envoy (cf. Acts 19:22). The church at Philippi, then, knew him well and loved him.

In the Old Testament certain outstanding people—Moses (Ex 14:31), Joshua (Josh 24:29), David (2 Sam 3:18), etc.—whom God used to advance his plans, were described as "servants of Yahweh". Paul and Timothy are "servants of Christ Jesus", that is, people who serve God by preaching his Gospel.

Our Lord Jesus Christ chose twelve Apostles with Peter at their head and commissioned them to make disciples of all nations, whom they were to sanctify and govern. Certain others were invited to assist them in this ministry; and because it had to last until the end of time, the Apostles appointed people to succeed them in their role in the Church, which is a hierarchically structured institution (cf. Vatican II, *Lumen gentium*, 20). Within a few years of their receiving their commission the Apostles already had a number of helpers in the ministry: the Apostle describes them here as "bishops and deacons". The Greek word *episkopos* means "watchman, guardian, overseer" and *diakonos* "servant, keeper". Although in this period these names did not carry the exact meaning they now have, they do indicate that the local church already had a form of hierarchical structure (cf. note on Acts 11:30). At the time this letter was written, "deacons" or servants seem to have been regarded, already, as sacred ministers, helpers of the bishops (cf. Acts 6:1ff).

**a.** Or *slaves* **b.** Or *overseers*

Rom 1:7
Rom 1:8
1 Cor 1:4

[2]Grace to you and peace from God our Father and the Lord Jesus Christ.

**Thanksgiving. Paul's affection and love**

[3]I thank my God in all my remembrance of you, [4]always in every prayer of mine for you all making my prayer with joy, [5]thankful

---

It is worth pointing out that the names of the various forms of Church office always have to do with service, ministry. The bishops are men chosen "to take charge of the community, presiding in God's stead over the flock of which they are the shepherds in that they are teachers of doctrine, ministers of sacred worship and holders of office in government" (*Lumen gentium*, 20). And deacons, for their part, "strengthened by sacramental grace, are dedicated to the people of God, in conjunction with the bishop and his body of priests, in the service of the liturgy, of the Gospel and of works of charity" (*Lumen gentium*, 29).

No mention is made in this letter of the "priests" or "elders" referred to in other Pauline letters (cf. 1 Tim 5:17; Tit 1:5). In the Apostle's time the terminology used did not clearly distinguish the various grades of holy order. It is possible that the "bishops" referred to here belong to the same level of the hierarchy as the "elders" (priests) of other letters—sacred ministers on a lower level than the Apostles and their co-workers (Timothy, Titus, etc.), who presided over the Christian communities. Their role would have been similar to that which parish priests later fill.

On the greeting "grace and peace", see the note on Eph 1:2.

**1:2.** See the second part of the note on Rom 1:7.

**1:3–5.** "Your partnership": in the original this reads "your communion". In the New Testament this term has a wide meaning, mainly denoting closeness of thought, action and lifestyle. It is sometimes used in connexion with collections made in favour of the needy (cf. Rom 15:26; 2 Cor 9:13).

Despite the fact that the faithful at Philippi were in general people of modest means and were themselves experiencing hardship (cf. 2 Cor 8:2), they never spared any effort when others were in need, and always did what they could to help the spread of the Church, by both almsgiving (cf. 2 Cor 8:3–4) and personal commitment (cf. 2 Cor 8:5), prayer and help to the ministers of the Gospel, as the Apostle knew from personal experience (cf. Phil 4:14–16).

St Paul recognizes their difficulties are due to their generous response to the demands of the faith—a gift of God (cf. v. 29); that is why he continually prays that they may always have the grace they need.

**1:4.** "With joy": the Apostle's joy is one of the outstanding features of this epistle; the good spirit of the Philippians makes him particularly happy: the very thought of them brings him joy. Further on, in 3:1; he tells them to rejoice in the Lord; and in 4:4 he twice repeats this exhortation to a joy that comes from closeness to the Lord (cf. notes on Phil 4:4; 4:5–7).

The same exhortation to true joy is very often to be found in early Christian writings: "Clothe yourself with cheerfullness, which always finds favour with God and is acceptable to him. Take all your

for your partnership in the gospel from the first day until now.
[6]And I am sure that he who began a good work in you will bring 1 Cor 1:6–8
it to completion at the day of Jesus Christ. [7]It is right for me to

---

delight in this, for every cheerful man does good, has good thoughts, and despises melancholy" (*Shepherd of Hermas*, 10, 3, 1).

Joy is a fruit of the Holy Spirit (cf. Gal 5:22) and a virtue intimately connected with supernatural charity, from which it derives (cf. *Summa theologiae*, 2–2, 23, 4). It is a gift a soul in grace experiences, irrespective of its personal situation or circumstances. It comes from union with God and recognition of his loving Providence towards all creation and especially towards his children. Joy gives the Christian peace and objectivity in everything he does.

**1:6.** The Old Testament teaches that God is "merciful and gracious, slow to anger, and abounding in steadfast love and faithfulness" (Ex 34:6; cf. Ps 119:137). His faithfulness means that he always is true to his word, always keeps the promises he makes to his people (cf. Deut 34:4); therefore man can abandon himself into God's hands without fear, for there he will find a safe refuge (cf. Ps 31:5–6). God, who initiated the work of salvation by giving Christians the gift of faith and filling them with sanctifying grace, will continue to enrich them with his grace until they at last encounter Christ in heaven (cf. 1 Cor 1:4–9).

On the basis of this verse of Scripture, the Church's Magisterium, in reaction to the Pelagian heresy, taught that the beginnings of faith, as also increase of faith and the act of faith whereby we believe, are all the result of grace and man's free response to that gift (cf. Second Council of Orange, can. 5). Centuries later, the Council of Trent repeated this teaching: just as God began this good work, he will bring it to completion, if we for our part cooperate (cf. *De iustificatione*, chap. 13).

By reflecting on this truth, St Francis de Sales tells us, we shall come to realize how much we ought to trust in God: "Our Lord is ever watchful of the actions of his children; he gets them to walk ahead of him and gives them a helping hand if they meet up with difficulty. He said as much through Isaiah: 'For I, the Lord your God, hold your right hand; it is I who say to you, Fear not, I will help you' (Is 41:13). So, in addition to having good morale, we should put all our trust in God and in his help, for, provided we don't lose the state of grace, he will complete in us the good work of our salvation which he has already begun" (*Treatise on the Love of God*, 3, 4).

To this trust in divine help must be added a personal effort to respond to grace, for, in the words of St Augustine, "God who created you without your cooperation will not save you without your cooperation" (*Sermon,* 169, 13).

"The day of Christ Jesus": see the note on 1 Cor 1:8–9.

**1:7.** St Paul's calling to the apostolate was entirely a matter of the grace of God (cf. Rom 1:1; 1 Cor 1:1; Col 1:25; etc.); however, staying faithful to this vocation meant that he had to work very hard and cope with all kinds of difficulties. He spared no effort to spread Christ's teaching, defend it from its enemies, and strengthen the faith of his converts (cf. 2 Cor 11:23–33).

"Partakers with me of grace": every Christian is called to play a part in the apostolate. "To the apostles and their

feel thus about you all, because I hold you in my heart, for you are
Rom 1:9 all partakers with me of grace, both in my imprisonment and in
2 Cor 1:23 the defence and confirmation of the gospel. 8 For God is my
witness, how I yearn for you all with the affection of Christ Jesus.
Rom 2:18; 1 Cor 5:8 9 And it is my prayer that your love may abound more and more,

---

successors Christ has entrusted the office of teaching, sanctifying and governing in his name and by his power. But the laity are made to share in the priestly, prophetical and kingly office of Christ; they have therefore, in the Church and in the world, their own assignment in the mission of the whole people of God. In the concrete, their apostolate is exercised when they work at the evangelization and sanctification of men; it is exercised too when they endeavour to have the Gospel spirit permeate and improve the temporal order, going about it in a way that bears clear witness to Christ and helps forward the salvation of men. The characteristic of the lay state being a life led in the midst of the world and of secular affairs, laymen are called by God to make of their apostolate, through the vigour of their Christian spirit, a leaven in the world" (Vatican II, *Apostolicam actuositatem*, 2).

**1:8.** "With all the affection of Christ Jesus": St Paul is so identified with our Lord that he can say that he has the same sentiments towards them as Christ has. This supernatural love is quite compatible with human affection, but it raises it on to a higher level. This entire epistle is an excellent proof of how the two kinds of love—human and divine—interweave. Charity "joins closely to God those in whom it reigns", Leo XIII teaches, "and causes them to receive from God the life of the soul and to live with him and for him. Love of neighbour has to go hand in hand with charity and love of God, for (we must recognize that) all mankind share in God's infinite goodness and are made in his image and likeness" (*Sapientiae christianae*, 51–52).

Helping others is the surest sign of true love, for, writes St Teresa of Avila, "we cannot be sure if we are loving God, although we may have good reasons for believing that we are, but we can know quite well if we are loving our neighbour. And be certain that, the farther advanced you find you are in this, the greater the love you will have for God; for so dearly does His Majesty love us that He will reward our love for our neighbour by increasing the love which we bear to himself, and that in a thousand ways" (*Interior Castle*, 5, 3, 8).

This love is the basis of apostolic effectiveness: "A sign of love will be the concern to give the truth and to bring people into unity. Another sign of love will be a devotion to the proclamation of Jesus Christ, without reservation or turning back" (Paul VI, *Evangelii nuntiandi*, 79).

**1:9–11.** "Discernment": a deeply Christian view of things, which enables one to see the events of everyday life in a supernatural light and therefore understand them properly—very much the same idea as conveyed by the "wisdom" so often referred to in the Old Testament.

Up to this point St Paul's prayers and exhortations have had to do with steady growth in charity. Since charity is a supernatural virtue, "one needs to ask God to increase it, since God alone can bring that about in us" (St Thomas Aquinas, *Commentary on Phil*, ad loc.). Growth in charity means our attaining greater "knowledge" of God. "The lover", St

with knowledge and all discernment, [10]so that you may approve Heb 5:14
what is excellent, and may be pure and blameless for the day of
Christ, [11]filled with the fruits of righteousness which come Jas 3:18
through Jesus Christ, to the glory and praise of God.

**Paul's own circumstances**

[12]I want you to know, brethren, that what has happened to me has 2 Tim 2:9
really served to advance the gospel, [13]so that it has become known

---

Thomas Aquinas says, "is not satisfied with superficial knowledge of the beloved, but strives to gain an intimate knowledge of everything pertaining to him, so as to penetrate his very soul" (*Summa theologiae*, 1–2, 28, 2). Eagerness to know God brings one closer and closer to Jesus Christ, in an effort to absorb his teachings and put into practice the saving truths they contain—to act "with all discernment", knowing what is the best thing to do in every situation.

A personal relationship with God through prayer, identification with Christ by frequent reception of the sacraments, and the action of the Holy Spirit indwelling in the soul in grace, give the Christian a special insight that enables him to distinguish good from evil in the concrete situations that arise. The gift of wisdom "allows us to know God and rejoice in his presence; it enables us to judge accurately the situations and events of this life [...].

"Not that the Christian should neglect to see all that is good in humanity, appreciate its healthy joys or participate in its enthusiasm and ideals. On the contrary, a true Christian will vibrate in unison with all the good he finds in the world. And he will live in the midst of it with a special concern, since he knows, better than anyone, the depth and the richness of the human spirit.

"A Christian's faith does not diminish his spirit or limit the noble impulses of his soul: rather it makes them grow with the realization of their true and authentic meaning" (St Josemaría Escrivá, *Christ Is Passing By*, 133).

**1:12–14.** *Praetorium* was the name given to the residence of the Roman governor in each province of the empire; in its most formal sense it referred to the praetorian guard in Rome, who were responsible for the protection of the emperor. On the question of where the Apostle was imprisoned when he wrote this letter, see pages 83–84 above. These verses contain items of news; but St Paul does not think about himself; he is wholly focused on Christ; he does not refer to his health or the difficulties of his confinement, but to how his situation has helped to spread the Gospel.

By his work and example it has become clear to the whole praetorian guard that the cause of his imprisonment is his fidelity to the preaching of the Christian message. What he does tell us shows how effective Christian witness is. By their example, Christ's disciples "stir up irresistible questions in the hearts of those who see how they live: Why are they like this? Why do they live in this way? What or who is it that inspires them? Why are they in our midst? Such a witness is already a silent proclamation of the Good News and a very powerful and effective one [...]. Nevertheless this always remains insufficient, because even the finest witness will prove ineffective in the long run if it is not [...] made explicit

throughout the whole praetorian guard[c] and to all the rest that my
imprisonment is for Christ; [14]and most of the brethren have been
made confident in the Lord because of my imprisonment,* and are
much more bold to speak the word of God without fear.
[15]Some indeed preach Christ from envy and rivalry, but others
from good will. [16]The latter do it out of love, knowing that I am

---

by a clear and unequivocal proclamation of the Lord Jesus" (Paul VI, *Evangelii nuntiandi*, 21–22).

The Apostle both preaches the word and gives good example; this encourages his brethren in the faith to put their trust in the Lord and shed any fear they might have about speaking out about God. Apostolate should not be inhibited by apparently adverse circumstances.

This passage also shows the great salvific value of suffering: St Paul's imprisonment has "served to advance the Gospel" (v. 12). Firstly, because despite its difficulties it provides an opportunity for the Gospel message to reach very many people. Additionally, because difficulties and hardship play an important part in personal sanctification and in the sanctification of others and allow one in a special way to identify with Christ. "If one becomes a sharer in the sufferings of Christ," Pope John Paul II teaches, "this happens because Christ *has opened his suffering to man*, because he himself in his redemptive suffering has become, in a certain sense, a sharer in all human sufferings. Man, discovering through faith the redemptive suffering of Christ, also discovers in it his own sufferings; he *rediscovers them, through faith*, enriched with a new content and new meaning" (*Salvifici doloris*, 20). The supernatural effectiveness of suffering for Christ derives from the fact that "those who share in the sufferings of Christ preserve in their own sufferings a very special *particle of the infinite treasure* of the world's Redemption, and can share this treasure with others" (ibid., 27).

Thus, difficulties or apparently adverse circumstances should not be seen as obstacles but as a precious opportunity for apostolate. Acceptance of suffering and practice of self-denial are necessary to personal sanctification and apostolate. As St Josemaría Escrivá so forcefully put it, "Purify your intentions. Do everything for the love of God and embrace your daily cross joyfully. This is something I have repeated thousands of times because I believe that these ideas should be engraved on every Christian heart. When we advance beyond the stage of simply tolerating difficulties or sufferings (whether physical or moral) and, instead, love them and offer them to God in reparation for our sins and the sins of all mankind, then, I assure you, they do not distress us.

"It is no longer just any cross we are carrying. We discover that it is the Cross of Christ and we have the consolation of knowing that our Redeemer has taken it upon himself to bear its weight" (*Friends of God*, 132)

"To speak the word of God without fear": the New Vulgate simply says "the word", which is probably the original reading, but "of God" is added because it appears in many important Greek and Latin codexes; besides, it makes the meaning clearer.

**1:15–18.** "From envy and rivalry": we do not know whom he is referring to, but it does not seem to be Judaizers, as is the

**c.** Greek *in the whole praetorium*

put here for the defence of the gospel; [17]the former proclaim
Christ out of partisanship, not sincerely but thinking to afflict me
in my imprisonment. [18]What then? Only that in every way,
whether in pretence or in truth, Christ is proclaimed; and in that
I rejoice.
[19]Yes, and I shall rejoice. For I know that through your prayers Job 13:16 2 Cor 1:11
and the help of the Spirit of Jesus Christ this will turn out for my
deliverance, [20]as it is my eager expectation and hope that I shall 1 Cor 6:20
not be at all ashamed, but that with full courage now as always
Christ will be honoured in my body,* whether by life or by death.
[21]For to me to live is Christ, and to die is gain. [22]If it is to be life Gal 2:20

---

case in the epistles to the Galatians and the Romans. St Paul, who gives no thought to himself, rejoices as long as the Gospel is preached, even if the preachers have bad intention (v. 18). Christians should always be happy to see others working for Christ.

Jesus says this quite clearly in the Gospel: "'Teacher, we saw a man casting out demons in your name, and we forbade him, because he was not following us.' But Jesus said, 'Do not forbid him; for no one who does a mighty work in my name will be able soon after to speak evil of me. For he that is not against us is for us'" (Mk 9:38–40). The basis of this teaching lies in the fact that an apostle is only an instrument of God in the service of souls; he has no proprietary rights over souls. "[Let us remember] that souls belong to God; that no one on earth has that right of ownership over souls; and that the Church's apostolate, by which it announces and brings about salvation, is not based on personal prestige of individuals but on the grace of God" (St Josemaría Escrivá, *Friends of God*, 267).

**1:19.** His imprisonment for preaching Christ, and even his pain at others' preaching out of rivalry, does not take away the Apostle's peace; for he realizes that this pain identifies him with Christ. "And the reason for this is that when we do any good action that promotes the salvation of others, this makes for our own salvation" (St Thomas Aquinas, *Commentary on Phil*, ad loc.). St James makes the same point: "whoever brings back a sinner from the error of his way will save his own soul from death and will cover a multitude of sins" (Jas 5:20).

**1:20.** "Christ will be honoured in my body": whether he lives (because that *will* allow him to keep up his apostolic work) or whether he has to face martyrdom: in either case he is able to bear witness to Christ.

Every Christian is linked to Christ through Baptism (cf. Rom 6:5) and this union is strengthened by the Eucharist (cf. 1 Cor 10:16–17). A believer, therefore, should aspire to identify with Jesus to such an extent that he can say with the Apostle, "it is no longer I who live, but Christ who lives in me" (Gal 2:20). Everything anyone has is a gift from God; and a Christian's life in the body, with any suffering he experiences, and even death, identifies him in some way with Christ's own life: this identification is the goal of every Christian.

**1:21–26.** St Paul expresses a desire to "depart" and be with Christ: the Greek

in the flesh, that means fruitful labour for me. Yet which I shall
2 Cor 5:8 choose I cannot tell. 23I am hard pressed between the two. My
desire is to depart and be with Christ, for that is far better. 24But
to remain in the flesh is more necessary on your account.
25Convinced of this, I know that I shall remain and continue with
you all, for your progress and joy in the faith, 26so that in me you
may have ample cause to glory in Christ Jesus, because of my
coming to you again.

---

verb he uses has the sense of casting off (like a boat before it leaves harbour) or upping stakes (like an army decamping): he sees death as a liberation from earthly ties, which allows him immediately to "be with Christ". These words indicate that those who die in grace do not have to wait until the Last Judgment to enjoy God in heaven. This was the teaching of the Church, based on Sacred Scripture, at the Second Council of Lyons: "the souls of those who after holy Baptism have acquired no stain of sin at all, and those who having incurred the stain of sin are cleansed ... are received immediately into heaven" (*Profession of Faith of Michael Paleologue*).

The Apostle is in two minds. But his desire to be with Christ does not inhibit his generous work for the good of souls: he wants to stay in the world, in order to continue working for the conversion of the Gentiles and to look after the Christian communities which he has founded, which are going from strength to strength.

In spite of his uncertainty about his future, St Paul is inclined to think that he will be allowed to continue his work to the spiritual advantage of the Philippians and the other churches.

**1:21.** Death is "gain", because, for a person who dies in the grace of God, it means entering into the joy of the Lord, seeing him face to face (cf. 1 Cor 13:12) and enjoying "what no eye has seen, nor ear heard, nor the heart of man conceived, what God has prepared for those who love him" (1 Cor 2:9). This desire to enjoy God in heaven caused St Teresa of Avila to say: "I am living and yet I am not really living, for I place my hopes on such a higher life that I am dying because I do not die" (*Poems*, 2).

"Christ himself, our teacher of salvation, shows us how useful it is to leave this life; when his disciples became sad because he told them that he was going away, he said to them, 'If you loved me, you would have rejoiced, because I go to the Father' (Jn 14:28), thereby teaching them that, when those we love leave this world, we should rejoice rather than be sad" (St Cyprian, *De mortalitate*, 7). Faith shows us that death is the definitive step into eternal life. However, to have a well grounded hope of attaining that goal we need to remember that for us "to live is Christ" here on earth also. For one thing, supernatural life is the life of grace, and this has been won for us by Christ; also, knowing and loving Christ should be our life-purpose. A Christian has to try to see that his life is fruitful in terms of holiness, and that he uses all ordinary events and all his activities to draw others towards Christ.

"So, if you have encountered Christ," John Paul II exhorts, "live for Christ, live with Christ, and bear witness to him; proclaim this in the first person singular: 'For me to live is Christ.' That is what true

## 2. TEACHINGS

**Appeal for steadfastness**

27Only let your manner of life be worthy of the gospel of Christ, Col 1:10
so that whether I come and see you or am absent, I may hear of 1 Thess 2:12
you that you stand firm in one spirit, with one mind striving side
by side for the faith of the gospel, 28and not frightened in anything

---

liberation also consists of—proclaiming Jesus Christ freed from attachments and present in men who are transformed and become a new creation" (*Homily, Santo Domingo Cathedral*, October 1984).

**1:27.** The Greek term translated here as "let your manner of life be" has a more specific meaning—"Live like good citizens." The inhabitants of Philippi enjoyed Roman citizenship and were very proud of this (cf. p. 101 above). However, in addition to whichever positions they have in society, Christians are citizens of heaven (cf. Phil 3:20), and therefore they should lead a life "worthy of the gospel of Christ", like good citizens of the Kingdom of God, where Christ reigns as king (cf. Jn 18:37), by loyally obeying his laws—the new law of grace contained in the Gospel.

However, being a citizen of heaven is quite compatible with being a citizen of human society: "to acknowledge God is in no way to oppose the dignity of man, since such dignity is grounded and brought to perfection in God. Man has in fact been placed in society by God, who created him as an intelligent and free being; but over and above this he is called as a son to intimacy with God and to share in his happiness. (The Church) further teaches that hope in a life to come does not take away from the importance of the duties of this life on earth but rather adds to it by giving new motives for fulfilling those duties" (Vatican II, *Gaudium et spes*, 21).

A truly Christian life in the middle of the world speaks to all, Christians or no, of the presence of God and of his plans for the salvation of all mankind. Moreover, "what does much to show God's presence clearly is the brotherly love of the faithful who, being all of one mind and spirit work together for the faith of the Gospel (cf. Phil 1:18) and stand out as a sign of unity" (ibid.). This is essential to the effort to spread the Kingdom of God, for "every kingdom divided against itself is laid waste" (Lk 11:17). The early Christians really did put this teaching into practice: they were "of one heart and soul" (Acts 4:32).

**1:28.** Today, as in St Paul's time, the Gospel has its enemies, who try to dislodge faith from the human heart. Christians should not let themselves be intimidated by these people: the fact that there are enemies around should lead them to try to be ever stronger in the faith. "It is particularly necessary that each person enter into himself, most vigilantly to keep the faith deeply rooted in his heart, guarded against all dangers and especially against certain deceptive ways of thinking. The better to safeguard this virtue, we consider it especially useful and very suited to our times that everyone should carefully study Christian doctrine, to the best of his ability, nourishing his mind with as much knowledge as possible of those truths that pertain to religion and can be grasped by human reason" (Leo XIII, *Sapientiae christianae*, 17).

by your opponents. This is a clear omen to them of their
destruction, but of your salvation, and that from God. 29For it has
been granted to you that for the sake of Christ you should not only
Acts 16:22 believe in him but also suffer for his sake, 30engaged in the same
conflict which you saw and now hear to be mine.

### Unity and humility

2 1So if there is any encouragement in Christ, any incentive of
love, any participation in the Spirit, any affection and

---

In addition to being well-instructed in the faith, a Christian needs to be able to defend it when attacked: "In an emergency imperilling faith everyone is bound to declare his faith openly, either to instruct and support other believers or to put down the scorn of unbelievers" (St Thomas Aquinas, *Summa theologiae*, 2–2, 3, 2, ad 2). Again, Leo XIII reminds us: "Giving way to the enemy or keeping quiet when on every side people clamour to oppress the truth is a line of conduct proper to a coward or else to someone who is unsure of the truths he professes to hold. In either case it is shameful and offensive to God, opposed to the salvation of the individual and of society; the only service it does is to the enemies of the Christian person, for the cowardice of the good encourages the audacity of the bad" (*Sapientiae christianae*, 18).

**1:29–30.** St Paul was not spared persecution or difficulties in his mission work. The Philippians had witnessed his imprisonment in their own city (cf. Acts 16:19–36), and now they are hearing about a further term spent in gaol. He exhorts them to follow his own example (cf. v. 30), and to see their sufferings on Christ's behalf as a grace, a gift from God (cf. v. 29).

Setbacks, the fatigue of work, difficulties in interior struggle and in apostolate are opportunities which God offers us in order to identify more closely with Christ by fearlessly embracing his cross. "How lovingly Jesus embraces the wood which is to bring him to death! Is it not true that as soon as you cease to be afraid of the Cross, of what people call the cross, when you set your will to accept the Will of God, then you find happiness, and all your worries, all your sufferings, physical or moral, pass away? Truly the Cross of Jesus is gentle and lovable. There, sorrows cease to count; there is only the joy of knowing that we are co-redeemers with him" (St Josemaría Escrivá, *The Way of the Cross*, II).

**2:1–4.** Verse 1 begins with a very awkwardly constructed clause, which the New Vulgate and the RSV translate literally. It is a conditional, rhetorical clause, rather than an affirmative statement, and its meaning is clarified by the rest of the sentence.

St Paul is making an affectionate appeal to the Christian good sense of the faithful; he seems to be saying: "if you want to console me in Christ, complete my joy by paying attention to the advice I am now going to give you" (cf. St Thomas Aquinas, *Commentary on Phil,* ad loc.).

The Apostle recommends that they should always act humbly and with an upright intention (vv. 3–4) if they want charity to reign among them (v. 2). In

sympathy, [2]complete my joy by being of the same mind, having
the same love, being in full accord and of one mind. [3]Do nothing Rom 12:10 Gal 5:26
from selfishness or conceit, but in humility count others better
than yourselves. [4]Let each of you look not only to his own 1 Cor 10:24, 33
interests, but also to the interests of others.

---

their work and social life ordinary Christians should be upright in all their dealings. They should go about everything, even apparently unimportant things, in a humble way, doing them for God. But they should also remember that their behaviour has an effect on others. "Don't forget that you are also in the presence of men, and that they expect from you, from you personally, a Christian witness. Thus, as regards the human dimension of our job, we must work in such a way that we will not feel ashamed when those who know us and love us see us at our work, nor give them cause to feel embarrassed" (St Josemaría Escrivá, *Friends of God*, 66).

This fact that our behaviour can encourage others and set a headline for them means that we need to act very responsibly: "Let us try therefore, brethren," St Augustine says, "not only to be good but to conduct ourselves well in the eyes of others. Let us try to see that there is nothing that our conscience upbraids us for, and also, bearing in mind our weakness, do all that we can, to avoid disedifying our less mature brother" (*Sermon*, 47, 14).

**2:3–11.** Verse 3 exhorts us to see others as better than ourselves. Our Lord, although he was our superior in all respects, did not see his divinity as something to boast about before men (v. 6). In fact, he humbled himself and emptied himself (vv. 7–8), was not motivated by conceit or selfishness (cf. v. 3), did not look to his own interests (cf. v. 4), and "became obedient unto death" (v. 8), thereby carrying out the Father's plan for man's salvation. By reflecting on his example we shall come to see that suffering for Christ is a sign of salvation (cf. 1:28–29): after undergoing the sufferings of his passion and death, Christ was publicly exalted above all creation (cf. vv. 9–11).

Our Lord offers us a perfect example of humility. "The coming of our Lord Jesus Christ, the Sceptre of God's Majesty, was in no pomp of pride and haughtiness—as it could so well have been—but in self-abasement [...]. You see, dear friends, what an example we have been given. If the Lord humbled himself in this way, what ought we to do, who through him have come under the yoke of his guidance?" (St Clement of Rome, *Letter to the Corinthians*, 13).

**2:3–4.** "'In every man,' writes St Thomas Aquinas, 'there are some grounds for others to look on him as superior, according to the Apostle's words, "Each of us must have the humility to think others better men than himself" (Phil 2:3). It is in this spirit that all men are bound to honour one another' (*Summa theologiae*, 2–2, 103, 2). Humility is the virtue that teaches us that signs of respect for others—their good name, their good faith, their privacy—are not external conventions, but the first expressions of charity and justice.

"Christian charity cannot confine itself to giving things or money to the needy. It seeks, above all, to respect and understand each person for what he is, in his intrinsic dignity as a man and child of God" (St Josemaría Escrivá, *Christ Is Passing By*, 72).

### Hymn in praise of Christ's self-emptying

5Have this mind among yourselves, which was in Christ Jesus,
Is 52:3 6who, though he was in the form of God,* did not count equality
2 Cor 8:9 with God a thing to be grasped, 7but emptied himself,* taking the

---

**2:5.** "The Apostle's recommendation, 'Have this mind among yourselves, which was in Christ Jesus', requires all Christians, so far as human power allows, to reproduce in themselves the sentiments that Christ had when he was offering himself in sacrifice—sentiments of humility, of adoration, praise, and thanksgiving to the divine majesty. It requires them also to become victims, as it were; cultivating a spirit of self-denial according to the precepts of the Gospel, willingly doing works of penance, detesting and expiating their sins. It requires us all, in a word, to die mystically with Christ on the Cross, so that we may say with the same Apostle: 'I have been crucified with Christ' (Gal 2:19)" (Pius XII, *Mediator Dei*, 22).

**2:6–11.** In what he says about Jesus Christ, the Apostle is not simply proposing him as a model for us to follow. Possibly transcribing an early liturgical hymn adding some touches of his own, he is—under the inspiration of the Holy Spirit—giving a very profound exposition of the nature of Christ and using the most sublime truths of faith to show the way Christian virtues should be practised.

This is one of the earliest New Testament texts to reveal the divinity of Christ. The epistle was written around the year 62 (or perhaps before that, around 55) and if we remember that the hymn of Philippians 2:6–11 may well have been in use prior to that date, the passage clearly bears witness to the fact that Christians were proclaiming, even in those very early years, that Jesus, born in Bethlehem, crucified, died and buried, and risen from the dead, was truly both God and man.

The hymn can be divided into three parts. The first (vv. 6 and the beginning of 7) refers to Christ's humbling himself by becoming man. The second (the end of v. 7 and v. 8) is the centre of the whole passage and proclaims the extreme to which his humility brought him: as man he obediently accepted death on the cross. The third part (vv. 9–11) describes his exaltation in glory. Throughout St Paul is conscious of Jesus' divinity: he exists from all eternity. But he centres his attention on his death on the cross as the supreme example of humility. Christ's humiliation lay not in his becoming a man like us and cloaking the glory of his divinity in his sacred humanity: it also brought him to lead a life of sacrifice and suffering which reached its climax on the cross, where he was stripped of everything he had, like a slave. However, now that he has fulfilled his mission, he is made manifest again, clothed in all the glory that befits his divine nature and which his human nature has merited.

The man-God, Jesus Christ, makes the cross the climax of his earthly life; through it he enters into his glory as Lord and Messiah. The Crucifixion puts the whole universe on the way to salvation.

Jesus Christ gives us a wonderful example of humility and obedience. "We should learn from Jesus' attitude in these trials," St Josemaría Escrivá reminds us. "During his life on earth he did not even want the glory that belonged to him. Though he had the right to be treated as God, he took the form of a servant, a slave (cf. Phil 2:6–7). And so the Christian knows that all glory is due to God and that he must not use the sublimity and greatness of the Gospel to further his own interests or human ambitions. "We should learn from Jesus. His attitude in rejecting all human glory is in perfect balance with the greatness of his unique mission as the beloved Son of God who becomes incarnate to save men" (*Christ Is Passing By*, 62).

**2:6–7.** "Though he was in the form of God" or "subsisting in the form of God": "form" is the external aspect of something and manifests what it is. When referring to God, who is invisible, his "form" cannot refer to things visible to the senses; the "form of God" is a way of referring to Godhead. The first thing that St Paul makes clear is that Jesus Christ is God, and was God before the Incarnation. As the *Nicene-Constantinopolitan Creed* professes it, "the only begotten Son of God, born of the Father before time began, light from light, true God from true God".

"He did not count equality with God as something to be grasped": the Greek word translated as "equality" does not directly refer to equality of nature but rather the equality of rights and status. Christ was God and he could not stop being God; therefore, he had a right to be treated as God and to appear in all his glory. However, he did not insist on this dignity of his as if it were a treasure which he possessed and which was legally his: it was not something he clung to and boasted about. And so he took "the form of a servant". He could have become man without setting his glory aside—he could have appeared as he did, momentarily, at the Transfiguration (cf. Mt 17:1ff); instead he chose to be like men, in all things but sin (cf. v. 7). By becoming man in the way he did, he was able, as Isaiah prophesied in the Song of the Servant of Yahweh, to bear our sorrows and to be stricken (cf. Is 53:4).

"He emptied himself", he despoiled himself: this is literally what the Greek verb means. But Christ did not shed his divine nature; he simply shed its glory, its aura; if he had not done so it would have shone out through his human nature. From all eternity he exists as God and from the moment of the Incarnation he began to be man. His self-emptying lay not only in the fact that the Godhead united to himself (that is, to the person of the Son) something which was corporeal and finite (a human nature), but also in the fact that this nature did not itself manifest the divine glory, as it "ought" to have done. Christ could not cease to be God, but he could temporarily renounce the exercise of rights that belonged to him as God—which was what he did.

Verses 6–8 bring to the Christian's mind the contrast between Jesus and Adam. The devil tempted Adam, a mere man, to "be like God" (Gen 3:5). By trying to indulge this evil desire (pride is a disordered desire for selfadvancement) and by committing the sin of disobeying God (cf. Gen 3:6), Adam drew down the gravest misfortunes upon himself and on his whole line (present potentially in him): this is symbolized in the Genesis passage by his expulsion from Paradise and by the physical world's rebellion against his lordship (cf. Gen 3:16–24). Jesus Christ, on the contrary, who enjoyed divine glory from all eternity, "emptied himself": he chooses the way of humility, the opposite way to Adam's (opposite, too, to the way previously taken by the devil). Christ's obedience thereby makes up for the disobedience of the first man; it puts mankind in a position to more than recover the natural

Heb 12:2 form of a servant,[d] being born in the likeness of men. 8And being
found in human form he humbled himself and became obedient

---

and supernatural gifts with which God endowed human nature at the creation. And so, after focusing on the amazing mystery of Christ's humiliation or self-emptying (*kénosis* in Greek), this hymn goes on joyously to celebrate Christ's exaltation after death.

Christ's attitude in becoming man is, then, a wonderful example of humility. "What is more humble", St Gregory of Nyssa asks, "than the King of all creation entering into communion with our poor nature? The King of kings and Lord of lords clothes himself with the form of our enslavement; the Judge of the universe comes to pay tribute to the princes of this world; the Lord of creation is born in a cave; he who encompasses the world cannot find room in the inn [...]; the pure and incorrupt one puts on the filthiness of our nature and experiences all our needs, experiences even death itself" (*Oratio I in beatitudinibus*).

This self-emptying is an example of God's infinite goodness in taking the initiative to meet man: "Fill yourselves with wonder and gratitude at such a mystery and learn from it. All the power, all the majesty, all the beauty, all the infinite harmony of God, all his great and immeasurable riches, God whole and entire! was hidden for our benefit in the humanity of Christ. The Almighty appears determined to eclipse his glory for a time, so as to make it easy for his creatures to approach their Redeemer" (St Josemaría Escrivá, *Friends of God*, 111).

**2:8.** Jesus Christ became man "for us men and for our salvation", we profess in the Creed. Everything he did in the course of his life had a salvific value; his death on the cross represents the climax of his redemptive work for, as St Gregory of Nyssa says, "he did not experience death due to the fact of being born; rather, he took birth upon himself in order to die" (*Oratio catechetica magna*, 32).

Our Lord's obedience to the Father's saving plan, involving as it did death on the cross, gives us the best of all lessons in humility. For, in the words of St Thomas Aquinas, "obedience is the sign of true humility" (*Commentary on Phil*, ad loc.). In St Paul's time death by crucifixion was the most demeaning form of death, for it was inflicted only on criminals. By becoming obedient "unto death, even death on a cross", Jesus was being humble in the extreme. He was perfectly within his rights to manifest himself in all his divine glory, but he chose instead the route leading to the most ignominious of deaths.

His obedience, moreover, was not simply a matter of submitting to the Father's will, for, as St Paul points out, he made himself obedient: his obedience was active; he made the Father's salvific plans his own. He chose voluntarily to give himself up to crucifixion in order to redeem mankind. "Debasing oneself when one is forced to do so is not humility", St John Chrysostom explains; "humility is present when one debases oneself without being obliged to do so" (*Hom. on Phil*, ad loc.).

Christ's self-abasement and his obedience unto death reveals his love for us, for "greater love has no man than this, that a man lay down his life for his friends" (Jn 15:13). His loving initiative merits a loving response on our part: we should show that we desire to be one

**d.** Or *slave*

unto death, even death on a cross. 9Therefore God has highly Acts 2:33
exalted him and bestowed on him the name which is above every
name, 10that at the name of Jesus every knee should bow, in
heaven and on earth and under the earth, 11and every tongue Heb 12:11
confess that Jesus Christ is Lord, to the glory of God the Father.

---

with him, for love "seeks union, identification with the beloved. United to Christ, we will be drawn to imitate his life of dedication, his unlimited love and his sacrifice unto death. Christ brings us face to face with the ultimate choice: either we spend our life in selfish isolation, or we devote ourselves and all our energies to the service of others" (St Josemaría Escrivá, *Friends of God*, 236).

**2:9–11.** "God highly exalted him": the Greek compounds the notion of exaltation, to indicate the immensity of his glorification. Our Lord himself foretold this when he said "he who humbles himself will be exalted" (Lk 14:11).

Christ's sacred humanity was glorified as a reward for his humiliation. The Church's Magisterium teaches that Christ's glorification affects his human nature only, for "in the form of God the Son was equal to the Father, and between the Begetter and the Only-begotten there was no difference in essence, no difference in majesty; nor did the Word, through the mystery of incarnation, lose anything which the Father might later return to him as a gift" (St Leo the Great, *Promisisse me memini*, chap. 8). Exaltation is public manifestation of the glory which belongs to Christ's humanity by virtue of its being joined to the divine person of the Word. This union to the "form of a servant" (cf. v. 7) meant an immense act of humility on the part of the Son, but it led to the exaltation of the human nature he took on.

For the Jews the "name that is above every name" is the name of God (Yahweh), which the Mosaic Law required to be held in particular awe. Also, they regarded a name given to someone, especially if given by God, as not just a way of referring to a person but as expressing something that belonged to the very core of his personality. Therefore, the statement that God "bestowed on him the name which is above every name" means that God the Father gave Christ's human nature the capacity to manifest the glory of divinity which was his by virtue of the hypostatic union: therefore, it is to be worshipped by the entire universe.

St Paul describes the glorification of Jesus Christ in terms similar to those used by the prophet Daniel of the Son of man: "To him was given dominion, and glory and kingdom, that all peoples, nations and languages should serve him; his dominion is an everlasting dominion, which shall not pass away, and his kingdom one that shall not be destroyed" (Dan 7:14). Christ's lordship extends to all created things. Sacred Scripture usually speaks of "heaven and earth" when referring to the entire created universe; by mentioning here the underworld it is emphasizing that nothing escapes his dominion. Jesus Christ can here be seen as the fulfilment of Isaiah's prophecy about the universal sovereignty of Yahweh: "To me every knee shall bow, every tongue shall swear" (Is 45:23). All created things come under his sway, and men are dutybound to accept the basic truth of Christian teaching: "Jesus Christ is Lord." The Greek word *Kyrios* used here by St Paul is the word used by the Septuagint, the early Greek version of the

**The children of God, the light of the world**

2 Cor 7:15 [12]Therefore, my beloved, as you have always obeyed, so now, not
only as in my presence but much more in my absence, work out
2 Cor 7:15 your own salvation with fear and trembling; [13]for God is at work
in you, both to will and to work for his good pleasure.

---

Old Testament, to translate the name of God (*Yahweh*). Therefore, this sentence means "Jesus Christ is God."

The Christ proclaimed here as having been raised on high is the man-God who was born and died for our sake, attaining the glory of his exaltation after undergoing the humiliation of the cross. In this also Christ sets us an example: we cannot attain the glory of heaven unless we understand the supernatural value of difficulties, ill-health and suffering: these are manifestations of Christ's cross present in our ordinary life. "We have to die to ourselves and be born again to a new life. Jesus Christ obeyed in this way, even unto death on a cross (Phil 2:18); that is why God exalted him. If we obey God's will, the cross will mean our own resurrection and exaltation. Christ's life will be fulfilled step by step in our own lives. It will be said of us that we have tried to be good children of God, who went about doing good in spite of our weakness and personal shortcomings, no matter how many" (St Josemaría Escrivá, *Christ Is Passing By*, 21).

**2:12–18.** St Paul now points out that reflection on Christ's example should lead Christians to make a genuine and generous effort to attain salvation. When he was in their midst, they did try to do this; he is no longer with them, but they should still be pressing forward (v. 12). In doing so, they are always being helped by grace, which will lead them to implement God's plans for them (v. 13).

With God's help Christians should light up the world by the example of their honest, simple lives (v. 14). The Apostle points out that his work will be effective if they conduct themselves as children of God and bear witness to others concerning the word of salvation (vv. 16–17). The Philippians' response to grace more than repays him for all his efforts and fills his heart with joy (v. 18).

**2:12–13.** Perseverance in faith and charity until the end of one's life is a gift from God. This perseverance is possible provided one does not frustrate the graces which God continues to provide. In this connexion the Council of Trent stresses that "all ought to have most secure hope in the help of God. For unless men are unfaithful to his grace, God will bring the good work to perfection, just as he began it, working both the will and the performance" (*De iustificatione*, chap. 13).

"For his good pleasure": the grace God gives a person to enable him to perform supernatural acts is an expression of his benevolence; he wants all men to be saved. Man can do nothing that leads to eternal life unless he be moved by grace. And yet grace does not overpower our freedom: it is *we* who love, and *we* who act. Man's inability to perform meritorious actions on his own should not cause him to lose heart. On the contrary, it is an additional reason why we should be grateful to God, for he is always ready to give us the help of grace; grace enables us to do good works, which are efficacious for meriting heaven. St Francis de Sales gives this example to show the wonderful way God's love works: "when an affectionate mother is

[14]Do all things without grumbling or questioning, [15]that you 1 Pet 4:9
may be blameless and innocent, children of God without blemish Deut 32:5
in the midst of a crooked and perverse generation, among whom

teaching her little child to walk, she helps him and holds him if necessary, directing him to safer places and more level ground, holding him by the hand and keeping him there, or lifting him up in her arms. Our Lady similarly watches over the steps her children take" (*Treatise on the Love of God*, book 3, chap. 4).

God's solicitude towards us should not, however, be an excuse for inaction on our part. He is always desirous of entering our soul (cf. Rev 3:20), but he will not do so if we refuse to listen to his voice; if we bar our heart to him. Hence St Paul's advice: "work out your own salvation with fear and trembling" (v. 12). This is an urgent invitation to second the action of God's grace in our soul. The "fear" and "trembling" are the fear of a good child who does not want to displease someone who loves him (cf. 2 Cor 7:15); this filial fear is closely connected with the joy of serving God (cf. Ps 2:11) and it is sweetened by the sure knowledge that God himself is bent on our being holy; "we must [...] not be dispirited. We must not be stopped by any kind of human calculation. To overcome the obstacles we have to throw ourselves into the task so that the very effort we make will open up new paths" (St Josemaría Escrivá, *Christ Is Passing By*, 160).

**2:14–15.** In the midst of people who sometimes turn their backs on God, a Christian should always act in a "blameless and innocent" way that befits a child of God. By so doing his work and social dealings will be "lights in the world", showing everyone the way, with the light of Christ. "Don't let your life be barren. Be useful. Make yourself felt. Shine forth with the torch of your faith and your love. With your apostolic life, wipe out the trail of filth and slime left by the unclean sowers of hatred. And set aflame all the ways of the earth with the fire of Christ that you bear in your heart" (St Josemaría Escrivá, *The Way*, 1).

The first Christians did not go in fear of the world, despite being surrounded by depravity and wickedness. Although the equals of their fellow-citizens, their way of acting exerted a supernatural influence on the society of which they formed part. They were putting into practice their Master's teaching: "Let your light so shine before men, that they may see your good works and give glory to your Father who is in heaven" (Mt 5:16).

"The difference between Christians and the rest of mankind is not a matter of nationality, or language, or customs. Christians do not live apart in separate cities of their own, they do not speak any special dialect, or practise any separate way of life [...]. To put it briefly, the relationship of Christians is to the world as that of soul to body. As the soul is diffused through every part of the body, so are Christians through all the world" (*Letter to Diognetus*, 5, 1 and 2; 6, 1).

Today, as then, Christians continue to be a leaven of spiritual and truly human life. Nothing human is a matter of indifference to them.

In addition to the many human reasons which motivate this way of acting, the faithful also draw inspiration from their faith: "Every Christian should make Christ present among men; he ought to act in such a way that those who know him sense 'the fragrance of Christ' (cf. 2 Cor 2:15). People should be able to

you shine as lights in the world, [16]holding fast the word of life, so
that in the day of Christ I may be proud that I did not run in vain
or labour in vain. [17]Even if I am to be poured as a libation upon
the sacrificial offering of your faith, I am glad and rejoice with
Phil 3:1; 4:4 you all. [18]Likewise you also should be glad and rejoice with me.

## 3. PLANS AND NEWS

### Timothy's mission

Job 13:16 [19]I hope in the Lord Jesus to send Timothy to you soon, so that I
1 Cor 16:10 may be cheered by news of you. [20]I have no one like him, who
will be genuinely anxious for your welfare. [21]They all look after

---

recognize the Master in his disciples" (St Josemaría Escrivá, *Christ Is Passing By*, 105).

**2:17.** In some of the sacrifices regulated by the Mosaic Law (cf. Ex 29:40; Num 15:5, 7; 28:14–15) as also in many types of pagan sacrifice, a libation was poured over the sacrificial victim. In pagan rites this consisted in pouring wine over the holocaust while it was actually burning on the altar. St Paul's words here refer to this rite. Up to this he has offered his life as a sacrifice so that the faith might spread to all men; now he is ready to go further—to shed his blood as a libation to make his sacrifice complete. Should it prove necessary to die a martyr's death, that would not sadden him; he would be very happy.

Many saints have felt the same way. St Ignatius of Antioch, for example, asked the Christians of Rome to sing in thanksgiving to God when the time came for him to be thrown to the lions: "Suffer me to be a libation poured out to God, while there is still an altar ready for me. Then you may form a loving choir around it and sing hymns of praise in Jesus Christ to the Father" (*Letter to the Romans*, 2, 2). Total self-surrender and unreserved commitment to his vocation should categorize an apostle's life, for he should always bear in mind that "no ideal becomes a reality without sacrifice" (St Josemaría Escrivá, *The Way*, 175). Self-denial, therefore is absolutely essential if one is to fully identify with Christ. However, "Many who would willingly let themselves be nailed to a cross before the astonished gaze of a thousand onlookers cannot bear with a Christian spirit the pinpricks of each day! Think, then, which is the more heroic" (*The Way*, 204).

**2:19–24.** Since this is a family letter, the Apostle now changes the subject and begins to tell the Philippians something about his plans: he is thinking of visiting Philippi, but before that, once it seems his case is likely to go well, he will send Timothy to them. The virtues for which he praises his co-worker—the support he gives him (Paul), and his concern for others (cf. v. 20), his self-forgetfulness (v. 21), his humility and commitment to the Gospel (v. 22)—are virtues which all Christians should have, for all have a God-given calling to apostolate.

Among the qualities for which St Paul praises Timothy, perhaps the most outstanding is the way he identifies with

their own interests, not those of Jesus Christ. [22]But Timothy's
worth you know, how as a son with a father he has served with me
in the gospel. [23]I hope therefore to send him just as soon as I see
how it will go with me; [24]and I trust in the Lord that shortly I
myself shall come also.

**Epaphroditus' mission**

[25]I have thought it necessary to send to you Epaphroditus my Phil 4:18
brother and fellow worker and fellow soldier, and your messenger
and minister to my need, [26]for he has been longing for you all, and
has been distressed because you heard that he was ill. [27]Indeed he
was ill, near to death. But God had mercy on him, and not only on

---

the Apostle's own sentiments and concerns; in this he sets an example of how Christians (particularly priests and all who have responsibility for souls) should be at one with the lawful pastors of the Church. The hierarchical constitution of the Church requires that all be united and obedient to those who have a mission of government. The authority of the Church, the hierarchy, "was established by Christ. It is his representative, the authoritative organ of his word, the expression of his great pastoral charity. Hence obedience has faith as its starting point. It is exercised in the school of evangelical humility. It is a participation in the wisdom, unity, idealism and charity which are ruling factors in the corporate life of the Church. It confers upon him who commands and upon him who obeys the merit of being like Christ who 'became obedient unto death'" (Paul VI, *Ecclesiam suam*, 44).

**2:25–30.** Imprisonment obviously entailed suffering and made it difficult for Paul to carry on his apostolate. Yet God's plans envisaged his being in that situation: "In the messianic programme of Christ, which is at the same time the programme *of the Kingdom of God*, suffering is present in the world in order to release love, to give birth to works of love towards neighbour, to transform the whole of human civilization into a 'civilization of love'" (John Paul II, *Salvifici doloris*, 30). St Paul's imprisonment stirred the love and generosity of the Philippians to send Epaphroditus to minister to his needs. It is very touching to see the sensitive way the first Christians practised fraternity among themselves, and the respect and affection they had for their pastors. "The world of human suffering unceasingly calls for, so to speak, another world—the world of human love; and in a certain sense man owes to suffering that unselfish love which stirs in his heart and in his actions" (ibid., 28).

This passage also reveals another aspect of the fraternity of these early Christians: they really looked after one another: this interest even extended to others' physical health and worries. "And so, if we know Jesus, we realize that we can live only by giving ourselves to the service of others. A Christian can't be caught up in personal problems; he must be concerned about the universal Church and the salvation of all souls [...]. Our neighbours' problems must be our problem. Christian fraternity should be something very deep in the soul, so that we are indifferent to no one" (St Josemaría Escrivá, *Christ Is Passing By*, 145).

him but on me also, lest I should have sorrow upon sorrow. 28I am
the more eager to send him, therefore, that you may rejoice at seeing
him again, and that I may be less anxious. 29So receive him in the
Acts 20:24 Lord with all joy; and honour such men, 30for he nearly died for the
work of Christ, risking his life to complete your service to me.

## 4. THE CHRISTIAN LIFE

### A warning about Judaizers

3 1Finally, my brethren, rejoice in the Lord. To write the same
things to you is not irksome to me, and is safe for you.
Rev 22:15 2Look out for the dogs, look out for the evil-workers, look out for
those who mutilate the flesh. 3For we are the true circumcision, who
Rom 2:29 worship God in spirit,[e] and glory in Christ Jesus, and put no
2 Cor 11:18, 22 confidence in the flesh. 4Though I myself have reason for

---

**3:1.** In the second part of this verse the Apostle seems to be referring to an earlier letter, dealing with the same subject—the need for watchfullness so as not to be led astray by Judaizers. According to St Polycarp's testimony (cf. *Letter to the Philippians*, 3, 2), St Paul wrote "letters" to the Philippians. However, no other letter has come down to us (see page 102 above). It is possible that this chapter may incorporate the essence of one of these letters. St Paul did not mind repeating himself: with Christ the fullness of God's Revelation was reached (cf. Vatican II, *Dei Verbum*, 4), but that revelation needs to be proclaimed on an ongoing basis and, besides, it makes sense to emphasize ideas again and again: that is what teachers and parents do, and it is the advice the Apostle will later give his disciple Timothy (cf. 2 Tim 4:2).

On joy, see the note on Philippians 4:4.

**3:2–3.** It was quite common for Roman houses to have a notice at the entrance which read "*Cave canem*", Beware of the dog. St Paul uses these words as a colourful way of telling the Philippians to be on their guard against Judaizers—"evil-workers" who instead of helping to build Christ's building were demolishing it.

In the Old Testament circumcision showed that one belonged to the people of Israel; it guaranteed the promises of salvation made by God on Sinai. The Judaizers were arguing that all Gentiles who came to the faith should first be circumcised. The Apostle calls them "those who mutilate the flesh", because the circumcision they were promoting was something purely external, to do with the flesh, whereas after Christ the only true circumcision is an internal one, circumcision of the heart, the work of the Holy Spirit, which is effected by Baptism (cf. Rom 2:28–29).

**3:4–11.** St Paul had no opposition in Philippi; the Philippians in fact, were exemplary in their conduct. But prudence leads him to warn them about those who have been causing trouble in other churches, just in case they venture into Philippi also. His adversaries cannot

**e.** Other ancient authorities read *worship by the Spirit of God*

confidence in the flesh also. If any other man thinks he has reason
for confidence in the flesh, I have more: 5circumcised on the eighth Gen 17:10
day, of the people of Israel, of the tribe of Benjamin, a Hebrew born Acts 26:5
of Hebrews; as to the law a Pharisee, 6as to zeal a persecutor of the
church, as to righteousness under the law blameless.

**The righteousness of God exceeds that of the Law**

7But whatever gain I had, I counted as loss for the sake of Christ. Mt 13:44, 46
8Indeed I count everything as loss because of the surpassing worth Lk 14:33
of knowing Christ Jesus my Lord. For his sake I have suffered the
loss of all things, and count them as refuse, in order that I may
gain Christ 9and be found in him, not having a righteousness of Rom 3:21; 10:3

---

argue that he is ignorant of the Law and the traditions of the chosen people. Just as on another occasion he felt he had to make it known that he was a Roman citizen (cf. Acts 16:37; 22:25–29), now, because he thinks it will help the spread of the Gospel, he spells out his Jewish pedigree (cf. 2 Cor 11:22).

Similarly, it is not only lawful for a Christian to claim his civic rights or those connected with his family or work position: justice or the common good may *demand* that he exercise them.

**3:8.** St Paul has a great love for his people. In Romans he shows that he would be ready to accept any sacrifice "for the sake of my brethren, my kinsmen of the flesh" (Rom 9:3f). However, he recognizes that everything in which he gloried before his conversion is worthless in comparison with the grace of knowledge of Christ: that is the hidden treasure, the precious pearl referred to in Gospel parables (cf. Mt 13:44–46). For "once a person experiences the riches of Christ the Lord, he looks down on everything else: property, wealth and honours he views as filth. For there is nothing that can compare with that supreme treasure, nothing that can be placed beside it" (*St Pius V Catechism*, 4, 11, 15).

**3:9.** St Paul makes the distinction between "a righteousness of my own", attainable by personal effort, and that which comes from God. The former is the righteousness a person can attain by fulfilling the Mosaic Law; it is a good thing, but it is insufficient to give one the full revelation of God in Christ, insufficient to give one a share in the glory of his Resurrection (vv. 10–11). For that, one needs to have righteousness from God, that is, supernatural grace: "not the justice by which he is himself just, but the justice by which he makes us just, namely, the justice which we have as a gift from him and by which we are renewed in the spirit of our mind. And not only are we considered just, but we are truly said to be just, and we are just" (Council of Trent, *De iustificatione*, chap. 7). For a more detailed explanation of the concept of the righteousness that comes from God, see the note on Romans 1:17.

**3:10–12.** The calling to holiness which every Christian receives is not a reward for personal merit: it comes from God's initiative; God desires all men to be saved and to come to the knowledge of the truth (cf. 1 Tim 2:4), that is, to know God himself. The Apostle bears witness to this when he says that "Christ Jesus has made

Rom 6:3ff my own, based on law, but that which is through faith in Christ,
Gal 6:17 the righteousness from God that depends on faith; [10]that I may
1 Pet 4:13 know him and the power of his resurrection, and may share his
sufferings, becoming like him in his death, [11]that if possible I may
attain the resurrection from the dead.

### The spiritual athlete

Rev 20:4f [12]Not that I have already obtained this or am already perfect; but
I press on to make it my own, because Christ Jesus has made me

---

me his own." However, he also says that, in order to grow in knowledge of Christ and enjoy God in heaven, one needs to strive to share in Christ's sufferings. "The Christian is certainly bound both by need and by duty to struggle with evil through many afflictions and to suffer death; but, as one who has been made a partner in the paschal mystery and has been configured to the death of Christ, he will go forward, strengthened by hope, to the resurrection" (Vatican II, *Gaudium et spes*, 22). This struggle, which sometimes calls for heroism, is usually pitched in the incidents of one's ordinary day. Heroism in the everyday battle proves the sincerity of our love and is a sure way to holiness.

"Certainly our goal is both lofty and difficult to attain. But please do not forget that people are not born holy. Holiness is forged through a constant interplay of God's grace and man's response. As one of the early Christian writers says, referring to union with God, 'Everything that grows begins small. It is by constant and progressive feeding that it gradually grows big' (St Mark the Hermit, *De lege spirituali*, 172). So I say to you, if you want to become a thorough-going Christian—and I know you do, even though you often find it difficult to conquer yourself or to keep climbing upwards with this poor body—then you will have to be very attentive to the minutest of details, for the holiness that our Lord demands of you is to be achieved by carrying out with love of God your work and your daily duties, and these will almost always consist of ordinary little things" (St Josemaría Escrivá, *Friends of God*, 7).

"That if possible I may attain the resurrection of the dead": St Paul is referring here to the glorious resurrection of the just, whom the power of the risen Christ will rescue from the domain of death. At the second coming of the Lord, both the souls of the blessed in heaven and the souls of those who are still in purgatory undergoing the temporal punishment due to sins they committed will be re-united with their now glorified bodies. The reprobate will also rise, but their destiny is to suffer for ever the pains of hell in body and soul (cf. Second Council of Lyons, *Profession of Faith of Michael Paleologue*).

Man's supernatural last end consists in knowing God as he is and enjoying him in heaven. When he attains this, man finds complete fulfilment. His life on earth has been a route leading to this perfection, a perfection which can only be fully attained by resurrection in glory. The Apostle recognizes that he needs the help of grace to be "perfect" (that is, faithful unto death) and thereby attain the prize promised by God: perseverance right to the end is not entirely a function

his own.* [13]Brethren, I do not consider that I have made it my Lk 9:62
own; but one thing I do, forgetting what lies behind and straining
forward to what lies ahead, [14]I press on toward the goal for the 1 Cor 9:24f
prize of the upward call of God in Christ Jesus. [15]Let those of us

---

of the merit a person has built up; it is a gift from God (cf. *De iustificatione*, chap. 13). However, God does not dispense man from generously responding to grace in order to attain holiness. As St Teresa of Avila says. "It matters a great deal, it is essential [...], that one have very great, very determined, resolution not to halt until one attains it, come what may, whatever happens, however much one suffers, however much people may gossip, whether I get there or not, even if I die on the way or am not able to face all the effort involved, even if the world collapses around me" (*Way of Perfection*, 35, 2).

**3:12–14.** Growth in holiness always demands an effort. St Paul here uses a vivid comparison—races in the stadium. He describes ascetical struggle in terms of enjoyable supernatural sport. Realizing that he has not reached perfection, he strains to win: Christ already made him his own (cf. v. 12) by entering his life on the Damascus road; from that moment onwards he has striven single-mindedly to serve God.

Our Lord helps everyone to discover his or her particular supernatural vocation. In response to that calling a person should seek to serve God in such a way that "everything good he does, interiorly or externally, he does for the glory and pleasure of God, like a loyal slave who gives everything he gets to his master. Moreover," St John of Avila goes on, "even though he has worked as a servant for many years past, he is not easy-going or careless [...]. He always has that 'hunger and thirst for righteousness' (Mt 5:6): he puts little weight on everything he has done, thinking of how much he has received and how much is due to the Lord he serves" (*Audi, filia*, 92).

In making one's way towards perfection it is important to be always trying to advance spiritually. "What does walking mean?", St Augustine asked himself; "I shall answer very briefly: it means going forward [...]. Examine yourself. You should always be unhappy with what you are, if you want to attain what you are not yet. For when you were content with yourself, you stayed where you were, because if you say 'Enough', you are finished that very minute. Always grow, always walk on, always advance; do not stop on the way, do not turn back, do not go off course. One who does not advance is standing still; one who returns to the things he already abandoned is going backwards; one who goes off course commits apostasy. It is better to hobble along the road than run on any other route" (*Sermon,* 169, 15, 18).

**3:15.** "Those of us who are mature": St Paul is referring to well-instructed Christians who have all the training needed for winning victory, even though they may not yet have attained it (cf. v. 12). If someone, out of ignorance or presumption, is not yet convinced of the need to strive and advance rapidly, God will show him what he must do. The Apostle has no intention of diluting his teaching, for he is the servant of that message, not its master.

Christian teaching does make demands on people which they at first find difficult to accept or fulfil; but this does not exempt an apostle from the duty to com-

1 Cor 2:6 who are mature be thus minded; and if in anything you are
otherwise minded, God will reveal that also to you. 16Only let us
Gal 6:16 hold true to what we have attained.

### Citizens of heaven

1 Cor 4:16; 11:1 17Brethren, join in imitating me, and mark those who so live as
you have an example in us. 18For many, of whom I have often told

---

municate that teaching in its entirety. If someone finds it difficult to accept, God will help him to see the truth.

**3:16.** The Greek text could be translated as "let us keep pressing ahead without breaking ranks"—a reference to soldiers marching in formation, as a phalanx. Keeping this formation was regarded at the time as an essential tactic for success in battle.

We should remember that the church at Philippi was made up mainly of veterans of Roman legions and their families: Paul's use of military language would have helped to get his message across to this kind of audience. He is pointing out how important it is for every Christian to live in accord with Christian faith and moral teaching, in solidarity with his brethren.

**3:17.** The Apostle's teaching goes further than to list a series of truths and rules for moral behaviour: he backs this up with his own life in the service of the Gospel, and, through it, all men; this is what makes his preaching arresting and convincing.

"There is no better teaching than the teacher's own example," St John Chrysostom exclaims, commenting on this passage; "by taking this course the teacher is sure of getting his disciple to follow him. Speak wisely, instruct as eloquently as you can […], but your example will make a greater impression, will be more decisive […]. When your actions are in line with your words, nobody will be able to find fault with you" (*Hom. on Phil,* ad loc.).

This, then, is the standard Christians should aim at. It will help those they come in contact with to learn how to be hard-working, noble, loyal and sincere people, or at least to tend in that direction.

One can see from this verse, as from many other passages in his letters, that St Paul refers to himself now as "me", now as "us". In the second case he is probably also referring to his co-workers; these they should also imitate, for like him they are imitators of Christ (cf. 1 Cor 4:17). It is quite likely that he is thinking particularly of Timothy, whose name he put alongside his own at the head of this letter—and whom he praised in glorious terms in the previous chapter (cf. Phil 2:19, 22).

Imitation of the saints is a very good way to equip oneself to serve others. "Most earnestly, then, we exhort you", Pius XII says, "be very solicitous for the salvation of those whom Providence has entrusted to your apostolic labours, maintaining throughout the closest union with our divine Redeemer, by whose strength we can do all things (cf. Phil 4:13). It is our ardent desire, beloved sons, that you may emulate those saintly men of old who, by the immensity of their achievement, bore witness to the power of divine grace. Would that each of you could on the evidence of the faithful attribute to himself in humble sincerity the words of the Apostle: 'I will most gladly spend

you and now tell you even with tears, live as enemies of the cross Rom 16:18
of Christ. [19]Their end is destruction, their god is the belly, and Gal 6:12; Col 3:2
they glory in their shame, with minds set on earthly things.* [20]But Col 3:1
our commonwealth is in heaven, and from it we await a Saviour,
the Lord Jesus Christ, [21]who will change our lowly body to be like Rom 8:29
his glorious body, by the power which enables him even to subject 1 Cor 15:43, 49
all things to himself. Col 3:4

**Exhortation to perseverance and joy** 2 Cor 1:14

4 [1]Therefore, my brethren, whom I love and long for, my joy and 1 Thess 2:19
crown, stand firm thus in the Lord, my beloved.
[2]I entreat Euodia and I entreat Syntyche to agree in the Lord.
[3]And I ask you also, true yokefellow, help these women, for they Lk 10:20

---

and be spent for your souls' (2 Cor 12:15)" (*Menti nostrae*, 31).

**3:18–19.** St Paul points to the bad example given by those (cf. v. 2) who, by upholding false doctrines or abusing their Christian freedom, lead a life steeped in vice; they let themselves be controlled by their sensual appetites and they set their hearts on things which enslave them, which should rather make them blush. They are enemies of Christ's cross.

"They glory in their own shame": they take pride in behaviour which is shameful. This may also be an allusion to circumcision, for Judaizers were proud of a mark which decency keeps covered.

**3:20–21.** "It is nature, flawed by sin, that begets all the citizens of the earthly city, whereas it is grace alone which frees nature from sin, which begets citizens of the heavenly city" (*The City of God,* 15, 2). Christians are "citizens of heaven" and therefore are called to live a life that is joyful and full of hope, as befits children of God.

The effort to live in a manner worthy of members of the commonwealth of heaven is aided by hope in the second coming of our Lord Jesus Christ in glory. The Parousia, as well as the passion and death of Christ and his subsequent resurrection, are constant themes in the Apostle's preaching. Reflection on these mysteries helps us to have hope and gives us encouragement in our everyday struggle.

Christ's resurrection is the cause of our resurrection, for "Christ has been raised from the dead, the first fruits of those who have fallen asleep. For as by a man came death, by a man has come also the resurrection of the dead" (1 Cor 15:20–21). An essential prerequisite for attaining resurrection in glory is the effort to identify with Christ, in both joy and suffering, in both life and death. "If we have died with him, we shall also live with him; if we endure, we shall also reign with him" (2 Tim 2:11–12). Christ is the Lord of all creation; his authority extends over the entire universe (cf. Col 1:15–20). If we make the effort that fidelity requires, he will take our body, which is weak and subject to illness, death and decay, and transform it into a glorious body.

**4:3.** True "yokefellow": the same Greek word seems to have been used as a personal name—Syzygus; St Paul may

have laboured side by side with me in the gospel together with
Clement and the rest of my fellow workers, whose names are in
2 Cor 13:11 the book of life.
Heb 10:37 4Rejoice in the Lord always; again I will say, Rejoice. 5Let all
Jas 5:8–9 Mt 6:25–34 men know your forbearance. The Lord is at hand. 6Have no

---

be making a play on words, addressing a colleague of his (this is the only reference we have to him) to ask him to help Euodia and Syntyche. By so doing he will be living up to his name, sharing the burden of the Gospel.

"My fellow workers": many men and women helped St Paul in his apostolic work: some—Timothy, Titus—had received the sacrament of Order by the laying-on of hands, but most of them were ordinary members of the faithful. The Second Vatican Council, in a passage dealing with the apostolate of lay people in the world, refers to this verse and stresses that all have a duty to do apostolate: "All the laity have the exalted duty of working for the greater spread of the divine plan of salvation to all men, of every epoch and all over the earth" (*Lumen gentium*, 33).

**4:4.** What St Paul says here is particularly impressive if one bears in mind that he is writing this letter from prison. In order to have joy it does not matter if we are living in difficult conditions. "For a Christian, joy is a treasure. Only by offending God do we lose it, because sin is the fruit of selfishness, and selfishness is the root of sadness. Even then, a bit of joy survives under the debris of our soul—the knowledge that neither God nor his Mother ever forgets us. If we repent, if an act of sorrow springs from our heart, if we purify ourselves in the holy sacrament of penance, God comes out to meet and forgive us. Then there can be no sadness whatsoever" (St Josemaría Escrivá, *Christ Is Passing By*, 178).

The kind of profound joy that fills the soul with peace does not derive from the satisfaction of physical or material needs but from faithfullness to God and his commandments by embracing the Cross. "This is the difference between us and those who do not know God," St Cyprian says: "they complain in adversity; but difficulties do not draw us away from virtue or from the true faith. On the contrary, our virtue and faith are reinforced in affliction" (*De mortalitate*, 13).

In the Old Testament, God, speaking through Nehemiah, said, "Do not be grieved, for the joy of the Lord is your strength" (Neh 8:10). Joy, in fact, is a powerful ally in the struggle to achieve victory (cf. 1 Mac 3:2ff), to conquer evil with good, for it is something closely connected with grace. "The true worth of what a Christian does is determined by the active presence of God's grace in him and his deeds. In a Christian's heart, therefore, peace is inseparable from joy [...]. When the joy that is in a Christian heart is poured out on others, it gives them hope and optimism; it spurs them to be generous in their daily toil and infects the entire society. My children, only if you have in you this divine grace which is joy and peace, will you be able to do anything useful for others" (John Paul II, *Address*, 10 April 1979).

**4:5–7.** "The Lord is at hand": the Apostle reminds the faithful of the nearness of our Lord; he wants to encourage them to rejoice and to be understanding towards one another. These words must surely have brought to their minds the exclama-

anxiety about anything, but in everything by prayer and supplication with thanksgiving let your requests be made known to
God. 7And the peace of God, which passes all understanding, will Jn 14:27
keep your hearts and your minds in Christ Jesus.
8Finally, brethren, whatever is true, whatever is honourable, what- Rom 12:17
ever is just, whatever is pure, whatever is lovely, whatever is gracious, if there is any excellence, if there is anything worthy of praise,
think about these things. 9What you have learned and received and Rom 16:20
heard and seen in me, do; and the God of peace will be with you. 1 Cor 14:33 1 Thess 5:23

---

tion *Marana tha* (Come, Lord), which was often on their lips at liturgical celebrations (cf. note on 1 Cor 16:21–24). In the sort of hostile environment that many of them lived in, they needed to put their hope in their Saviour, Jesus Christ, who will come from heaven to judge the living and the dead (cf. Phil 3:20; 1 Thess 4:16f; 2 Thess 1:5). St Paul does not mean to specify when the *Parousia* or second coming of Christ will take place (cf. "Introduction to St Paul's Letters to the Thessalonians" in *The Navarre Bible: Thessalonians*; *EB*, 414–461; note on Mt 24:36). Like the first Christians, we should make sure it does not catch us unprepared. Besides, the Lord is always near us, always caring for us in his providence (cf. Ps 119:151). There is no reason for us to feel ill at ease. He is our Father, he is near to all who call on him (cf. Ps 145:18); he listens to our prayers, ever ready to instruct us and to give us whatever we need to overcome difficulties that arise. All that he asks is that we trustingly tell him our situation, speaking to him with the simplicity of a child.

Constant dialogue with God in prayer is, as St Paul suggests, a good way to prevent anything robbing us of peace of soul, for prayer "regulates our affections", St Bernard teaches, "directs our actions, corrects our faults, guides our conduct, beautifies and orders our life; it brings with it knowledge of things divine and things human also. It determines what we ought to do and reflects on what we have done, in such a way that our heart never becomes wanton or in need of discipline" (*Book of Consideration*, 1, 7).

**4:8–9.** The Christian soul is never closed or indifferent to noble human aspirations. "Redeemed by Christ and made a new creature by the Holy Spirit, man can, indeed he must, love the things of God's creation: it is from God that he has received them, and it is as flowing from God's hand that he looks upon them and reveres them. Man thanks his divine benefactor for all these things, he uses them and enjoys them in a spirit of poverty and freedom: thus he is brought to a true possession of the world, as having nothing yet possessing everything: 'All [things] are yours; and you are Christ's; and Christ is God's' (1 Cor 3:22–23)" (Vatican II, *Gaudium et spes*, 37).

The Second Vatican Council has highlighted the permanent relevance of St Paul's teaching in this and in other passages: "In the pursuit of this aim priests will be helped by cultivating those virtues which are rightly held in high esteem in human relations. Such qualities are goodness of heart, sincerity, strength and constancy of mind, careful attention to justice, courtesy and others which the apostle Paul recommends [...] (Phil 4:8)" (*Presbyterorum ordinis*, 3).

### Thanks for help received

[10]I rejoice in the Lord greatly that now at length you have revived
your concern for me; you were indeed concerned for me, but you
1 Tim 6:6 had no opportunity. [11]Not that I complain of want; for I have
learned, in whatever state I am, to be content. [12]I know how to be
abased, and I know how to abound; in any and all circumstances

---

In the same connexion, in a passage where it is encouraging the apostolate of the laity the Council says: "Catholics should strive to cooperate with all men of good will in the promotion of all that is true, just, holy, all that is worthy of love (cf. Phil 4:8)" (*Apostolicam actuositatem*, 14).

Earthly realities and the noble things of this world have a divine value; they are good; they help man to reach God. For, as St Irenaeus wrote, "through the Word of God, everything comes under the influence of the work of Redemption; the Son of God has been crucified on behalf of all, and has traced the sign of the cross on all things" (*Proof of the Apostolic Preaching*). "We cannot say that there are things—good, noble or indifferent—which are exclusively worldly. This cannot be after the Word of God has lived among the children of men, felt hunger and thirst, worked with his hands, experienced friendship and obedience and suffering and death" (St Josemaría Escrivá, *Christ Is Passing By*, 112). Therefore, "your daily encounter with Christ takes place where your fellow men, your yearnings, your work and your affections are. It is in the midst of the most material things of the earth that we must sanctify ourselves, serving God and all mankind" (St Josemaría Escrivá, *Conversations*, 113).

**4:10–20.** Gratitude is a very characteristic feature of Christian life; in this passage we can see the noble soul of St Paul, ever appreciative of any sign of affection and thoughtfullness.

It also shows what great confidence St Paul had in the Philippians; from them alone did he accept help, for his general policy was not to accept material aid so as to leave no one in any doubt about the purity of his intentions in preaching the Gospel (cf. 1 Cor 9:18; 2 Cor 12:14–18). This meant that he was also practising the virtue of poverty, being content with what he had.

Financial resources do make a person's life easier and by helping us meet our material needs they allow us to cultivate friendship with God and go to the help of others, but these resources are not an end in themselves; they are only a means. Therefore there is nothing essentially bad about not having money or property: one can get to heaven without them. However, if a person is well-to-do and is attached to his wealth, that is bad. That is what St Paul is saying. "If you want to be your own masters at all times, I advise you to make a very real effort to be detached from everything, and to do so without fear or hesitation. Then, when you go about your various duties, whether personal, family or otherwise, make honest use of legitimate human resources with a view to serving God, his Church, your family, your profession, your country, and the whole of mankind. Remember that what really matters is not whether you have this or lack that, but whether you are living according to the truth taught us by our Christian faith, which tells us that created goods are only a means, nothing more. So, do not be beguiled into imagining that they are in

I have learned the secret of facing plenty and hunger, abundance 2 Cor 12:10
and want. [13]I can do all things in him who strengthens me. 2 Tim 34:17
[14]Yet it was kind of you to share my trouble. [15]And you
Philippians yourselves know that in the beginning of the gospel, 2 Cor 11:9
when I left Macedonia, no church entered into partnership with
me in giving and receiving except you only; [16]for even in Acts 17:1
Thessalonica you sent me help[f] once and again. [17]Not that I seek 1 Cor 9:11
the gift; but I seek the fruit which increases to your credit. [18]I have Ex 29:18

---

any way definitive" (St Josemaría Escrivá, *Friends of God*, 118).

**4:13.** "In him who strengthens me": the proposition "in" often refers to the place "where", in which case the text would mean that the person who lives in Christ, who is identified with him, can do all things. However, in biblical Greek it frequently has a causal meaning, in which case the Apostle would be saying that he can do all things because God lends him his strength.

The difficulties which can arise in apostolic work or in one's search for personal holiness are not an insuperable obstacle, for we can always count on God's support. So, we need to let ourselves be helped; we need to go to the Lord whenever we are tempted or feel discouraged ("Thou art the God in whom I take refuge": Ps 43:2), humbly recognizing that we need his help, for we can do nothing on our own. St Alphonsus encourages us always to put our trust in God: "The proud person relies on his strength and he falls; but the humble person, who puts all his trust in God, holds his ground and does not succumb, no matter how severely he is tempted" (*The Love of God*, 9).

"I have asked you", St Josemaría Escrivá says, "to keep on lifting your eyes up to heaven as you go about your work, because hope encourages us to catch hold of the strong hand which God never ceases to reach out to us, to keep us from losing our supernatural point of view. Let us persevere even when our passions rear up and attack us, attempting to imprison us within the narrow confines of our selfishness; or when puerile vanity makes us think we are the centre of the universe. I am convinced that unless I look upward, unless I have Jesus, I shall never accomplish anything. And I know that the strength to conquer myself and to win comes from repeating that cry, 'I can do all things in him who strengthens me' (Phil 4:13), words which reflect God's firm promise not to abandon his children if they do not abandon him" (St Josemaría Escrivá *Friends of God*, 213).

**4:17–19.** Using a metaphor taken from commercial life, the Apostle gives us an insight into the value of generosity. He is not asking the Philippians for donations: he can survive without them; he is seeking the good that will redound to them on account of their alms-giving (cf. v. 17): and, given their own limited financial resources, they are in fact being particularly generous (cf. 2 Cor 8:2).

Since God is the one who rewards men for their actions, then clearly a person who gives alms ultimately benefits more than he who receives alms. As a reward for their almsgiving the Philippians will receive nothing less than the eternal glory

**f.** Other ancient authorities read *money for my needs*

received full payment, and more; I am filled, having received from Epaphroditus the gifts you sent, a fragrant offering, a sacrifice acceptable and pleasing to God. [19]And my God will supply every need of yours according to his riches in glory in Christ Jesus. [20]To our God and Father be glory for ever and ever. Amen.

**Words of farewell**

Phil 1:13 [21]Greet every saint in Christ Jesus. The brethren who are with me greet you. [22]All the saints greet you, especially those of Caesar's household.

Gal 6:18 [23]The grace of the Lord Jesus Christ be with your spirit.

---

won for us by Christ Jesus. And so St Leo the Great recommends that "whoever gives alms should do so with detachment and joy, for the less he keep back for himself, the greater will be his gain" (*Tenth Lenten Sermon*).

**4:21–22.** "Those of Caesar's household": these would have been civil servants, employees of the imperial government, who had been converted to Christianity. The Philippians would have been pleased to receive such greetings, because it would show them that the Gospel was gaining ground even in those circles. On where this letter was written from, see pp. 83–84, above.

# Introduction to the Letter to the Colossians

## THE CITY OF COLOSSAE

In St Paul's time Colossae was a small city in Asia Minor. It was situated in a region called Phrygia, in a valley of the Lycus river, a tributary of the Meander. Located in the same valley were Laodicea, about 15 kilometres (11 miles) to the northeast, and Hierapolis, 20 kilometres to the north.

Herodotus[1] and Xenophon[2] tell us that Colossae was a very important city in ancient times. By St Paul's day Laodicea had become the main city in the Lycus valley;[3] now, all that remains of Colossae is some unimportant ruins near the Turkish city of Konya.

Most of the inhabitants of the city, as of the whole region, were Gentiles, although it also had a sizeable Jewish community, as is suggested by the fact that residents of Phrygia were among those who listened to Peter's address in Jerusalem on the day of Pentecost (cf. Acts 2:10).

St Paul visited this region at least twice. The first time was during his second journey, on the way from Lystra and Iconium to Galatia (cf. Acts 15:6); the second, during his third journey, when he stayed there a short while to strengthen the morale of the disciples in Phrygia (cf. Acts 18:23). However, there is no reference in Acts to his actually visiting Colossae, and the Apostle seems to imply that he did not know the Colossians personally (cf. Col 2:1), although he does say that he plans to visit them soon: in his letter to Philemon, a well-to-do Colossian, he asks him to prepare to receive him (cf. Philem 22). We do not know if he ever managed to carry out this plan.

The origins of the Church in Colossae lie in St Paul's long stay in Ephesus during his second apostolic journey, when as a result of his preaching, as Acts tells us, "all the residents of Asia heard the word of the Lord, both Jews and Greeks" (Acts 19:10). Among those who listened to the Apostle's daily preaching in the hall of Tyrannus (cf. Acts 19:9) there would have been some Colossians who became converts; these, after receiving Baptism, would have begun to play their part in the spread of the Gospel. One of these was Philemon (cf. Philem 1 and 19), another Epaphras (cf. Col 4:12), whom St Paul would commission to preach in his home city (cf. Col 1:7) and in neighbouring Hierapolis and Laodicea (cf. Col 4:13).

**1.** *History*, 7, 30. **2.** *Anabasis*, 1, 2, 6. **3.** Strabo, *Geography*, 12, 8, 3.

The Colossae community, then, had not been directly founded by St Paul but by Epaphras; however, it was very attached to the Apostle. Most of its members were of Gentile origin (cf. Col 1:21; 2:13), although some were Jews (cf. Col 2:16; 3:11).

St Paul was very familiar with the faith and brotherly love of the Colossians (cf. Col 1:4), and with the difficulties they were experiencing. He is not physically with them, but his heart is with them (cf. Col 2:5), he strives for their spiritual advancement (cf. Col 2:1–2) and never ceases to pray for them (cf. Col 1:9). The Letter to the Colossians is a good example of the Apostle's pastoral solicitude.

## PLACE AND DATE OF COMPOSITION OF THE LETTER

As he says in the letter, St Paul wrote this letter from prison (cf. Col 4:3, 10, 18). Early Christian tradition considers him to have written it during his first Roman imprisonment in the period 61–63.

Since the beginning of the twentieth century, there have been some scholars who argued that this letter was written when Paul was in prison in Ephesus. The only early text which says this is an ancient prologue to New Testament writings. If he was writing from Ephesus, it would explain St Paul's hope of soon passing through Colossae (cf. Philem 22). But there is no evidence that Aristarchus and Luke—who send the Colossians greetings in the letter (cf. Col 4:10, 14)—were with Paul in Ephesus; whereas we do know that they accompanied him to Rome (cf. Acts 27:2). Another theory suggests Caesarea as the place where the letter was written; but Paul's imprisonment in Caesarea does not fit in with the situation described in the letter.

From the letter itself we can see that the Apostle enjoyed a degree of freedom in the prison in question: he was able to receive visitors—for example, Epaphras (cf. Col 1:14)—and to engage in spreading the Gospel with the help of his co-workers (cf. Col 4:7ff). These circumstances certainly obtained during his first Roman imprisonment: all that time, although he was guarded by a soldier (cf. Acts 28:16), he was living in rented accommodation and was able to receive as many visitors as came, which meant that he could preach the Gospel "quite openly and unhindered" (cf. Acts 28:30–31). Moreover, the fact that he had with him all the companions he names, is much easier to understand in terms of that Roman imprisonment.

The letter was brought to the Colossians by Tychicus (cf. Col 4:7), who was accompanied by Onesimus (cf. Col 4:9). The latter bears another letter to his master, Philemon—written, therefore, at the same time as Colossians—in which St Paul looks forward to being released very soon (cf. Philem 22). The epistle, then, must have been written towards the end of the Apostle's first imprisonment in Rome, possibly around the beginning of the year 63, a few months before his case lapsed. This we know to have occurred in the spring of that year.

## PAULINE AUTHORSHIP

It is generally agreed that the Letter to the Colossians was written by St Paul (which does not mean that he may not have used an amanuensis: cf. Col 4:18); the earliest sources of Tradition testify to this, and what are very probably references to passages of this letter appear in works written at the end of the first century and in the early years of the second[4]—which indicate that the letter was known at that time. In the second century St Irenaeus[5] and Tertullian[6] expressly attribute it to St Paul, as does the Muratorian Fragment.

Thus it is fair to say that from earliest times Christians acknowledged the Pauline authorship of this epistle. It was only from the nineteenth century onwards that some scholars began to question its authenticity, arguing from the content of the letter itself. Essentially they base their views on two points—the fact that the vocabulary of the letter contains new words, not found elsewhere in Pauline epistles; and the very considerable advance in theological thinking evidenced in it—which these scholars feel could not have occurred in the Apostle's lifetime.

It is true that Colossians contains elements of developed theology, especially in its teaching on Christ's pre-eminence over all creation. In other letters St Paul had explored in depth God's plan of redemption as it affected mankind, but in this letter all created beings are seen as sharing in the fruits of Redemption.[7] However, this change of perspective is not a sufficient argument against Pauline authorship. One needs to remember that the letter was written in a polemical context, to confront heresies which were threatening the Christians of Colossae. It is not surprising that these erroneous teachings should have caused St Paul to reflect further and should have led him, under the influence of the Holy Spirit, to attain new insights into these mysteries.[8]

The particular background against which the letter was written would justify the Apostle using terminology which those spreading false theories

**4.** St Clement of Rome, in his *Letter to the Corinthians*, 1, 49, 2, puts forward the same idea as is found in Colossians 14; similarities can likewise be seen between Colossians 1:16 and the Epistle of Barnabas, 12:7 and between Colossians 1:23 and St Ignatius of Antioch, *Letter to the Ephesians*, 10:3. **5.** *Against Heresies*, 3, 14, 1. **6.** *De resurrectione carnis*, 23; *Liber de praescriptionibus,* 7. **7.** The only other place where this idea was previously developed to any degree was in Romans 8:19–22. **8.** Besides there is nothing really "original" in this letter: most of its ideas are to be found in other Pauline texts, but in a less structured way. On the pre-existence of Christ, cf. 1 Cor 1:23–24 (Christ is "the wisdom of God") and 1 Cor 2:7 ("we impart a secret and hidden wisdom of God, which God decreed before the ages for our glorification"). In 2 Corinthians 4:4 Christ is already described as being "the likeness of God" (Col 1:15). In 1 Corinthians 8:6 our Lord is already linked to the act of creation (Col 1:16). The notion of Christ's death reconciling the whole world to God (Col 1:20) is already present in 2 Corinthians 5:18–19. See also the previous note.

were themselves using: this would make his meaning clearer and help to remove doubts. The circumstances, then, explain why St Paul uses terms not found in his earlier writing.

## THE REASON FOR THE LETTER

While St Paul was in prison in Rome, around the year 61 or 62, he was visited by Epaphras, who brought him good news which filled him with joy; but he also told him about dangers threatening his beloved Christians in Phrygia. Epaphras, a faithful disciple and a hard-working pastor of the communities at Colossae, Hierapolis and Laodicea, told the Apostle that teachings at odds with the Gospel were making inroads, especially at Colossae.

From the scriptural and non-scriptural data available to us now, it is apparent that these teachings were being promoted by false apostles of Judaizing tendency who had been influenced by various philosophical ideas current at the time. These teachings claimed that the universe was ruled by certain heavenly powers, intermediaries between God and mankind—spiritual powers ranged in hierarchies, each with a sphere of influence on the affairs of men and the fate of the cosmos. Apparently these false teachers were trying to fit the mystery of Christ into this cosmological scheme of things.

Epaphras' report must have been enough to make St Paul see the seriousness of the situation and to realize that here was a religio-philosophical system poles apart from Christianity. It was in fact a prelude to the movement which from the start of the second century was to be known as Gnosticism.

In addition to propagating these pre-Gnostic teachings, the Judaizers in question were also trying to impose a rigid form of asceticism. They stressed certain precepts of Judaism, such as sabbath observance, the celebration of certain feasts, and the necessity of circumcision—adding other obligations derived from the new teachings; for example, because they saw matter as something evil, they laid down severe fasts, abstinence from certain types of food and avoidance of certain modes of behaviour which they regarded as too worldly.

Due to the fact that they attributed the creation and government of the universe to heavenly spirits, they superstitiously rendered these homage.

These doctrinal and ascetical ideas had been attracting some of the more restless souls in the young communities of Asia Minor. It was not the first time St Paul came up against this type of thing, and he was quick to see what a damaging effect it could have.

These problems that had arisen in Colossae, like those of earlier years in Galatia, provided St Paul with the opportunity to deal with key truths of faith and morality, especially the mystery of Christ.

## STRUCTURE AND CONTENT

1. *Introduction* (1:1–14). After a brief greeting (1:1–2) St Paul, moved by the news Epaphras has brought him, thanks God for the way the faithful of Colossae are responding to God's gifts (1:3–8) by their faith in Jesus Christ, their love for one another, and their hope in heaven. Their spiritual health owes much to Epaphras and his preaching of the Gospel.

The Apostle never ceases praying for them that they may steadily grow in holiness (1:9–11) and receive the gifts of knowledge and understanding which will protect them against false teaching. The Lord, he tells them, expects them to bear fruit of good works.

He urges them to be grateful to God for the wonders he has worked in them (1:12–14).

2. *Doctrinal exposition* (1:15—2:23). The main body of the epistle begins with a boldly drawn outline of the central points of Christian doctrine.

*Hymn to Christ's lordship over all creation* (1:15–29). The Apostle focuses on the mystery of Christ and his redemptive mission. In the beautiful hymn of 1:15–20 he reflects on Jesus Christ's lordship over creation—over all created things and over the Church; there is nothing that does not receive the redeeming influence of the blood of his Cross.

He goes on to consider the fruits of this salvific action (1:21–23), which calls for response in the form of steadfastness in the faith.

St Paul's own contribution has been that of fulfilling his God-given mission to proclaim to the Gentiles the mystery of God—his eternal plan of salvation for all mankind. The possibility of having to undergo suffering to do God's will does not alarm him; he is in fact quite happy to suffer (1:24–29).

*Defence of the faith* (2:1–23). He expresses his solicitude for the Colossians and for all those whom he does not know personally (2:1–3). Although he is not with them physically he is so in spirit; therefore, while rejoicing to learn of their faith, he warns them not to be led astray by false philosophy (2:4–8), the errors of which he identifies.

To counter the danger which complicated cosmological theories might do to the Colossians' faith, he explains the essential basis of Christ's primacy: "In him the whole fullness of deity dwells bodily", for he is both true God and true man (2:9–10).

Another erroneous idea being promoted by the false apostles is the necessity of circumcision for Gentiles who embrace Christianity. Against this, St Paul tells them that only Baptism, "the circumcision of Christ", has the power to give us supernatural life and to forgive sins (2:14–12), and the reason for this is that through Christ's death we have been liberated from the slavery of sin and the Law and, therefore, it is no longer necessary to observe the countless precepts which Judaism added to the Decalogue over the years, making the Law something impossible to adhere to—a kind of sentence of condemnation (2:13–14). He makes it quite clear that angelic powers, to which the heretics were giving such importance, are totally subordinate to Jesus Christ (2:15).

The false teachers were also trying to impose a rigid kind of asceticism involving abstention from certain types of food, and the celebration of certain Jewish festivals (2:16–17). Also, due to their mistaken notions of how the cosmos is structured and governed, they rendered superstitious homage to angels, to the detriment of the worship that is due to God alone (2:18–20). Because they regarded matter as evil, they avoided touching or tasting things which are in themselves good, having been made by God for the benefit of mankind (2:21–22). St Paul takes issue with all these abuses on the grounds that they are in conflict with proper expressions of religious devotion (2:23).

3. *Moral consequences* (3:1—4:6). The principle on which Christian moral conduct is based is union with Christ, which begins with Baptism—which is true spiritual resurrection—and is brought to perfection by a life of prayer and by the other sacraments. The Christian, therefore, must constantly be seeking the "things that are above", where Christ is. Christian life, therefore, cannot be reduced to avoidance of sin; it consists, rather, in something more positive—sharing in the very life of Christ (3:1–4); that is the moral direction, the Apostle says, in which the Christian should go.

The first step is to shun the vices of the "old nature", the old man (3:5–9), and put on the "new nature" by practising Christian virtues (3:10–13), the most important of which is charity (3:14). Therefore, to progress spiritually Christ must reign in one's heart (3:15).

Assiduous meditation on the word of God is essential to the nourishment of Christian life (3:16). Everything a Christian does should be sanctified by love of Christ (3:17).

Having outlined the basic principle of Christian morality, the Apostle then deals with duties which derive from it in specific situations—those of husband and wife (3:18–19), parents and children (3:20–21), and masters and slaves (3:22—4:1).

Finally, he calls on all to play an active part in the apostolate: with the backing of prayer, the Christian should try to attract everyone to the faith through his good example marked by human and supernatural grace (4:2–6).

4. *Conclusion* (4:7–18). The letter will be carried by Tychicus, and Onesimus will go with him. Both of them will give the Colossians more detailed information about Paul's situation (4:7–9). Paul's companions send greetings (4:10–17) and the Apostle writes a few words of farewell in his own hand (4:18).

## PRINCIPAL DOCTRINAL TOPICS

The central stem from which the entire teaching of this epistle develops is the mystery of Christ: the Son, eternal God, like the Father, at a particular moment in time assumed a human nature. The Apostle expresses this truth in these words: "In him the whole fulness of deity dwells bodily" (Col 2:9).

Apropos of the errors currently being spread at Colossae, St Paul deals specifically with the creation and government of the universe and God's saving plan for mankind, a plan which extends, in some way, to all earthly realities. In the light of these principles he elaborates a sublime hymn extolling the mystery of Christ.

Christ is Creator with the Father; but he has taken on a created nature; this gives him pre-eminence among men. He has a key role in the creation of all things; as also in the new creation, that is, regeneration in the order of grace; this second creation he accomplishes by sacrificing himself on the Cross, a sacrifice which repairs the damage done to nature through sin. Therefore, he is "head" of all the universe, of all earthly realities, and of the Church.

One of the aspects of teaching underlined here is the *lordship* of Christ, his total sovereignty as the Lord (*Kyrios*) who exercises his authority over all creation, invisible as well as visible (cf. Col 1:16–20 and Eph 1:10–21). Christ's lordship over the angelic world (cf. Col 2:10; Eph 1:2ff) and over the Church is given particular emphasis.

### CHRIST IS OVER ALL CREATION

St Paul takes issue directly with the convoluted theories disturbing the faith of the neophytes at Colossae and categorically states that the Lord Jesus is supreme over all created beings, in heaven or on earth; his dominion is absolute and he is infinitely higher than any created entity (cf. Col 1:15–20). The Apostle explains that this is so because "in him all the fullness (*pleroma*) of God was pleased to dwell and through him to reconcile to himself all things" (Col 1:19–20). It is not that he merely has sovereignty within a certain sphere: he fills everything: "in him the whole fullness of deity dwells bodily" (Col 2:9).

The Apostle goes right to the nub of the question, putting everything in proper focus: compared with Christ, what are celestial beings, whether thrones or dominions or principalities or powers: they are created entities—creatures created for Christ and through Christ (cf. Col 1:16).

What exactly are these celestial hierarchies? St Paul does not go into detail: whatever importance they have is altogether relative: they are simply created things. What is important—and this is the key—is the fact that Christ Jesus, God and man, is Lord (*Kyrios*) over them all and over the whole of creation.

As the enigmatic text of Colossians 2:15 puts it, "he disarmed the principalities and powers, and made a public example of them, triumphing over them" (cf. note on Col 2:15). Thus, there is nothing that is outside the dominion of Christ.

Christ, then, is not just one of the many beings which populate the universe: he is the head, the principle by which salvation reaches all.

Similarly, Christ's supremacy over the cosmos derives not only from *who* he is—he is God and man—but also from *what* he is: he is the Saviour. Salvation has already been accomplished by Christ, but its application is an on-going process, for its fruits must reach each and every member of mankind, and its ultimate climax will come when all things are recapitulated in Christ.

## CHRIST IS THE HEAD OF THE CHURCH

Since St Thomas Aquinas it has been customary to identify three elements in Christ's headship over the Church—pre-eminence, perfection and life-force.[9]

Colossians contains two basic texts concerning Christ as head of the Church—1:18 and 2:19. The first of these identifies a headship in terms of pre-eminence (Christ is the first); while the second speaks more clearly of his being the life-force of the Church. Both aspects, however, are intimately linked in both texts.

Colossians 1:15–20 is a hymn which extols Christ as absolutely supreme over all creation and over each of its levels. In the course of the hymn it is stated that "he is [also] the head of the body, the church" (Col 1:18). The subject of this sentence, "he", is the undivided Christ, the God–man. This verse adds to the proclamation of Christ's supremacy over creation, the notion that he is head of the Church. The "head" is the most noble, the supreme, part of every living thing, whether physical or moral; there is no doubt, therefore, about what this "being head" involves. Moreover, in the Hellenistic literature of the time, especially in treatises on medicine, the "head" was seen as the centre of vitality and the control element of the entire human or animal body, that is, its life-force.

In the second chapter of Colossians, when St Paul deals with the need to be united to the head, he says that by him the whole body, through its joints and ligaments, is nourished and knit together with a growth that comes from God (cf. Col 2:19). This passage is very much in line with the ideas about physiology we have just referred to—about the head performing the vitalizing function for the rest of the body.

The notion of the Church as Christ's body is wonderfully expressive about how the mystery of salvation works. It explains the supernatural life and

**9.** Cf. *Summa theologiae*, 3, 8, 1, c.

growth of each and every member of the entire Christian community: thanks to the organic unity which the Church has as the body of Christ, the members are enabled to grow in charity, each supporting the others while performing its own special function as a living member of the organism. Salvation thus works its way organically and systematically to reach all the members of the Church.

And so the image of the Church as body of Christ tells us how the Church as a whole and each of its members in particular are involved in, affected by, Christ's life-giving role. The different members of the Church are not merely passive elements in this vital process: they both receive grace, the life-force, and act as conductors of the supernatural energy which comes from Christ the head, thus enabling all the members of the community/ecclesial body to benefit from it. The Church/body of Christ is therefore seen to be, in the economy of salvation, not only a passive, acted-on, subject: it also has an active role—but one which is closely dependent on Christ the head.

Indeed, through the intimate union which obtains between body and head, the body extends the action of the head: without the cooperation of the body, the head would in some way be incomplete as far as its life-giving activity is concerned. Therefore, the Christian can in a certain sense "complete" the redemptive passion of Christ himself: "Now I rejoice in my sufferings for your sake, and in my flesh I complete what is lacking in Christ's afflictions for the sake of his body, that is, the church" (Col 1:24).

The image of the Church as the body of Christ implies the idea that just as in a living organism the head performs the thinking, organizing and directive function, something similar happens with Christ the head and the Church the body: the Church is governed by Christ, carries out Christ's intentions and in some way extends and "completes" his life-giving activity.

## CHRIST IS OVER ALL TEMPORAL REALITIES

This section of our introduction deals with a specific dimension of Christ's supremacy. Since the members of the Church are involved in temporal realities, "profane" affairs, it is important to note the richness of the revealed teaching in Colossians and Ephesians concerning Christ's lordship, a lordship which embraces not only heaven, not only the most intimate dimensions of the human person, but also all earthly affairs, all everyday human interests and involvements: for, Christ "is before all things, and in him all things hold together" (Col 1:17). Therefore, temporal realities are, in themselves, capable of being "christianized": in fact they should be christianized, sanctified. The key to the attitude a Christian should have to all the affairs and activities of mankind is to be found in a famous verse in this epistle: "Whatever you do, in word or deed, do everything in the name of the Lord Jesus, giving thanks to God the Father through him" (Col 3:17).

This is not simply a matter of invoking the name of Jesus as one goes about one's business, but of directing every human activity to Christ. In the last analysis, human actions—be they sacred or profane—acquire a "Christian" dimension, that is, a supernatural dimension, when they are imbued with the spirit of Jesus Christ, with Christian moral values, and are done with upright purpose.

Earthly realities are the medium, the setting, which allows a person to achieve his ultimate goal, that is, salvation. Christ should be placed at the summit of all these realities, as their head, their source of salvation and the point at which they converge, for he is the ultimate goal towards which all the activities of mankind should be directed.

# THE LETTER OF PAUL TO THE COLOSSIANS

*The Revised Standard Version, with notes*

## 1. INTRODUCTION

### Greeting

1 [1]Paul, an apostle of Christ Jesus by the will of God, and Eph 1:1
Timothy our brother,
[2]To the saints and faithful brethren in Christ at Colossae: Rom 1:7
Grace to you and peace from God our Father.

### Thanksgiving for the Colossians' response to the Gospel

[3]We always thank God, the Father of our Lord Jesus Christ, when Eph 1:16 1 Cor 13:13
we pray for you, [4]because we have heard of your faith in Christ Eph 1:15
Jesus and of the love which you have for all the saints, [5]because of Eph 1:13 1 Pet 1:4

---

**1:1–2.** The city of Colossae, as has already been mentioned in the Introduction, lay in the valley of the Lycus river, in Phrygia, a region in the west central part of Anatolia (modern Turkey).

Timothy—whose mother was Jewish and whose father was Greek—was already a Christian when St Paul met him in Lystra (cf. Acts 16:1–2). He readily agreed to go with Paul and from that point onwards he was one of the Apostle's most faithful co-workers. Sometimes we see him accompanying Paul (cf. Acts 20:4), and at other times Paul is sending him off on a special mission (cf. Acts 19:22). When St Paul is writing to the Colossians from his Roman prison, Timothy is by his side and joins him in sending greetings.

Later on, the Apostle will entrust Timothy with the overseeing of the church of Ephesus, and in that capacity he will send him two letters, which form part of the canon of the New Testament.

On the greeting "grace and peace", see the note on Eph 1:2.

**1:3–16.** Epaphras, who was probably born in Colossae, must have come to know St Paul during his stay in Ephesus and been converted after receiving instruction from the Apostle. After being baptized he preached the Gospel to his fellow-citizens. The combination of grace and his own effort make his preaching very effective. However, due to certain false apostles of a Judaizing tendency, errors of a pre-Gnostic and syncretist type began to gain ground among the Colossians, to the detriment of their faith (cf. p. 124 above).

St Paul writes the epistle after receiving a report from Epaphras on the Church in Colossae (v. 9). Although the news Epaphras brought was on the whole good (vv. 3–5), the Apostle feels that the false doctrines being spread among the Colossians are a danger to their faith: the faith that they hold, which they learned from Epaphras, a loyal minister of Jesus Christ, is the true one.

**1:3–5.** St Paul expresses his gratitude to God for all the graces and benefits he has given the Colossians and for the way they have responded to them. He picks out the three theological virtues—faith, charity, and hope—and emphasizes the importance of hope as a support for faith and fraternal love. In this regard, St Josemaría Escrivá says in a homily, "I have seen many souls with such hope in God that they are aflame with love, with a fire that makes the heart beat strong and keeps it safe from discouragement and dejection,

the hope laid up for you in heaven. Of this you have heard before
Eph 1:13 in the word of the truth, the gospel 6which has come to you, as
1 Tim 3:16 indeed in the whole world it is bearing fruit and growing—so
among yourselves, from the day you heard and understood the
grace of God in truth, 7as you learned it from Epaphras our
beloved fellow servant. He is a faithful minister of Christ on our[a]
behalf 8and has made known to us your love in the Spirit.
Eph 1:16 9And so, from the day we heard of it, we have not ceased to
Phil 1:9 pray for you, asking that you may be filled with the knowledge of
his will in all spiritual wisdom and understanding, 10to lead a life
Eph 2:10; 4:1 worthy of the Lord, fully pleasing to him, bearing fruit in every

---

even though along the way they may suffer and at times suffer greatly" (*Friends of God*, 205).

**1:7.** "On our behalf" (cf. RSV note): many important manuscripts read this as "on your behalf", but "on our behalf" parallels the "for us" of the New Vulgate, meaning that Epaphras is a minister of Christ who faithfully substitutes for Paul in his apostolic work among the Colossians.

**1:8.** "Your love in the Spirit": this may refer either to the theological virtue of charity or to the love which the faithful, under the influence of the Holy Spirit, have for the Apostle.

**1:9–11.** Knowledge that the brethren are advancing on the way to holiness gives Paul joy and also leads him to intensify his prayer for them and encourage them to keep up their effort. St John Chrysostom explains this with a graphic example: "Just as at the racecourse the shouts to encourage the riders increase the nearer they get to the finish, so the Apostle vigorously encourages those faithful who are closest to perfection" (*Hom. on Col*, 2, ad loc.).

The Apostle asks God to fill the Colossians with knowledge of his will (v. 9), and he puts particular emphasis on their needing the Holy Spirit to enlighten them with his gifts of wisdom and understanding, to enable them to distinguish good teaching from the misleading teaching of the false apostles; this insight should express itself in all kinds of good works: as St Thomas comments, "it is not enough to have knowledge, for he who knows what is the right thing to do and fails to do it commits sin (cf. Jas 4:17); therefore, one must need to perform virtuous actions" (*Commentary on Col*, ad loc.). Christians therefore should always rely on God to strengthen them to do good; if they do so, they will always be happy.

"To lead a life" (v. 10): literally, "to make your way", a typical Hebrew expression often used in Holy Scripture. Leading a life worthy of the Lord means keeping his commandments, acting in a way that reflects the dignity of God who created us and made us his children through grace, and who watches all our doings with fatherly affection; it means being very faithful to our Christian calling, which leaves us in our place

**a.** Other ancient authorities read *your*

good work and increasing in the knowledge of God. 11May you be
strengthened with all power, according to his glorious might, for
all endurance and patience with joy, 12giving thanks to the Father,
who has qualified us[b] to share in the inheritance of the saints in
light. 13He has delivered us from the dominion of darkness and
transferred us to the kingdom of his beloved Son, 14in whom we
have redemption, the forgiveness of sins.

1 Cor 1:5
Eph 3:16
Acts 26:18
Eph 1:18
Lk 22:53
Eph 6:12
Eph 1:7

---

(cf. 1 Cor 7:21–24) but requires us to bear "fruit in every good work".

**1:12–14.** "The dominion of darkness": the condition of enslavement to the devil of a person in the state of sin. As is frequent in Holy Scripture (cf. Is 58:10; Jn 12:35; 1 Jn 1:5; 2:8; 2 Cor 6:14; Rom 13:11–14; Eph 5:7–13), the simile of movement from darkness to light is used to refer to "redemption" or the change from a condition of sin to one of righteousness and friendship with God, which is effected by infusion of sanctifying grace (cf. St Thomas, *Commentary on Col*, ad loc.).

"Light": this is a symbol of the risen Christ and also of the abundance of graces which he won for mankind in his Easter Mystery. It also describes the whole ensemble of supernatural benefits which grace brings with it—goodness, righteousness (or holiness) and truth (cf. Eph 5:9), which lead to the glory of heaven (cf. 2 Cor 4:6). Hence the "rite of light", so richly a symbol of supernatural realities, which has formed part of baptismal liturgy since the first centuries.

The struggle between light and the power of darkness is referred to in many passages of Holy Scripture (cf. Jn 1:5, 9–11). Darkness means both evil and the power of the Evil One. Before the redemption took place, all men—as a consequence of original sin and their personal sins—were slaves to sin; this slavery darkened their minds and made it difficult for them to know God, who is the true light. Christ our Lord, by carrying out the redemption and obtaining forgiveness for our sins (cf. v. 14), rescued us from the kingdom of darkness, from the tyranny of the Evil One, and brought us into the kingdom of light, the kingdom of truth and justice, of love and of peace (cf. *Preface for the Solemnity of Christ the King*), enabling us to enjoy "the glorious freedom of the children of God" (Rom 8:21).

"His beloved Son": the Hebrew expression "Son of his love", which is paralleled in the Greek, is one of the ways Jesus Christ is referred to in the New Testament (cf. Mt 12:6; Lk 20:13). A variation, "my Son, the Beloved", is spoken by the voice from heaven, that is, by the Father, at Jesus' baptism (cf. Mt 3:17; Mk 1:11; Lk 3:22) and at the Transfiguration (cf. Mt 17:5; Mk 9:7; Lk 9:35).

By speaking in this way St Paul, like St John, is underlining the fact that "God is love" (1 Jn 4:8). God's love for us was made manifest by his sending his only Son into the world so that we might live through him (cf. 1 Jn 4:9). By dying on the Cross he won life for us; by redeeming us with his blood he obtained forgiveness for our sins (cf. Col 1:14; Eph 2:4ff): "He revealed to us that God is love, and he gave us the 'new commandment' of love (Jn 13:34), at the same time communicating to us the certainty that the path

**b.** Other ancient authorities read *you*

### Hymn in praise of Christ, the head of all creation

Heb 1:3 15He is the image of the invisible God, the first-born* of all
Jn 1:3; Eph 1:21 creation; 16for in him all things were created, in heaven and on
Heb 1:2f earth, visible and invisible, whether thrones or dominions or

---

of love is open for all people, so that the effort to establish universal brotherhood is not a vain one (cf. *Gaudium et spes*, 38). By conquering through his death on the Cross evil and the power of sin, by his loving obedience he brought salvation to all" (John Paul II, *Reconciliatio et paenitentia*, 10).

On the meaning of "redemption" and "forgiveness of sins", see the note on Eph 1:7–8.

**1:12.** We Christians should be grateful to God for his great mercy in deigning to free us from the power of the devil, forgiving our sins and making us worthy to "share in the inheritance of the saints". We have benefitted in so many ways: "In addition to the gift itself, he also gives us the power we need to receive it [...]. God has not only honoured us by making us share in the inheritance, but has made us worthy to possess it. And so we receive a double honour from God—firstly, the position itself; and secondly, the capacity to measure up to it" (Chrysostom, *Hom. on Col*, ad loc.).

Our sharing in "the inheritance of the saints" enables us to draw on the treasury of spiritual goods which the Church is continually applying to its members—prayers, sacrifices and all kinds of meritorious actions, which benefit every Christian. This "inheritance of the saints" —in which we begin to share in this present life—will be found in its full and permanent form by those who attain everlasting joy. The grace of conversion originates in God's loving kindness. "Prior to God's gift of grace, although not every man might be sinful there is nothing that he does or can do which would merit forgiveness or the grace of God. You must realize", St John of Avila says, "that it is God who has brought you out of darkness into his wonderful light [...]. And what caused him to do so was not your past merits or any service you have rendered him, but his kindness alone and the merits of our only mediator, Jesus Christ our Lord" (*Audi, filia*, 65).

**1:15–20.** Now we come to a very beautiful hymn in praise of Christ's sublime dignity as God and as man. This was a truth deserving emphasis in view of the danger to the faith which the false apostles' teaching represented (cf. note on vv. 7–8). However, quite apart from the particular situation in Colossae, the sublime teaching contained in this canticle holds good for all times; it is one of the most important Christological texts in St Paul's writings.

The real protagonist of this passage is the Son of God made man, whose two natures, divine and human, are always linked in the divine person of the Word. However, at some points St Paul stresses his divinity (vv. 16, 17, 18b and 19) and at others his humanity (vv. 15, 18a, 18c and 20). The underlying theme of the hymn is Christ's total pre-eminence over all creation.

We can distinguish two stanzas in the hymn. In the first (vv. 15–17) Christ's dominion is stated to embrace the entire cosmos, stemming as it does from his action as Creator: "in him all things were created" (v. 16). This same statement is made in the prologue to the fourth

Gospel (cf. Jn 1:3), and it is implied in the book of Genesis, which tells us that creation was effected by God's word (cf. Gen 1:3, 6, 9 etc.). Since Christ is the Word of God, he is above all things, and therefore St Paul stresses that all angels — irrespective of their hierarchy or order —come under his sway.

Christ's pre-eminence over natural creation is followed by his primacy in the economy of supernatural salvation, a second creation worked by God through grace. The second stanza (vv. 18–20) refers to this further primacy of Christ: by his death on the cross, Christ has restored peace and has reconciled all things—the world and mankind—to God. Jews and Gentiles both are called to form part of one body, the Church, of which Christ is the head; and all the celestial powers are subject to his authority.

This passage is, then, a sublime canticle celebrating Christ, the head by virtue of his surpassing excellence and his salvific action. "The Son of God and of the Blessed Virgin", Pius XII teaches, "must be called the head of the Church for the special reason of his pre-eminence. For the head holds the highest place. But none holds a higher place than Christ as God for he is the Word of the Eternal Father and is therefore justly called 'the first-born of all creation'. None holds a higher place than Christ as man, for he, born of the immaculate Virgin, is the true and natural Son of God, and by reason of his miraculous and glorious resurrection by which he triumphed over death he is 'the first-born from the dead'. And none stands higher than he who, being the 'one mediator between God and man' (1 Tim 2:5), admirably unites earth with heaven; who, exalted on the Cross as on his throne of mercy, has drawn all things to himself" (*Mystici Corporis*, 15).

**1:15.** By the unaided use of reason man can work out that God exists, but he could never, on his own, have grasped the essence of God: in this sense God is said to be invisible (cf. St Thomas, *Commentary on Col,* ad loc.). This is why it is said in St John's Gospel that "no one has ever seen God" (Jn 1:18).

In Sacred Scripture we are told that man was created "in the image of God" (Gen 1:26). However, only the second person of the Blessed Trinity, the Son, is the perfect image and likeness of the Father. "The image [likeness] of a thing may be found in something else in two ways; in one way it is found in something of the same specific nature—as the image of the king is found in his son; in another way it is found in something of a different nature, as the king's image on the coin. In the first sense the Son is the image of the Father; in the second sense man is called the image of God; and therefore in order to express the imperfect character of the divine image in man, man is not simply called 'the image' but is referred to as being 'according to the image', whereby is expressed a certain movement or tendency to perfection. But it cannot be said that the Son of God is 'according to the image', because he is the perfect image of the Father" (*Summa theologiae*, 1, 35, 2, ad 3). And so, "for something to be truly an image, it has to proceed from another as similar to it in species, or at least in some aspect of the species" (*Summa theologiae*, 1, 35, 1, c.). To say that the Son is "image of the invisible God" means that the Father and the Son are one-in-substance—that is, both possess the same divine nature—with the nuance that the Son proceeds from the Father. It also conveys the fact that they are two distinct persons, for no one is the image of himself.

principalities or authorities—all things were created through him
and for him. 17He is before all things, and in him all things hold

---

The supreme revelation of God is that effected by the Son of God through his Incarnation. He is the only one who can say, "He who has seen me has seen the Father" (Jn 14:9). His sacred humanity, therefore, reflects the perfections of God, which he possesses by virtue of the hypostatic union—the union of divine nature and human nature which occurs in his person, which is divine. The second Person of the Trinity restored man to his original dignity. The image of God, imperfect though it be, which there is in every man and woman, was blurred by Adam's sin; but it was restored in Christ: God's true self-image takes on a nature the same as ours, and thanks to the redemption wrought by his death, we obtain forgiveness of sins (v. 14).

Jesus Christ is the "first-born of all creation" by virtue of the hypostatic union. He is, of course, prior to all creation, for he proceeds eternally from the Father by generation. This the Church has always believed, and it proclaims it in the Creed: "born of the Father before time began ..., begotten, not made, of one being [consubstantial] with the Father" (*Nicene-Constantinopolitan Creed*).

In Jewish culture, the first-born was first in honour and in law. When the Apostle calls Jesus "the first-born of all creation", he is referring to the fact that Christ has pre-eminence and headship over all created things, because not only does he pre-date them but they were all created "through him" and "for him" (v. 16).

**1:16–17.** Jesus Christ is God; this is why he has pre-eminence over all created things. The relationships between Christ and creation are spelled out by three prepositions. "In him all things were created": *in* Christ: he is their source, their centre and their model or exemplary cause. "All things were created through him and for him": *through* him, in other words, God the Father, through God the Son, creates all things; and *for* him, because he is the last end, the purpose or goal of everything.

St Paul goes on to say that "in him all things hold together": "the Son of God has not only created everything: he conserves everything in being; thus, if his sovereign will were to cease to operate for even an instant, everything would return into the nothingness from which he drew everything that exists" (Chrysostom, *Hom. on Col,* ad loc.).

All created things, then, continue in existence because they share, albeit in a limited way, in Christ's infinite fullness of existence or perfection. His dominion extends not only over celestial things but also over all material things, however insignificant they may seem: it embraces everything in heaven and in the physical universe.

The sacred text also points to Christ's supremacy over invisible creation, that is, over the angels and celestial hierarchies (cf. Heb 1:5). If St Paul stresses this fact, it is to expose the errors of those who were depicting Jesus as a creature intermediary between corporeal beings and spiritual created beings, and, therefore, lower than the angels.

**1:18.** "He is the head of the body, the church": this image shows the relationship of Christ with the Church, to which he sends his grace in abundance, bearing

together. [18]He is the head of the body, the church; he is the Eph 1:22
beginning, the first-born from the dead, that in everything he* Col 1:15
might be pre-eminent. [19]For in him all the fullness of God was Jn 1:16

---

life to all its members. "The head," St Augustine says, "is our very Saviour, who suffered under Pontius Pilate and now, after rising from the dead, is seated at the right hand of the Father. And his body is the Church [...]. For the whole Church, made up of the assembly of the faithful—for all the faithful are Christ's members—has Christ, as its head, who rules his body from on high" (*Enarrationes in Psalmos*, 56, 1).

St Paul unequivocally teaches that the Church is a body. "Now if the Church is a body it must be something one and undivided, according to the statement of St Paul: 'We, though many, are one body in Christ' (Rom 12:5). And not only must it be one and undivided, it must also be something concrete and visible, as our Predecessor of happy memory, Leo XIII, says in his Encyclical *Satis cognitum*: 'By the very fact of being a body the Church is visible.' It is therefore an aberration from divine truth to represent the Church as something intangible and invisible, as a mere 'pneumatic' entity joining together by an invisible link a number of communities of Christians in spite of their difference in faith.

"But a body requires a number of members so connected that they help one another. And, in fact, as in our mortal organism when one member suffers the others suffer with it, and the healthy members come to the assistance of those who are ailing, so in the Church individual members do not live only for themselves but also help one another, alleviating their suffering and helping to build up the entire body" (Pius XII, *Mystici Corporis*, 7).

"He is the beginning, the first-born from the dead": this can be said because he was the first man to rise from the dead, never again to die (cf. 1 Cor 15:20; Rev 1:5), and also because thanks to him it enabled men to experience resurrection in glory (cf. 1 Cor 15:22; Rom 8:11), because they are justified through him (cf. Rom 4:25).

So, just as the previous verses looked to Christ's pre-eminent role in creation, the hymn now focuses on his primacy in a new creation—the rebirth of mankind, and all creation in its train, in the supernatural order of grace and glory. Christ rose from the dead to enable us also to walk in newness of life (cf. Rom 6:4). Therefore, in every way Jesus Christ is "preeminent."

**1:19.** The word *plêrôma* translated here as "fullness", has two meanings in Greek: one, an active meaning, describes something that "fills" or "completes"; for example, a ship's full load can be referred to as its *plêrôma*. The other meaning is passive, "that which is filled" or "that which is complete", so that a ship can be said to be *plêrôma* when it is fully loaded. In this passage St Paul is using the word in both senses: Christ is the fullness (passive sense) of the Godhead (cf. Col 2:9), because he is full of all the perfections of the divine essence; and he is the fullness (active sense), because he fills the Church and all creation.

St John Chrysostom suggests that "the word 'fullness' is to be taken to mean the divinity of Jesus Christ [...]. This term has been chosen the better to show that the very essence of the God-

Eph 1:10 pleased to dwell, [20]and through him to reconcile to himself all
things, whether on earth or in heaven, making peace by the blood
of his cross.

**The effect of Christ's saving action**

Eph 2:1, 12 [21]And you, who once were estranged and hostile in mind, doing
evil deeds, [22]he has now reconciled in his body of flesh by his

---

head resides in Jesus Christ" (*Hom. on Col*, ad loc.).

Since Christ possesses the divine nature, he also possesses the fullness of the supernatural gifts, for himself and for all mankind. Hence St Thomas' comment that *plêrôma* "reveals the dignity of the head in so far as it has the fullness of all grace" (*Commentary on Col,* ad loc.). In this sense, Christ is the fullness of the Church, for as its head he vivifies his body with all kinds of unmerited gifts.

Finally, the entire created universe can be termed the "fullness" (*plêrôma*) of Christ, because everything that exists in heaven and on earth has been created and is maintained in existence by him (cf. vv. 16–17); they are ever-present to him and are ruled by him (cf. Is 6:3; Ps 139:8; Wis 1:7; etc.). Thus, the world, which was created good (cf. Gen 1:31) tends towards its fulfilment insofar as it clearly reflects the imprint God gave it at the start of creation.

**1:20.** Since Christ is pre-eminent over all creation, the Father chose to reconcile all things to himself through him. Sin had cut man off from God, rupturing the perfect order which originally reigned in the created world. By shedding his blood on the cross, Christ obtained peace for us; nothing in the universe falls outside the scope of his peace-giving influence. He who in the beginning created all things in heaven and on earth has re-established peace throughout creation.

This reconciliation of all things, ushered in by Christ, is fostered by the Holy Spirit who enables the Church to continue the process of reconciliation. However, we will not attain the fullness of this reconciliation until we reach heaven, when the entire created universe, along with mankind, will be perfectly renewed in Christ (cf. *Lumen gentium*, 48).

"The history of salvation—the salvation of the whole of humanity, as well as of every human being of whatever period —is the wonderful history of a reconciliation; the reconciliation whereby God, as Father, in the Blood and the Cross of his Son made man, reconciles the world to himself and thus brings into being a new family of those who have been reconciled.

"Reconciliation becomes necessary because there has been the break of sin from which derive all the other forms of break within man and about him. Reconciliation therefore, in order to be complete, necessarily requires liberation from sin, which is to be rejected in its deepest roots. Thus a close internal link unites *conversion* and *reconciliation*. It is impossible to split these two realities or to speak of one and say nothing of the other" (John Paul II, *Reconciliatio et paenitentia*, 13).

Jesus Christ also counts on the cooperation of every individual Christian to apply his work of redemption and peace to all creation. The founder of Opus Dei says, in this connexion: "We must love

death, in order to present you holy and blameless and irreproach- Mk 16:15
able before him, [23]provided that you continue in the faith, stable 1 Tim 3:16
and steadfast, not shifting from the hope of the gospel which you Eph 3:17
heard, which has been preached to every creature under heaven,
and of which I, Paul, became a minister.

## 2. PAUL'S MISSION

### Proclamation of the Mystery

[24]Now I rejoice in my sufferings for your sake, and in my flesh I 2 Cor 1:5f
complete what is lacking* in Christ's afflictions for the sake of his Eph 3:1, 13

---

the world and work and all human things. For the world is good. Adam's sin destroyed the divine balance of creation; but God the Father sent his only Son to re-establish peace, so that we, his children by adoption, might free creation from disorder and reconcile all things to God" (*Christ Is Passing By*, 112).

**1:21.** "Hostile in mind": literally, "enemies in mind and thought"; for, even if they did not formally declare themselves to be enemies of God, they were enemies in fact due to the way they acted.

**1:22.** "In his body of flesh": the physical body of Christ, through which he offered himself to the Father on the cross and brought about the reconciliation of men with God and with each other. Christ's sacred humanity is, therefore, an instrument of salvation: through his passion and death our Lord conquered sin and obtained the graces we need to be cleansed of our faults and to be presented "holy and blameless and irreproachable before him."

The sacred text shows that the Incarnation of the Word is something diametrically opposed to a disembodied spiritualism, which is quite foreign to the spirit of the Gospel. In a homily given in a Mass on the campus of Navarre University in 1967, St Josemaría Escrivá explained that "authentic Christianity, which professes the resurrection of all flesh, has always quite logically opposed 'dis-incarnation', without fear of being judged materialistic. We can, therefore, rightfully speak of a 'Christian materialism', which is boldly opposed to those materialisms which are blind to the spirit" (*Conversations*, 115).

**1:24.** Jesus Christ our Lord perfectly accomplished the work the Father gave him to do (cf. Jn 17:4); as he said himself when he was about to die, "It is finished", it is accomplished (Jn 19:30).

From that point onwards objective redemption is an accomplished fact. All men have been saved by the redemptive death of Christ. However, St Paul says that he completes in his flesh "what is lacking in Christ's afflictions"; what does he mean by this? The most common explanation of this statement is summarized by St Alphonsus as follows: "Can it be that Christ's passion alone was insufficient to save us? It left nothing more to be done, it was entirely sufficient to save all men. However, for the merits of the Passion to be applied to us, according to St Thomas (*Summa theologiae*, 3, 49, 3), we need to

Eph 3:2, 7 body, that is, the church, [25]of which I became a minister according
to the divine office which was given to me for you, to make the
Rom 16:25f word of God fully known, [26]the mystery hidden for ages and
generations[c] but now made manifest to his saints. [27]To them God

---

cooperate (subjective redemption) by patiently bearing the trials God sends us, so as to become like our head, Christ" (St Alphonsus, *Thoughts on the Passion*, 10).

St Paul is applying this truth to himself. Jesus Christ worked and strove in all kinds of ways to communicate his message of salvation, and then he accomplished the redemption by dying on the Cross. The Apostle is mindful of the Master's teaching and so he follows in his footsteps (cf. 1 Pet 2:21), takes up his cross (cf. Mt 10:38) and continues the task of bringing Christ's teaching to all men.

Faith in the fact that we are sharing in the sufferings of Christ, John Paul II says, gives a person "the certainty that in the spiritual dimension of the work of Redemption *he is serving*, like Christ, *the salvation of his brothers and sisters.* Therefore he is carrying out an irreplaceable service. In the Body of Christ, which is ceaselessly born of the Cross of the Redeemer, it is precisely suffering permeated by the spirit of Christ's sacrifice that is *the irreplaceable mediator and author of the good things* which are indispensable for the world's salvation. It is suffering, more than anything else, which clears the way for the grace which transforms human souls. Suffering, more than anything else, makes present in the history of humanity the force of the Redemption" (*Salvifici doloris*, 27).

**1:26–27.** The "mystery", now revealed, is God's eternal plan to give salvation to men, both Jews and Gentiles, making all without distinction co-heirs of glory and members of a single body which is the Church (cf. Eph 3:6), through faith in Jesus Christ (cf. Rom 16:25–26).

In Christ, who has brought salvation to Gentile and Jew, the "mystery" is fully revealed. His presence in Christians of Gentile origin is in fact a very clear manifestation of the supernatural fruitfullness of the "mystery" and an additional ground for Christians' hope. Thanks to this presence people who do not form part of Israel are enabled to attain salvation. Previously subject to the power of darkness and slaves of sin (vv. 13–14), they have now died to sin through Baptism (cf. Rom 6:2–3) and Christ, through grace, dwells in their hearts (on the salvific "mystery", cf. notes on Eph 1:13–14 and Eph 1:9 and "Introduction to the Letters of St Paul", in *The Navarre Bible: Romans and Galatians*.

In his infinite love Christ lives in us through faith and grace, through prayer and the sacraments. Also, "he is present when the Church prays and sings, for he has promised 'where two or three are gathered in my name, there am I in the midst of them' (Mt 18:20)" (Vatican II, *Sacrosanctum Concilium*, 7).

"Christ stays in his Church, its sacraments, its liturgy, its preaching—in all that it does. In a special way Christ stays with us in the daily offering of the Blessed Eucharist [...]. The presence of Christ in the host is the guarantee, the source and the culmination of his presence in the world.

**c.** Or *from angels and men*

chose to make known how great among the Gentiles are the riches Eph 3:9
of the glory of this mystery, which is Christ in you, the hope of
glory. [28]Him we proclaim, warning every man and teaching every Eph 4:13
man in all wisdom, that we may present every man mature in
Christ. [29]For this I toil, striving with all the energy which he Phil 4:13
mightily inspires within me.

**Paul's concern for the faithful**

2 [1]For I want you to know how greatly I strive for you, and for Col 1:9
those at Laodicea, and for all who have not seen my face, [2]that
their hearts may be encouraged as they are knit together in love,
to have all the riches of assured understanding and the knowledge Is 45:3
of God's mystery, of Christ, [3]in whom are hid all the treasures of Prov 2:3f
wisdom and knowledge. [4]I say this in order that no one may
delude you with beguiling speech. [5]For though I am absent in Rom 16:18 2 Pet 2:3
body, yet I am with you in spirit, rejoicing to see your good order
and the firmness of your faith in Christ. 1 Cor 5:3

---

"*Christ is alive in Christians.* Our faith teaches us that man, in the state of grace, is divinized—filled with God. We are men and women, not angels. We are flesh and blood, people with sentiments and passions, with sorrows and joys. And this divinization affects everything human; it is a sort of foretaste of the final resurrection" (St Josemaría Escrivá, *Christ Is Passing By*, 102–103).

**1:28.** "In all wisdom": St Paul is exhorting and teaching each and every one, communicating wisdom, the true teaching of Jesus Christ. The text clearly shows St Paul's conviction that he is a faithful transmitter of teachings revealed by God. Possessed of such wisdom he is confident that he can lead his disciples to Christian perfection.

**2:2–3.** The term "mystery", which St Paul uses on other occasions (cf. 1:26; Eph 1:9), refers in this verse expressly to Christ: Christ is the complete manifestation of the divine plan or "mystery" designed to bring about the salvation of mankind. The name Jesus means Saviour and indicates his principal mission—to save the people of Israel (and through them all mankind) from their sins (cf. Mt 1:21).

The assertion that in Christ "are hid all the treasures of wisdom and knowledge" is based on the fact that Christ—God made man—is the incarnation of divine Wisdom itself, for Wisdom is one of the names applied in Sacred Scripture to the second Person of the Blessed Trinity. Hence St Athanasius' comment that "God no longer chose to make himself known, as in times past, by the reflection and shadow of wisdom to be seen in created things: he determined that Wisdom itself, in person, should become incarnate, should be made man and suffer death on the cross, so that from then on all the faithful might attain salvation through faith grounded on the cross" (*Oratio II contra Arianos*).

The infinite richness of wisdom and knowledge hidden in Christ means that meditation on his life and his teachings is an inexhaustible source of nourishment for the life of the soul. "There are great

## 3. FIRMNESS IN THE FAITH

**A warning about heresy**

Eph 4:17 Eph 3:17 2 Thess 2:15 Eph 5:6 Col 2:16 Jn 1:14 Eph 1:21f; 3:19

6As therefore you received Christ Jesus the Lord, so live in him,
7rooted and built up in him and established in the faith, just as you
were taught, abounding in thanksgiving.
8See to it that no one makes a prey of you by philosophy and
empty deceit, according to human tradition, according to the
elemental spirits of the universe, and not according to Christ. 9For
in him the whole fullness of deity dwells bodily, 10and you have
come to fullness of life in him, who is the head of all rule and

---

depths to be fathomed in Christ. For he is like an abandoned mine with many recesses containing treasures, of which, for all that men try to fathom them, the end and bottom is never reached; rather in each recess men continue to find new veins of new riches on all sides" (St John of the Cross, *Spiritual Canticle*, 37, 3).

**2:4–8.** These verses reveal the Apostle's pastoral solicitude for the faithful of Colossae. Although physically absent, he is with them in spirit. He rejoices and gives thanks to God for their steadfastness, but he leaves them in no doubt about the dangers which threaten their faith. Clearly he is referring to those who were adulterating the Colossians' faith by intruding erroneous ideas. By sophistry and deceit they were trying to convince the faithful that it was better to have recourse to angels rather than to Christ, arguing that angels were the chief mediators between God and men.

The Christian faith is not opposed to human scholarship and science; it rejects only vain philosophy, that is, philosophy which boasts that it relies on reason alone and which fails to respect revealed truths.

Over the centuries, people have often tried to adapt the truths of faith to the philosophies or ideologies which happen to be in vogue. In this connexion Leo XIII said: "As the Apostle warns, 'philosophy and empty deceit' can deceive the minds of Christians and corrupt the sincerity of men's faith; the supreme pastors of the Church, therefore, always see it as part of their role to foster as much as they can sciences which merit that name, and at the same time to ensure, by special watchfullness, that human sciences are taught in keeping with the criteria of Catholic faith—particularly philosophy, because proper methodology in the other sciences is largely dependent on [correctness in] philosophy" (*Aeterni Patris*, 1).

"The elemental spirits of the universe": see the note on Gal 4:3.

**2:9.** This is such an important verse that it deserves close analysis. "Dwell": the Greek word means a stable way of living or residing, as distinct from a transitory presence: in other words, the union of Christ's human nature with his divine nature is not just something which lasts for a while; it is permanent. "Deity": the Greek word can also be translated as "divinity"; in either case, the sentence means that God has taken up a human

authority. [11]In him also you were circumcised with a circumcision made without hands, by putting off the body of flesh in the circumcision of Christ; [12]and you were buried with him in

Rom 2:29
1 Pet 3:21
Rom 6:4
Eph 1:19

---

nature, in such a way that, although it was only the second divine Person, the Son, who became incarnate, by virtue of the unity of the divine essence, where one divine person is present the other two persons are also present.

This verse enuntiates the profound mystery of the Incarnation in a different way to John 1:14: "And the word became flesh and dwelt among us, full of grace and truth; we have beheld his glory; glory as of the only Son from the Father" (cf. also 1 Jn 1:1–2).

When the sacred text says that in Christ "the whole fullness of deity dwells bodily", it means, St John of Avila explains, "that it does not dwell in him merely by grace—as in the case of the saints (men and angels both), but in another way of greater substance and value, that is, by way of personal union" (*Audi, filia*, 84).

In Jesus Christ, then, there are two natures, divine and human, united in one person, who is divine. This "hypostatic union" does not prevent each nature from having all its own proper characteristics, for, as St Leo the Great defined, "the Word has not changed into flesh, nor has flesh changed into Word; but each remains, in a unity" (*Licet per nostros*, 2).

**2:10.** Since Christ is head of angels and men, the head of all creation (cf. Eph 1:10) and especially head of the Church (cf. Col 1:18), all fullness is said to reside in him (cf. note on Col 1:19). Hence, not only is he pre-eminent over all things but "he fills the Church, which is his body and fullness, with his divine gifts (cf. Eph 1:22–23), so that it may increase and attain to all the fullness of God (cf. Eph 3:19)" (Vatican II, *Lumen gentium*, 7).

Union with Christ makes Christians sharers in his "fullness", that is, in divine grace (of which he is absolutely full and we have a partial share), in a word, in his perfections.

That is why the members of the Church who "through the sacraments are united in a hidden and real way to Christ" (*Lumen gentium*, 7) can attain the fullness of the Christian life.

It was very appropriate for St Paul to be instructing the Colossians in these truths at this time, because it put them on their guard against preachers who were arguing for exaggerated worship of angels, to the detriment of Christ's unique, pre-eminent mediation.

**2:11–12.** This is a reference to another error which the Judaizers were trying to spread at Colossae and which was already treated in detail in the letters to the Galatians and the Romans—the idea that it was necessary for Christians to be circumcised. Physical circumcision affects the body, whereas what the Apostle, by analogy, calls "the circumcision of Christ", that is, Baptism, puts off the "body of flesh" (an expression which seems to refer to whatever is sinful in man). "We, who by means of (Christ) have reached God, have not been given fleshly circumcision but rather spiritual circumcision [...]; we receive it by the mercy of God in Baptism" (St Justin, *Dialogue with Trypho*, 43, 2). "By the sacrament of Baptism, whenever it is properly conferred in the way the Lord

baptism, in which you were also raised with him through faith in
Eph 2:1–5 the working of God, who raised him from the dead. 13And you,
who were dead in trespasses and the uncircumcision of your flesh,
God made alive together with him, having forgiven us all our
Eph 2:14f 1 Pet 2:24 trespasses, 14having cancelled the bond which stood against us
with its legal demands; this he set aside, nailing it to the cross.
Lk 11:22 15He disarmed the principalities and powers and made a public
example of them, triumphing over them in him.[d]

---

determined and received with the proper dispositions of soul, man becomes truly incorporated into the crucified and glorified Christ and is reborn to a sharing of the divine life, as the Apostle says: [Col 2:12 follows]" (Vatican II, *Unitatis redintegratio*, 22).

As on other occasions (cf. Rom 6:4), St Paul, evoking the rite of immersion in water, speaks of Baptism as a kind of burial (a sure sign that someone has died to sin), and of resurrection to a new life, the life of grace. By this sacrament we are associated with Christ's death and burial so as to be able to rise with him. "Christ by his resurrection signified our new life, which was reborn out of the old death which submerged us in sin. This is what is brought about in us by the great sacrament of Baptism: all those who receive this grace die to sin [...] and are reborn to the new life" (St Augustine, *Enchiridion*, 41–42).

**2:13–14.** This is one of the central teachings of the epistle—that Jesus Christ is the only mediator between God and men. The basic purpose of his mediation is to reconcile men with God, through the forgiveness of their sins and the gift of the life of grace, which is a sharing in God's own life.

Verse 14 indicates how Christ achieved this purpose—by dying on the Cross. All who were under the yoke of sin and the Law have been set free through his death.

The Mosaic Law, to which the scribes and Pharisees added so many precepts as to make it unbearable, had become (to use St Paul's comparison) like a charge sheet against man, because it imposed heavy burdens but did not provide the grace needed for bearing them. The Apostle very graphically says that this charge sheet or "bond" was set aside and nailed on the Cross—making it perfectly clear to all that Christ made more than ample satisfaction for our crimes. "He has obliterated them," St John Chrysostom comments, "not simply crossed them out; he has obliterated them so effectively that no trace of them remains in our soul. He has completely cancelled them out, he has nailed them to the cross [...]. We were guilty and deserved the most rigorous of punishments because we were all of us in sin! What, then, does the Son of God do? By his death on the cross he removes all our stains and exempts us from the punishment due to them. He takes our charge-sheet, nails it to the cross through his own person and destroys it" (*Hom. on Col,* ad loc.).

**2:15.** Jesus is the only mediator between God and man. The angelic principalities and powers are insignificant by comparison with him: God has overpowered them and publicly exposed them through the death of his Son. The sentence seems to evoke the idea of the parade of a victorious general complete with trophies, booty and prisoners.

**d.** Or *in it* (that is, the cross)

### Rejection of false asceticism

16Therefore let no one pass judgment on you in questions of food and drink or with regard to a festival or a new moon or a sabbath. Rom 14:1

---

Some scholars interpret this passage differently; the "public spectacle", according to their interpretation, would refer to the fact that the good angels had been mediators in the revelation of the Mosaic Law (cf. Gal 3:19) and were being venerated by some contemporary Jews (among them some converts from Colossae) with a form of worship bordering on superstition. God would have caused them to become "a public spectacle" when they acted as a kind of escort in Christ's victory parade. Thus, both interpretations lead to the conclusion that angels, who are Christ's servants, should not be rendered the worship due to him alone, even though they do play an important part in God's plan of salvation. One of the missions entrusted to them is that of continually interceding on behalf of mankind.

At the time this epistle was being written there was need to emphasize first that Jesus Christ is the only mediator. The mediation of angels depends on him (it is something revealed in fact in the Old Testament: cf. Tob 12:3, 12ff; Dan 9:21ff; 10:13; Ezek 49:3; Zech 1:9; etc.). The Blessed Virgin Mary's mediation, also subordinate to that of Christ, is something which becomes clearer as the events of the New Testament unfold. Mary's mediation is, however, on a higher level than that of the angels. Pope Pius XII says this, echoing earlier teachings: "If, as he does, the Word works miracles and infuses grace by means of the human nature he has taken on, if he uses the sacraments, and his Saints, as instruments for the saving of souls, how could he not use the office and action of his most blessed Mother to distribute the fruits of the Redemption? With a truly maternal spirit (our predecessor Pius IX of immortal memory says), having in her hands the business of our salvation, she concerns herself with all mankind, for she has been made by the Lord Queen of heaven and earth and is raised above all the choirs of Angels and all the degrees of the Saints in heaven; she is there at the right hand of her only Son, Jesus Christ, our Lord, in most effective supplication, obtaining whatever she asks; she cannot but be heard" (*Ad caeli Reginam*, 17).

"Principalities and powers": see the note on Eph 6:12.

**2:16–18.** The text points to the abuses which were in evidence at Colossae due to the inroads of pre-Gnostic heresies (cf. p. 124 above). These abuses had to do basically with three points—abstention from certain kinds of food, celebration of certain feasts (v. 16) and exaggerated veneration of angelic spirits (v. 18).

The days of the new moon (cf. Lev 23:24) were Jewish festivals which went back to the nomadic period. In Saul's time they had become traditional feasts celebrated with a sacred meal and the offering of sacrifice (cf. 1 Sam 20:24ff). Later, Ezekiel specified certain liturgical and sacrificial rites to be celebrated in the temple at the start of each month (cf. Ezek 46:3).

The "sabbath" was of course the weekly Jewish holy day, a day kept for Yahweh, which he himself had sanctified (Ex 20:11). It was a day devoted to rest and prayer and was marked by religious rites and ceremonies.

Abstinence from certain types of food and drink was carefully regulated in the Old Testament (cf. Lev 10:9; 11:1–47;

[17]These are only a shadow of what is to come; but the substance
belongs to Christ. [18]Let no one disqualify you, insisting on self-
abasement and worship of angels, taking his stand on visions,
Eph 2:21; 4:15 puffed up without reason by his sensuous mind, [19]and not holding

---

Num 6:3), as were the festivals to be celebrated in Yahweh's honour (cf. Num 28:1–26). These prescriptions were not meant to be permanent; they were designed to prepare the chosen people for the coming of the Messiah. In the new stage of salvation history inaugurated by Christ it is no longer necessary to continue to burden men's consciences with out-of-date regulations (cf. Gal 4:9–10).

St Paul explains this by using a simile: the Old Law is as it were the shadow of the New Law promulgated by Christ. A shadow indicates that a body is present. The Mosaic Law, the shadow, had the function of marking the way until the coming of Christ; but now that he has come and promulgated the New Law, it would not make sense to give greater importance to the shadow than to the body which casts it.

The Apostle corrects the abuses which have developed in connexion with fasting and abstinence, but he is not saying that these penitential practices are wrong, for Jesus himself practised them (cf. Mt 4:2) and taught his followers to do so (cf. Mt 16:16–18).

The Second Vatican Council also recommends that, especially during Lent, "the practice of penance should be encouraged in ways suited to the present day, to different regions, and to individual circumstances" (*Sacrosanctum Concilium*, 110). Also, John Paul II has reminded us that "*the Church's penitential discipline*, even though it has been mitigated for some time, cannot be abandoned without grave harm both to the interior life of individual Christians and of the ecclesial community, and also to their capacity for missionary influence. It is not uncommon for non-Christians to be surprised at the negligible witness of true penance on the part of Christ's followers. It is clear, however, that Christian penance will only be authentic if it is inspired by love and not by mere fear; if it consists in a serious effort to crucify the 'old man' so that the 'new' can be born by the power of Christ; if it takes as its model Christ, who though he was innocent chose the path of poverty, patience, austerity and, one can say, the penitential life" (*Reconcilatio et paenitentia*, 26).

**2:18.** The false apostles were saying that their teaching derived from revelations in the form of visions. With a show of humility they were actually arguing that it was a gross impertinence for men to try to make direct contact with God: God was invisible and inaccessible to men. Instead, worship should be offered to spirits, who stand in between the Godhead and the material world. The Apostle exposes these errors for what they are.

This superstitious worship of angels is completely different from the veneration which the Church gives to angels and saints: she see them as created beings who promote God's plan of salvation by interceding on men's behalf.

**2:19.** Jesus Christ is "the head of the body, the church" (Col 1:18). To go along with the heresies just referred to (cf. vv. 16–18) would have terrible consequences, because it would mean breaking our link with Christ, who is the head, the only source of the Church's life. For a body to be full of vitality, not only do its limbs and

fast to the Head, from whom the whole body, nourished and knit
together through its joints and ligaments, grows with a growth that
is from God.
[20]If with Christ you died to the elemental spirits of the Gal 4:3–9
universe, why do you live as if you still belonged to the world?
Why do you submit to regulations, [21]"Do not handle, Do not taste,
Do not touch" [22](referring to things which all perish as they are Is 29:13
used), according to human precepts and doctrines? [23]These have Mt 15:9
indeed an appearance of wisdom in promoting rigor of devotion Rom 13:14
and self-abasement and severity to the body, but they are of no 1 Cor 6:13
value in checking the indulgence of the flesh.[e] 1 Tim 4:3

## 4. NEW LIFE IN CHRIST

**Seeking the things that are above**

3 [1]If then you have been raised with Christ, seek the things that
are above, where Christ is, seated at the right hand of God. [2]Set Mt 6:33

---

organs have to be correctly in place; they also have to be properly coordinated with one another, and actually working. See the note on Eph 4:13–16.

**2:20–23.** On being baptized, every Christian dies with Christ to the spirits of the world (cf. note on Gal 4:3) and is freed from the slavery of the Law (cf. Rom 7:4–6) and of sin (cf. Rom 6:4–7). It serves no purpose, then, for one to continue to be hidebound by precepts which no longer apply—much less, to be afraid to use the good things of the world.

St Paul speaks somewhat sarcastically about the endless array of commandments the false teachers have been trying to impose—regulations deriving from their notion of matter as something evil and contact with matter as involving a risk of uncleanness. Verse 21 in particular probably uses the terminology of not only the most scrupulously observant Jews but also of other eastern religions. The Apostle rejects this whole approach because it is out of line with Christ's teaching (cf. Mt 15:11): it is a human invention, a false kind of piety which serves no purpose and yet enslaves its practitioners. True piety leads to growth in holiness and consists primarily in being attentive to the voice of the Lord and not hardening one's heart (cf. Ps 95:7–8).

**3:1–4.** The more ethical and exhortatory part of the letter begins at this point. It is a practical application of the teaching given in the earlier chapters, designed to suit the circumstances that have arisen in the Colossian church.

By his death and resurrection the Son of God frees us from the power of Satan and of death. "By Baptism men are grafted into the paschal mystery of Christ; they die with him, are buried with him, and rise with him" (Vatican II,

**e.** Or *are of no value, serving only to indulge the flesh*

Rom 6:2 your minds on things that are above, not on things that are on
1 Cor 15:43 earth. [3]For you have died, and your life is hid with Christ in God.
Gal 2:20 [4]When Christ who is our life appears, then you also will appear
1 Jn 3:2 with him in glory.

### Avoiding sin

Rom 8:13 Eph 4:19; 5:3–5 [5]Put to death therefore what is earthly in you: fornication, impurity, passion, evil desire, and covetousness, which is idolatry.

---

*Sacrosanctum Concilium*, 6). In other words, Christians have been raised to a new kind of life, a supernatural life, whereby they share, even while on earth, in the glorious life of the risen Jesus. This life is at present spiritual and hidden, but when our Lord comes again in glory, it will become manifest and glorious.

Two practical consequences flow from this teaching—the need to seek the "things that are above", that is, the things of God; and the need to pass unnoticed in one's everyday work and ordinary life, yet to do everything with a supernatural purpose in mind.

As regards the first of these the Second Vatican Council has said: "In their pilgrimage to the heavenly city Christians are to seek and relish the things that are above (cf. Col 3:1–2): this involves not a lesser, but a greater commitment to working with all men to build a world that is more human" (*Gaudium et spes*, 57). Work, family relationships, social involvements—every aspect of human affairs—should be approached in a spirit of faith and done perfectly, out of love: "The true Christian, who acts according to his faith", St Josemaría Escrivá comments, "always has his sights set on God. His outlook is supernatural. He works in this world of ours, which he loves passionately; he is involved in all its challenges, but all the while his eyes are fixed on heaven" (*Friends of God*, 206).

Ordinary life, everyday interests, the desire to be better and to serve others without seeking public recognition of one's merits—all this makes for holiness if done for love of God. A simple life "hid with Christ in God" (v. 3) is so important that Jesus himself chose to spend the greater part of his life on earth living like an ordinary person: he was the son of a tradesman. "As we meditate on these truths, we come to understand better the logic of God. We come to realize that the supernatural value of our life does not depend on accomplishing great undertakings suggested to us by our over-active imagination. Rather it is to be found in the faithful acceptance of God's will, in welcoming generously the opportunities for small, daily sacrifice" (St Josemaría Escrivá, *Christ Is Passing By*, 172).

This means that those who try to seek holiness by imitating Jesus in his hidden life will be people full of hope; they will be optimistic and happy people; and after their death they will share in the glory of the Lord: they will hear Jesus' praise, "Well done, good and faithful servant; you have been faithful over a little; I will set you over much; enter into the joy of your master" (Mt 25:21).

On the value of the hidden life, see the note on Lk 2:15.

**3:5–17.** The Christian, who in Baptism has risen with Christ, should not live for himself but for God. This means that every day he needs to put off his old nature and put on the new.

[6]On account of these the wrath of God is coming.[f] [7]In these you Eph 5:6
once walked, when you lived in them. [8]But now put them all Eph 4:25–31;5:4
away: anger, wrath, malice, slander, and foul talk from your Eph 4:22, 25
mouth. [9]Do not lie to one another, seeing that you have put off the
old nature with its practices [10]and have put on the new nature, Gen 1:26f Rom 12:2
which is being renewed in knowledge after the image of its Eph 4:23f
creator. [11]Here there cannot be Greek and Jew, circumcised and Gal 3:28
uncircumcised, barbarian, Scythian, slave, free man, but Christ is
all, and in all.

**Progress in the spiritual life**

[12]Put on then, as God's chosen ones, holy and beloved, com- Eph 4:2, 32 1 Pet 2:9
passion, kindness, lowliness, meekness, and patience, [13]forbearing Mt 6:14; 18:27

---

The "old nature", the "old man": one who lets himself be led by disorderly passions (cf. Rom 7:8), who lets his body do evil in the service of sin (v. 5; cf. Rom 6:12f). With the help of grace the old nature is being more and more broken down, while the new nature is constantly being renewed (cf. 2 Cor 6:16). Impurity and the other vices need to be uprooted so as to make room for goodness and its train of Christian virtues (vv. 12–13), especially charity (v. 14), which are features of the new nature.

Christ's disciple, who has been made a new person and who lives for the Lord, has a new and more perfect knowledge of God and of the world (v. 10). Thanks to this he see things from a more elevated viewpoint; he has a "supernatural insight". This enables him to love and understand everyone without distinction of race, nation or social status (v. 11), and to imitate Christ, who has given himself up for all. "The Only-begotten of the Eternal Father vouchsafed to become a son of man, that we might be made conformable to the image of the Son of God and be renewed according to the likeness of him who created us. Therefore let all those who glory in the name of Christians not only look upon our divine Saviour as the most sublime and most perfect model of all virtues, but also, by the careful avoidance of sin and the unremitting practice of holiness, so reproduce in their conduct his teaching and life, that when the Lord appears they may be like to him in glory, seeing him as he is (cf. 1 Jn 3:2)" (Pius XII, *Mystici Corporis*, 20).

**3:12–13.** Putting on the new nature is not just an external action, like putting on different clothes. It is a transfiguration involving the whole person—soul and body, mind and will. This interior change begins to operate when one makes a firm resolution to lead a fully Christian life; but it calls for an on-going effort, day in day out, to practise all the virtues. "Conversion is something momentary; sanctification is the work of a lifetime. The divine seed of charity, which God

**f.** Other ancient authorities add *upon the sons of disobedience*

one another and, if one has a complaint against another, forgiving
Rom 13:8ff each other; as the Lord has forgiven you, so you also must forgive.
Eph 4:3 14 And above all these put on love, which binds everything
1 Cor 12:13 together in perfect harmony. 15 And let the peace of Christ rule in
Phil 4:7 your hearts, to which indeed you were called in the one body. And

---

has sown in our souls, wants to grow, to express itself in action, to yield results which continually coincide with what God wants. Therefore, we must be ready to begin again, to find again—in new situations—the light and the stimulus of our first conversion" (St Josemaría Escrivá, *Christ Is Passing By*, 58).

The virtues which the Apostle lists here as characteristic of the new man are all expressions, in one way or another, of charity, which "binds everything together in total harmony" (v. 14). Meekness, patience, forgiveness and gratefullness all reflect an essential virtue—humility. Only a humble person can be forgiving and truly appreciative, because only he realizes that everything he has comes from God. This realization leads him to be understanding towards his neighbour, forgiving him as often as needs be; by acting in this way he is proving the genuineness of his faith and love.

See the note on Eph 4:20–24.

**3:14.** The comparison of the new nature to a new outfit is extended here by a further metaphor: charity is the belt which keeps everything together. Without it the other virtues would fall apart: supernatural virtue could not survive (cf. 1 Cor 13:1–3). St Francis de Sales uses simple examples to explain this truth: "Without cement and mortar, which knits the bricks together and strengthens the walls, the entire building is bound to collapse; a human body would simply disintegrate unless it had nerves, muscles and tendons; and if charity were absent, virtues simply could not stay together" (St Francis de Sales, *Treatise on the Love of God*, 11, 9).

"Love, as the bond of perfection and fullness of the law (cf. Col 3:14; Rom 13:10), governs, imbues, and perfects all the means of sanctification" (Vatican II, *Lumen gentium*, 42). Therefore, "if we want to achieve holiness—in spite of personal shortcomings and miseries which will last as long as we live—we must make an effort, with God's grace, to practise charity, which is the fullness of the law and the bond of perfection. Charity is not something abstract, it entails a real, complete, self-giving to the service of God and all men—to the service of that God who speaks to us in the silence of prayer and in the hubbub of the world and of those people whose existence is interwoven with our own. By living charity—Love—we live all the human and supernatural virtues required of a Christian" (St Josemaría Escrivá, *Conversations*, 62).

**3:15.** The "peace of Christ" is that which flows from the new order of grace which he has established; grace gives man direct access to God and therefore to that peace he so much yearns for. "Thou has made us for thyself and our hearts are restless till they rest in thee" (St Augustine, *Confessions*, 1, 1). This is not a peace the world can give (cf. Jn 14:27), because it is not a function of purely material progress or well-being, nor does it derive from the sort of peace that should obtain among nations. "Peace on earth, which men of every era have most eagerly

be thankful. [16]Let the word of Christ dwell in you richly, teach and Eph 5:19
admonish one another in all wisdom, and sing psalms and hymns
and spiritual songs with thankfulness in your hearts to God. [17]And 1 Cor 10:31 Eph 5:20
whatever you do, in word or deed, do everything in the name of the
Lord Jesus, giving thanks to God the Father through him.

---

yearned for, can be firmly established only if the order laid down by God is dutifully observed" (John XXIII, *Pacem in terris*, 1).

The peace of Christ, then, is "a peace that comes from knowing that our Father God loves us, and that we are made one with Christ. It results from being under the protection of the Virgin, our Lady, and assisted by St Joseph. This is the great light that illuminates our lives. In the midst of difficulties and of our personal failings, it encourages us to keep up our effort" (St Josemaría Escrivá, *Christ Is Passing By*, 22).

**3:16.** "The word of Christ": the whole corpus of our Lord's teachings, of which the Apostles are accredited witnesses. This should be ever-present to the Christian's soul and "dwell ... richly" in him, imbuing everything he does: the word of Christ is the best nourishment of one's life of prayer and an inexhaustible source of practical teaching; and it is to be found in the first instance in the books of the New Testament. St John Chrysostom says that these writings "are teachers which never cease to instruct us [...]. Open these books. What a treasury of good remedies they contain! [...]. All you need do is look at the book, read it and remember well the wise teachings therein. The source of all our evils is our ignorance of the sacred books" (*Hom. on Col,* ad loc.).

St Paul also reminds us that our appreciation should lead us to glorify the Lord with songs of joy and gratitude. We can use ready-made hymns for this purpose, and also the Psalms, which the Church has always used in its liturgy to praise God and to nourish the spiritual life. "Just as the mouth savours good food, so does the heart savour the Psalms" (St Bernard, *Sermons on the Song of Songs*, 7, 5).

See the note on Eph 5:19.

**3:17.** All genuinely human things can and should be sanctified (cf. 1 Cor 10:31), by being done perfectly and for love of God.

The Second Vatican Council has recalled this teaching: "Lay people [...], while meeting their human obligations in the ordinary conditions of life, should not separate their union with Christ from their ordinary life; through the very performance of their tasks, which are God's will for them, they actually promote the growth of their union with him. This is the path along which lay people must advance, fervently, joyfully" (*Apostolicam actuositatem*, 4).

This teaching was very much part of the message and life of the founder of Opus Dei: "I assure you, my children, that when a Christian carries out with love the most insignificant everyday action, that action overflows with the transcendence of God. That is why I have told you repeatedly, and hammered away once and again on the idea, that the Christian vocation consists in making heroic verse out of the prose of each day. Heaven and earth seem to merge, my children, on the horizon. But where they really meet is in your hearts, when you sanctify your everyday lives" (*Conversations*, 116).

### Morals in family life

Eph 5:22; 6:9 [18]Wives, be subject to your husbands, as is fitting in the Lord.*
1 Pet 2:18; 3:7 [19]Husbands, love your wives, and do not be harsh with them.
[20]Children, obey your parents in everything, for this pleases the
Lord. [21]Fathers, do not provoke your children, lest they become

---

The Second Vatican Council also sees in this passage of Colossians a basis for ecumenical dialogue with non-Catholics: "And if in moral matters there are many Christians who do not always understand the Gospel in the same way as Catholics, and do not admit the same solutions for the more difficult problems of modern society, they nevertheless want to cling to Christ's word as the source of Christian virtue and to obey the command of the Apostle: [Col 3:17 follows]" (*Unitatis redintegratio*, 23).

**3:18–19.** In the period when this epistle was written, especially in the East, women were regarded as inferior to men. St Paul does not make a direct attack on the customs of his time, but the way he focuses the question of the role of women provides the elements of an answer to it. He identifies what a woman's role in the family should be: it is true that the husband has an important part to play, but the wife also has a role to perform and one which is non-transferable. The wife is not the husband's slave: she is his equal in dignity and must be treated by him with respect and sincere love. It is taken for granted that the family needs a centre of authority, and that this authority belongs to the husband, in accordance with God's design (cf. 1 Cor 11:3, 12–14). "The place and task of the father in and for the family is of unique and irreplaceable importance [...]. In revealing and in reliving on earth the very fatherhood of God (cf. Eph 3:15), a man is called upon to ensure the harmonious and united development of all the members of the family" (John Paul II, *Familiaris consortio*, 25).

God gave Eve to Adam as his inseparable companion and complement (cf. Gen 2:18); she was therefore duty-bound to live in peace with him. Man and woman have different, though complementary, roles in family life; they are equal in dignity, by virtue of the fact that they are human persons: "The unity of marriage, distinctly recognized by our Lord, is made clear in the equal personal dignity which must be accorded to man and woman in mutual and unreserved affection" (Vatican II, *Gaudium et spes*, 49).

Therefore, a husband should make a special effort to love and respect his wife: "You are not her master", writes St Ambrose, "but her husband; she was not given to you to be your slave, but your wife [...]. Reciprocate her attentiveness to you and be grateful to her for her love" (*Exameron*, 5, 7, 19, quoted in *Familiaris consortio*, 25).

See the note on Eph 5:22–24 and 5:25–33.

**3:20–21.** Children should obey their parents in everything, as God has commanded (cf. Ex 20:12; Sir 3:8ff)—a commandment which shows that this is something which is part of human nature. Obviously for a child's obedience to "please the Lord" it must not involve doing anything that is opposed to God's will, for Jesus taught that "he who loves father or mother more than me is not worthy of me" (Mt 10:37).

For their part, parents must do everything they can to bring up their children

discouraged. 22Slaves, obey in everything those who are your 1 Tim 6:1 Tit 2:9
earthly masters, not with eyeservice, as men-pleasers, but in 1 Pet 2:18
singleness of heart, fearing the Lord. 23Whatever your task, work
heartily, as serving the Lord and not men, 24knowing that from the Rom 12:11
Lord you will receive the inheritance as your reward; you are Lev 25:43, 53
serving the Lord Christ. 25For the wrongdoer will be paid back for Rom 2:11
the wrong he has done, and there is no partiality.
4 1Masters, treat your slaves justly and fairly, knowing that you 1 Pet 2:18
also have a Master in heaven.

---

well. In every family there should be an "educational exchange between parents and children (cf. Eph 6:1–4; Col 3:20f) in which each gives and receives. By means of love, respect and obedience towards their parents, children offer their specific and irreplaceable contribution to the construction of an authentically human and Christian family (cf. *Gaudium et spes*, 48). They will be aided in this if parents exercise their unrenounceable authority as a true and proper 'ministry', that is, as a service to the human and Christian well-being of their children, and in particular as a service aimed at helping them acquire a truly responsible freedom" (*Familiaris consortio*, 21).

See the note on Eph 6:1–4.

**3:22–4:1.** God makes no distinction between slave and free man (cf. v. 11), "shows no partiality" (Gal 2:6). This establishes the Christian basis for the abolition of slavery. Although the Apostle is not dealing with this question directly, what he teaches implies the gradual peaceful disappearance of the slave condition. He tells masters that they must practise justice: they will have to render an account to God, the one and only true master. For their part, slaves should do their work well, trying to please God. The solution of this social problem ought not to be sought in strife between masters and slaves, but by going the way of charity. The Church's Magisterium teaches that "the great mistake [...] is to think that one social class is necessarily the enemy of the other, as if nature intended employers and workers to live in mutual conflict [...]. Each needs the other: capital cannot do without labour, nor labour without capital. Mutual agreement results in the beauty of good order; whereas perpetual conflict necessarily produces confusion and savage barbarity. Now, in preventing such strife, and in uprooting it, the efficacy of Christian institutions is marvellous and manifold" (Leo XIII, *Rerum novarum*, 15).

Christian teaching, then, puts labour relations into proper focus. John Paul II has reminded us that "there is no doubt that human work has an ethical value of its own, which clearly and directly remains linked to the fact that the one who carries it out is a person, a conscious and free subject, that is to say, a subject who decides about himself [...]. Such a concept practically does away with the very basis of the ancient differentiation of people into classes according to the kind of work done" (*Laborem exercens*, 6).

The social structure of the time was not inspired by these principles of justice and recognition of human dignity, yet the Apostle does not encourage slaves to feel resentment, for "the class struggle, whoever the person who leads it or on occasion seeks to give it a theoretical justification, is

Rom 12:12
Eph 6:18
1 Thess 5:17
Rom 15:30
1 Cor 16:9
2 Thess 3:1
Eph 6:20

Eph 5:15

Mk 9:50
1 Pet 3:15

**Prayer and upright conduct**

2Continue steadfastly in prayer, being watchful in it with
thanksgiving; 3and pray for us also, that God may open to us a
door for the word, to declare the mystery of Christ, on account of
which I am in prison, 4that I may make it clear, as I ought to
speak.
5Conduct yourselves wisely toward outsiders, making the most
of the time. 6Let your speech always be gracious, seasoned with
salt, so that you may know how you ought to answer every one.

---

a *social evil*" (*Reconciliatio et paenitentia*, 16). On the contrary, he tells them that they should "work heartily, as serving the Lord and not men" (v. 23): "an inner effort on the part of the human spirit, guided by faith, hope and charity, is needed in order that through these points the *work* of the individual human being may *be given the meaning which it has in the eyes of God* and by means of which work enters into the salvation process on a par with the other ordinary yet particularly important components of its texture" (*Laborem exercens*, 24).

See the note on Eph 6:5–9.

**4:2.** Perseverance in prayer is something which is often stressed in the New Testament (cf. Lk 18:1; Rom 12:12; 1 Thess 5:17). The reason for this is that there is a very close connexion between holiness and prayer—so close that one cannot exist without the other. The daily effort to orientate one's ordinary activities towards God is a powerful spur to personal prayer. "How many occasions present themselves in the course of the day for a soul desirous of its own sanctification and the salvation of others, to raise itself to God—secret anguish, powerful and obstinate temptations, countless offences and omissions, and, lastly, fear of divine judgment" (St Pius X, *Haerent animo*, 10). Our sense of need encourages us to persevere in humble, confident prayer which wins God's favour and makes us rely more on his grace.

However, it is not only in the midst of difficulties that we should pray. The things that cause us happiness and the good things we desire to do or to see done should often be the theme of our conversation with God. "This is your duty," St John Chrysostom reminds us; "give thanks to God in your prayers, both for the benefits you are conscious of having received and for those which God has given you without your realizing it. Thank him both for the favours you have sought from him and for those which he has done you despite yourselves. Thank him both for the heaven where he promises you happiness and for the hell from which he sets you free. In a word, thank him for everything—afflictions and joys, disasters and happiness" (*Hom. on Col*, ad loc.).

**4:5–6.** "Outsiders": non–Christians (cf. 1 Cor 5:12; 1 Thess 4:12); in v. 6 St Paul specifies how we should behave in their company: by our conversation, ("gracious, seasoned with salt") and through our example and friendship we should help them discover the wonder of the faith, the marvel of God's love, and show them that

**Conclusion**

[7]Tychicus will tell you all about my affairs; he is a beloved brother Eph 6:21
and faithful minister and fellow servant in the Lord. [8]I have sent Eph 6:22

Christian living is perfectly compatible with everyday life and normal human involvements (cf. Mt 5:13; Mk 9:50). Friendliness, infectious cheerfullness and good humour are a reflection of the inner peace which comes from the grace of God and awareness that he is our Father; these virtues make life more pleasant for everyone and do much to attract people to the warmth of Christ's Church.

Christians should "make the most of the time", that is, use all the opportunities that arise to advance their own sanctification and to attract outsiders to the faith. "Time has grown very short", St Paul tells the Corinthians (1 Cor 7:29). "Brief indeed is our time for loving, for giving, for making atonement. It would be very wrong, therefore, for us to waste it, or to cast this treasure irresponsibly overboard. We must not squander this period of the world's history which God entrusted to each one of us" (St Josemaría Escrivá, *Friends of God*, 39). We must not be like those workers in the Gospel parable who were without work all day long (cf. Mt 20:6), or that servant who avoided trading with his master's money (cf. Mt 25:18). "They all prove insensitive to the great task the Master has entrusted to each and every Christian, that of seeing ourselves as his instruments, and acting accordingly, so that we may co-redeem with him, and of offering up our entire lives in the joyful sacrifice of surrendering ourselves for the good of souls" (*Friends of God*, 49).

The Apostle's counsel in these verses is a faithful echo of our Lord's commandment, "Go, therefore, and make disciples of all nations" (Mt 28:19). St Paul is speaking about the apostolate which all Christians have to do: we have received the grace of God and the gift of faith, and we have to manifest it by word and by deed. For, as Vatican II teaches, "witness of life is not the sole element in the apostolate; the true apostle is on the lookout for occasions of announcing Christ by word, either to unbelievers to draw them towards the faith, or to the faithful to instruct them, strengthen them, incite them to a more fervent life; 'for Christ's love urges us on' (2 Cor 5:14), and in the hearts of all should the Apostle's words find echo: 'Woe to me if I do not preach the gospel' (1 Cor 9:16)" (*Apostolicam actuositatem*, 6).

To give people the right answer calls for prudence—not the false prudence of the flesh which is only selfish astuteness but the cardinal virtue of prudence, which helps one adapt one's language and tone to the person one is addressing and the subject under discussion. "Your conversation should not be too austere or harsh, nor should it be too soft or weak: it should have a nice balance of firmness and sweetness. Excessive authoritarianism does more harm than good; but excessive sweetness and pleasantness are quite as bad. In everything there should be just measure [...]. A good doctor, if he acts wisely, does not prescribe the same diet for all his patients; all the more reason is there for a pastor to change his language to suit the particular circumstances of his people" (Chrysostom, *Hom. on Col*, ad loc.).

**4:7–9.** This letter—like that written to the Ephesians—is being delivered by Tychicus. He will have lots of other things to tell them on Paul's behalf. With him will go Onesimus, the runaway slave who was

him to you for this very purpose, that you may know how we are
Philem 10 and that he may encourage your hearts, 9and with him Onesimus,
the faithful and beloved brother, who is one of yourselves. They
will tell you of everything that has taken place here.
Acts 15:37, 39; 19:20; 20:4; 27:2 10Aristarchus my fellow prisoner greets you, and Mark the
cousin of Barnabas* (concerning whom you have received
Philem 24 instructions—if he comes to you, receive him), 11and Jesus who is
called Justus. These are the only men of the circumcision among
my fellow workers for the kingdom of God, and they have been a
comfort to me. 12Epaphras, who is one of yourselves, a servant[g]
of Christ Jesus, greets you, always remembering you earnestly in
his prayers, that you may stand mature and fully assured in all the
will of God. 13For I bear him witness that he has worked hard for
2 Tim 4:9f Philem 24 you and for those in Laodicea and in Hierapolis. 14Luke the
Rom 16:5 beloved physician* and Demas greet you. 15Give my greetings to
1 Thess 5:27 the brethren at Laodicea, and to Nympha and the church in her
house. 16And when this letter has been read among you, have it
read also in the church of the Laodiceans; and see that you read
also the letter from Laodicea. 17And say to Archippus, "See that
Philem 2 you fulfil the ministry which you have received in the Lord."

1 Cor 16:21 18I, Paul, write this greeting with my own hand. Remember my
2 Thess 3:17 fetters. Grace be with you.

---

later converted to the faith and whom St Paul is sending back to his master, Philemon, a resident of Colossae (Philem 10).

**4:10–17.** St Paul sends greetings to the Colossians from his fellow-workers. The first three mentioned are of Jewish background ("men of the circumcision"); which suggests that the other three are not Jews.

The passage contains an interesting piece of information to the effect that Mark—the author of the second Gospel—is the cousin of Barnabas, which explains why Barnabas felt so responsible for him (cf. Acts 15:37–40). Jesus Justus appears nowhere else; he has two names, one Jewish, one Latin—as was very common among Jews at the time. Luke, the author of the third Gospel and of the Acts of the Apostles, is described here by his pro-fession: he is a medical doctor (v. 14). Demas, a co-worker of Paul at this time, will later desert him because he is "in love with this present world" (2 Tim 4:10). Nympha, whom Paul also greets here, had generously lent her house for liturgical gath-erings (cf. Rom 16:5; 1 Cor 16:19). Archippus may have been Philemon's son (cf. Philem 2); we are not told what his "ministry" was. Epaphras' greeting is highly indicative of the pastoral work done by this great cooperator of St Paul: see pp. 121, 122, 124 above.

**g.** Or *slave*

On the interchange of letters between Laodicea and Colossae, see "Introduction to the Epistle to the Ephesians", above.

**4:18.** St Paul has been dictating his letter to an amanuensis; and therefore, as was customary, he writes a few words in his own hand to show that the letter is genuinely his.

What he says about "remembering his fetters" is interesting. Like any other Christian, he realizes that he is not alone in the apostolic work God has given him to do. It is true that he places his reliance on God—and therefore feels strengthened by his grace (cf. Phil 4:13)—but he also needs the support of his brothers and sisters in the faith. There is a solidarity in the order of grace whereby the weakness of some is supported by the strength of others: it is easy to see that the first Christians really availed of the supernatural resource of the communion of saints.

# Introduction to the Letter to Philemon

Philemon was a well-to-do citizen of Colossae whom St Paul had converted to Christianity, very probably during his three-year stay in Ephesus (cf. Philem 19), given that the Apostle had never been to Colossae (cf. Acts 19:10; 20:31). After Philemon's conversion his house became the base for the tiny local church (cf. Philem 1). St Paul was very appreciative of this; he calls Philemon his fellow worker (cf. Philem 1) and treats him with great affection and confidence (Philem 8, 17, 19, 21).

## DATE AND REASON FOR THE LETTER

One of Philemon's slaves, whose name was Onesimus, had run away, perhaps because he had stolen something (cf. Philem 18). Afraid of being punished, he did not want to go back to his master and instead fled to Rome, where he met Paul, who was in detention at the time. Thanks to the Apostle's kindness and zeal, Onesimus very soon came to know the Gospel and was converted.

St Paul may have initially planned to keep Onesimus with him as a helper (cf. Philem 13–14), but he soon came to the view that Onesimus should go back to Philemon. Tychicus was about to leave for Colossae, bearing Paul's letter, so Paul used the opportunity to have Onesimus travel with him (cf. Col 4:7–9). And so both letters, Colossians and Philemon, were written at the same time, the date usually being taken as near the end of St Paul's first Roman imprisonment, that is, around the year 63. That is why the Letter to Philemon is included among the Captivity Letters, even though in the Bible it usually comes after Titus and before Hebrews.

## PAULINE AUTHORSHIP

The Church has always included the Letter to Philemon as part of the *corpus paulinum*, its collection of Pauline letters. This we know from the second-century Muratorian Fragment and the writings of Origen, Eusebius, Tertullian, St Jerome and St Athanasius. The letter was written by St Paul. Its style, the logic of its argument, its deep psychology, the good human and tender love evidenced in it—all point to its Pauline authorship, and no one has argued otherwise.

## CONTENT AND MESSAGE

Despite its brevity, this epistle is a masterpiece of the art of letter-writing. It is full of the sensitivity and refined charity so characteristic of St Paul; he writes not in a tone of command (which he could have used because of his authority) but in one of humble entreaty. He describes himself as "an old man" and a "prisoner" on account of the Gospel (cf. Philem 9).

Although this is mainly a private letter, it does contain some teaching which is important despite its brevity. This epistle has been described as the "magna carta" of Christian freedom. St Paul does not directly ask Philemon to set Onesimus free but to take him back "as a beloved brother" (cf. Philem 16), that is, as if he were Paul himself (cf. Philem 17). By adopting this approach the Apostle thinks that Philemon will do even more than he asks (cf Philem 21).

What does he mean by "more"? The letter leaves us in suspense just when we seem to be heading to its main theme. The Apostle does not discuss slavery directly—it was part of the social structure of the period—but he provides the principles which will later lead to its abolition, when Christian teaching comes to imbue the civil law of nations. These principles are based on the freedom which Christ gained for us on the cross, whereby we become truly children of God and brothers of those who share our faith. "The freedom brought by Christ should necessarily have repercussions on the social plane."[1] This is the content of the "more" which St Paul expects of Philemon: he should treat Onesimus as a true brother in the faith, as his equal, making no discrimination of any kind on the grounds of race or colour, class or condition.

**1.** SCDF, *Liberatis nuntius*, 13.

# THE LETTER OF PAUL TO PHILEMON

*The Revised Standard Version, with notes*

## Greeting

1 [1]Paul, a prisoner for Christ Jesus, and Timothy our brother, Eph 3:11
To Philemon our beloved fellow worker [2]and Apphia our sister Col 4:17
and Archippus our fellow soldier, and the church in your house:
[3]Grace to you and peace from God our Father and the Lord Rom 1:7–9
Jesus Christ. 2 Tim 2:3

## Thanksgiving

[4]I thank my God always when I remember you in my prayers, Col 1:3f
[5]because I hear of your love and of the faith which you have
toward the Lord Jesus and all the saints, [6]and I pray that the Phil 1:9
sharing of your faith may promote the knowledge of all the good
that is ours in Christ. [7]For I have derived much joy and comfort 2 Col 7:4
from your love, my brother, because the hearts of the saints have
been refreshed through you.

---

**1–3.** Timothy is mentioned as a "brother" during St Paul's imprisonment, as in earlier letters (cf. Phil 1:1; Col 1:1). It is easy to deduce that this letter was written during the Apostle's first imprisonment in Rome, and not while he was in detention at Caesarea. Given that it is a short, private letter, the reference to Appia and Archippus suggests that these may have been members of Philemon's family, possibly his wife and son. From the Letter to the Colossians we know that Archippus was an important figure in the church of Colossae (cf. Col 4:17).

**5.** After the greeting, St Paul thanks God for Philemon's love and faith towards the Lord Jesus and all the "saints". The last clause of the verse ("because I hear … saints") has great theological importance; a Christian must not only love and have faith in Christ: through him and in him he should love and believe in other Christians. Although Onesimus had run away from Philemon's house, Philemon should have faith in his former slave from the moment he becomes a Christian. Both of them, master and servant, are now brothers in Christ Jesus, and therefore they should trust one another. St Paul is making a theological point to Philemon, which he goes on to develop, especially in v. 16.

On the custom of Christians calling one another "saints", see the note on Rom 1:7.

**6.** This verse has a complicated structure. What it is saying is that, by sharing the same faith, Christians have entered into communion with Christ and with other believers; and that Paul is confident that Philemon's faith is going to be practical and active because it shows him that all the benefits Christians enjoy are closely connected with Christ. Grammatically, this connexion with Christ is expressed in an extremely tight way—using a single Greek proposition, *eis*—, with the result that the meaning is ambiguous: the last part of the verse can be translated in various ways. The more likely meanings are: 1. "I pray that the sharing of your faith may lead you to realize that all the good that is ours is for [the glory of] Christ"; 2. "… that all the good that is ours [we have] through [thanks to] Christ".

### A plea on behalf of Onesimus

[8]Accordingly, though I am bold enough in Christ to command you
to do what is required, [9]yet for love's sake I prefer to appeal to
1 Cor 4:15 you—I, Paul, an ambassador[a] and now a prisoner also for Christ
Col 4:9 Jesus—[10]I appeal to you for my child, Onesimus, whose father I
Gal 4:19 have become in my imprisonment. [11](Formerly he was useless to
you, but now he is indeed useful[b] to you and to me.) [12]I am
sending him back to you, sending my very heart. [13]I would have
Phil 2:30 been glad to keep him with me, in order that he might serve me on

---

**8–12.** At this point St Paul gives his main reason for writing—to intercede for Onesimus. Typically, he appeals to Philemon's charity, rather than demanding his cooperation (cf. 2 Cor 1:23), and to support this appeal he refers to his (Paul's) being "an old man" and a "prisoner" for love of Jesus Christ (v. 9).

The Apostle's generosity of spirit is plain to see: in spite of being imprisoned he is self-forgetful and he uses every opportunity that presents itself to win converts—as was the case with Onesimus; and now he intercedes on his behalf. If once he was "useless" to his master, Onesimus can now be very "useful"; there is here a play on words, because the name Onesimus means "useful": it is as if he were saying that maybe Onesimus did not formerly live up to his name, but now he does; he has been very useful to Paul and now that he is going back he will also be useful to Philemon, who should receive him as if he were the Apostle himself (v. 12).

We should never have fixed ideas about people; despite mistakes and shortcomings, everyone can improve and, with God's grace, undergo a true change of heart.

The New Testament writings clearly show that the first Christians' apostolate extended to all sectors of society, with the result that Christians were to be found everywhere. St John Chrysostom points this out as follows: "Aquila worked at a manual trade; the lady who sold purple ran a workshop; another [Christian] was in charge of a gaol; another a centurion, like Cornelius; another was sick, like Timothy; another, Onesimus, was a slave and a fugitive; yet none of them found any of this an obstacle, and all shone for their holiness—men and women, young and old, slaves and free, soldiers and civilians" (*Hom. on St Matthew*, 43).

**13–14.** This is another example of the Apostle's typical refinement. Although his first idea was to keep Onesimus with him to help him during his imprisonment, he prefers that he who has the force of law on his side (Roman law, in this instance) should freely decide what action to take (cf. his approach to making collections: 2 Cor 9:7).

In line with the teaching of Christ and his Apostles, the Second Vatican Council "urges everyone, especially those responsible for educating others, to try to form men and women with a respect for the moral order and who will obey lawful authority and be lovers of true freedom—men, and women, who direct their activities with a sense of responsibility, and strive for what is true and just in willing cooperation with others" (*Dignitatis humanae*, 8).

**a.** Or *an old man* **b.** The name Onesimus meant *useful* or (compare verse 20) *beneficial*

your behalf during my imprisonment for the gospel; [14]but I preferred 2 Cor 9:7
to do nothing without your consent in order that your goodness 1 Pet 5:2
might not be by compulsion but of your own free will.
[15]Perhaps this is why he was parted from you for a while, that 1 Tim 6:2
you might have him back for ever, [16]no longer as a slave but more
than a slave, as a beloved brother, especially to me but how much

---

St Paul's refinement was not inspired only by reasons of friendship nor was it a mere tactic: he wants people—in this case, Philemon—to come to free personal decisions, for freedom is a great gift which God has given to every person. "If only we lived like this, if only we knew how to imbue our behaviour with generosity, with a desire for understanding and peace! We would encourage the rightful independence of all. Everyone would take a responsible approach to the tasks that correspond to him in temporal matters" (St Josemaría Escrivá, *Christ Is Passing By*, 124).

**15–16.** At this point Paul's thinking becomes exceptionally theological and incisive. What at first sight could have been seen as something bad—Onesimus' running away—can now be viewed in another light, the sharper light of divine providence: God can draw good out of evil, for "in everything, God works for good with those who love him" (Rom 8:28); he has allowed this incident to happen so as to give Onesimus the chance to discover the Christian faith.

Therefore, Philemon should now recognize him as a brother, for faith in Jesus Christ makes us all children of the same Father (cf. Gal 3:27–28; Eph 6:9). "Look at Paul writing on behalf of Onesimus, a runaway slave; he is not ashamed to call him his child, his very heart, his brother, his partner. What can I say?", St John Chrysostom asks; "Jesus Christ lowered himself to the point of making our slaves his brothers. If they are brothers of Jesus Christ, then they are also our brothers" (*Hom. on Philem*, 2, ad loc.).

Due to this teaching slavery gradually died out. The teaching of the Church's Magisterium has contributed to a growing realization that all workers have innate dignity and rights as men and as sons and daughters of God. In an early encyclical of modern times Leo XIII called on employers to see that "it is truly shameful and inhuman to misuse men as though they were mere things designed just to be used in the pursuit of gain", and reminded them of their duties never "to look upon workers as their bondsmen but to respect in every man his dignity and worth as a man and a Christian" (*Rerum novarum*, 16).

Christianity, then, elevates and gives a new dignity to interpersonal relationships, thereby helping produce changes and improvements in social structures. Every Christian insofar as he can should contribute to bringing these changes about, but the methods used to do so must always be moral. Neglect to play one's part in social reform could even constitute a grave sin, a "social" sin against the virtue of justice.

John Paul II teaches that "the term *social* applies to every sin against justice in interpersonal relationships, committed either by the individual against the community or by the community against the individual. Also *social* is every sin against the rights of the human person, beginning

more to you, both in the flesh and in the Lord. [17]So if you consider
me your partner, receive him as you would receive me. [18]If he has
wronged you at all, or owes you anything, charge that to my
Gal 6:11 account. [19]I, Paul, write this with my own hand, I will repay it—
2 Thess 3:17 to say nothing of your owing me even your own self. [20]Yes,
brother, I want some benefit from you in the Lord. Refresh my
heart in Christ.

[21]Confident of your obedience, I write to you, knowing that
you will do even more than I say.

---

with the right to life and including the life of the unborn, or against a person's physical integrity. Likewise *social* is every sin against others' freedom, especially against the supreme freedom to believe in God and adore him; *social* is every sin against the dignity and honour of one's neighbour. Also *social* is every sin against the common good and its exigencies in relation to the whole broad spectrum of the rights and duties of citizens. The term *social* can be applied to sins of commission or omission—on the part of political, economic or trade union leaders, who though in a position to do so do not work diligently and wisely for the improvement and transformation of society according to the requirements and potential of the given historic moment; as also on the part of workers who through absenteeism or non-cooperation fail to ensure that their industries can continue to advance the well-being of the workers themselves, of their families, and of the whole of society" (*Reconciliatio et paenitentia*, 16).

**17–21.** Paul identifies himself with Onesimus because they share the same faith—and Paul is an extremely generous person. Here we can clearly see his great charity which leads him to love everyone much more than is his strict duty. "Be convinced that justice alone is never enough to solve the great problems of mankind. When justice alone is done, do not be surprised if people are hurt: the dignity of man, who is a son of God, requires much more. Charity must penetrate and accompany justice because it sweetens and deifies everything: 'God is love' (1 Jn 4:16). Our motive in everything we do should be the Love of God, which makes it easier for us to love our neighbour and which purifies all earthly love and raises it on to a higher level" (St Josemaría Escrivá, *Friends of God*, 172). It is not surprising, then, that the Apostle should ask Philemon to charge it to his account if Onesimus has wronged him or owes him anything (v. 18). And as if to confirm this commitment with affection and good humour he as it were signs a docket promising to pay any charge there may be. However, he immediately goes on to remind Philemon that if they worked out their accounts Philemon would be found to be in debt to Paul, because it was due to Paul that he became a Christian (v. 19). On this account Paul feels that he can ask him to forgive Onesimus: that sign of love and affection would really do Paul good in his present circumstances. But, he goes on to say (it is a suggestion that delicately respects Philemon's decision) that he hopes Philemon's obedience will lead him to do "even more" (v. 21). As suggested in the Introduction to this letter he is probably hoping that he will set Onesimus free. In the eyes of the law

**Words of farewell**

22At the same time, prepare a guest room for me, for I am hoping Phil 1:27; 2:24
through your prayers to be granted to you.
23Epaphras, my fellow prisoner in Christ Jesus, sends greetings Col 1:7
to you, 24and so do Mark, Aristarchus, Demas, and Luke, my Col 4:10, 14
fellow workers.
25The grace of the Lord Jesus Christ be with your spirit. Gal 6:18 2 Tim 4:22

---

Onesimus is still a slave; but as a Christian he is already a free man.

St Paul does not directly ask for Onesimus' freedom, although he does hint at it, encouraging his old master to set him free but leaving it up to him to decide (and thereby merit). He reminds Philemon how generous he, Paul, was towards him (vv. 18–19), in the hope that Philemon will reciprocate. "This is a repetition of the same testimony he expressed earlier in his letter", St John Chrysostom points out; "'knowing that you will do even more than I say': it is impossible to imagine anything more persuasive, any more convincing argument than this tender regard for his generosity which St Paul expresses; Philemon cannot but agree to his demand" (*Hom. on Philem,* ad loc.).

**22–25.** The letter ends as it began, in a tone of familiarity and trust.

It is easy to see what an important part Philemon's home and family played in the life of the young church of Colossae. "Families who lived in union with Christ and who made him known to others. Small Christian communities which were centres for the spreading of the Gospel and its message. Families no different from other families of those times, but living with a new spirit, which spread to all those who were in contact with them. That is what the first Christians were, and this is what we have to be—sowers of peace and joy, the peace and joy that Jesus has brought to us" (St Josemaría Escrivá, *Christ Is Passing By*, 30).

Those who are with St Paul at time of writing (they are mentioned also in Col 4:10–14) send their greetings and then comes the usual final blessing (cf. Gal 6:18).

# New Vulgate Text

## EPISTOLA AD EPHESIOS

**[1]** 1Paulus apostolus Christi Iesu per voluntatem Dei sanctis, qui sunt Ephesi, et fidelibusin Christo Iesu:
2gratia vobis et pax a Deo Patre nostro et Domino Iesu Christo. 3Benedictus Deus et Pater Domini nostri
Iesu Christi, / qui benedixit nos in omni benedictione spiritali in caelestibus in Christo, / 4sicut elegit
nos in ipso ante mundi constitutionem, / ut essemus sancti et immaculati in conspectu eius in caritate,
/ 5qui praedestinavit nos in adoptionem filiorum / per Iesum Christum in ipsum, / secundum
beneplacitum voluntatis suae, / 6in laudem gloriae gratiae suae, / in qua gratificavit nos in Dilecto, / 7in
quo habemus redemptionem per sanguinem eius, / remissionem peccatorum, / secundum divitias gratiae
eius, / 8quam superabundare fecit in nobis / in omni sapientia et prudentia / 9notum faciens nobis
mysterium voluntatis suae, / secundum beneplacitum eius, quod proposuit in eo, / 10in dispensationem
plenitudinis temporum: / recapitulare omnia in Christo, / quae in caelis et quae in terra, in ipso; 11in
quo etiam sorte vocati sumus, praedestinati secundum propositum eius, qui omnia operatur secundum
consilium voluntatis suae, 12ut simus in laudem gloriae eius, qui ante speravimus in Christo; 13in quo
et vos cum audissetis verbum veritatis, evangelium salutis vestrae, in quo et credentes signati estis
Spiritu promissionis Sancto, 14qui est arrabon hereditatis nostrae in redemptionem acquisitionis, in
laudem gloriae ipsius. 15Propterea et ego audiens fidem vestram, quae est in Domino Iesu, et
dilectionem in omnes sanctos, 16non cesso gratias agens pro vobis memoriam faciens in orationibus
meis, 17ut Deus Domini nostri Iesu Christi, Pater gloriae, det vobis Spiritum sapientiae et revelationis
in agnitione eius, 18illuminatos oculos cordis vestri, ut sciatis quae sit spes vocationis eius, quae divitiae
gloriae hereditatis eius in sanctis 19et quae sit supereminens magnitudo virtutis eius in nos, qui
credimus, secundum operationem potentiae virtutis eius, 20quam operatus est in Christo, suscitans illum
a mortuis et constituens ad dexteram suam in caelestibus 21supra omnem principatum et potestatem et
virtutem et dominationem et omne nomen, quod nominatur non solum in hoc saeculo sed et in futuro;
22et *omnia subiecit sub pedibus eius*, et ipsum dedit caput supra omnia ecclesiae, 23quae est corpus
ipsius, plenitudo eius, qui omnia in omnibus adimpletur. **[2]** 1Et vos, cum essetis mortui delictis et
peccatis vestris, 2in quibus aliquando ambulastis secundum saeculum mundi huius, secundum principem
potestatis aeris, spiritus, qui nunc operatur in filios diffidentiae; 3in quibus et nos omnes aliquando
conversati sumus in concupiscentiis carnis nostrae, facientes voluntates carnis et cogitationum, et
eramus natura filii irae sicut et ceteri. 4Deus autem, qui dives est in misericordia, propter nimiam
caritatem suam, qua dilexit nos, 5et cum essemus mortui peccatis, convivificavit nos Christo—gratia
estis salvati—6et conresuscitavit et consedere fecit in caelestibus in Christo Iesu, 7ut ostenderet in
saeculis supervenientibus abundantes divitias gratiae suae in bonitate super nos in Christo Iesu. 8Gratia
enim estis salvati per fidem; et hoc non ex vobis, Dei donum est: 9non ex operibus, ut ne quis glorietur.
10Ipsius enim sumus factura, creati in Christo Iesu in opera bona, quae praeparavit Deus, ut in illis
ambulemus. 11Propter quod memores estote quod aliquando vos gentes in carne, qui dicimini
praeputium ab ea, quae dicitur circumcisio in carne manufacta, 12quia eratis illo in tempore sine Christo,
alienati a conversatione Israel et extranei testamentorum promissionis, spem non habentes et sine Deo
in mundo. 13Nunc autem in Christo Iesu vos, qui aliquando eratis longe, facti estis prope in sanguine
Christi. 14Ipse est enim pax nostra, qui fecit utraque unum et medium parietem maceriae solvit,
inimicitiam, in carne sua, 15legem mandatorum in decretis evacuans, ut duos condat in semetipso in
unum novum hominem, faciens pacem, 16et reconciliet ambos in uno corpore Deo per crucem
interficiens inimicitiam in semetipso. 17Et veniens *evangelizavit pacem* vobis, *qui longe fuistis, et pacem
his, qui prope*; 18quoniam per ipsum habemus accessum ambo in uno Spiritu ad Patrem. 19Ergo iam non
estis extranei et advenae, sed estis concives sanctorum et domestici Dei, 20superaedificati super
fundamentum apostolorum et prophetarum, ipso summo angulari lapide Christo Iesu, 21in quo omnis
aedificatio compacta crescit in templum sanctum in Domino, 22in quo et vos coaedificamini in
habitaculum Dei in Spiritu. **[3]** 1Huius rei gratia ego Paulus vinctus Christi Iesu pro vobis gentibus—
2si tamen audistis dispensationem gratiae Dei, quae data est mihi pro vobis, 3quoniam secundum

revelationem notum mihi factum est mysterium, sicut supra scripsi in brevi, [4]prout potestis legentes
intellegere prudentiam meam in mysterio Christi, [5]quod aliis generationibus non innotuit filiis
hominum, sicuti nunc revelatum est sanctis apostolis eius et prophetis in Spiritu, [6]esse gentes coheredes
et concorporales et comparticipes promissionis in Christo Iesu per evangelium, [7]cuius factus sum
minister secundum donum gratiae Dei, quae data est mihi secundum operationem virtutis eius. [8]Mihi
omnium sanctorum minimo data est gratia haec: gentibus evangelizare investigabiles divitias Christi
[9]et illuminare omnes, quae sit dispensatio mysterii absconditi a saeculis in Deo, qui omnia creavit, [10]ut
innotescat nunc principatibus et potestatibus in caelestibus per ecclesiam multiformis sapientia Dei
[11]secundum propositum saeculorum, quod fecit in Christo Iesu Domino nostro, [12]in quo habemus
fiduciam et accessum in confidentia per fidem eius. [13]Propter quod peto, ne deficiatis in tribulationibus
meis pro vobis, quae est gloria vestra. [14]Huius rei gratia flecto genua mea ad Patrem, [15]ex quo omnis
paternitas in caelis et in terra nominatur, [16]ut det vobis secundum divitias gloriae suae virtute corroborari
per Spiritum eius in interiorem hominem, [17]habitare Christum per fidem in cordibus vestris, in caritate
radicati et fundati, [18]ut valeatis comprehendere cum omnibus sanctis quae sit latitudo et longitudo et
sublimitas et profundum, [19]scire etiam supereminentem scientiae caritatem Christi, ut impleamini in
omnem plenitudinem Dei. [20]Ei autem, qui potens est supra omnia facere superabundanter quam petimus
aut intellegimus, secundum virtutem, quae operatur in nobis, [21]ipsi gloria in ecclesia et in Christo Iesu
in omnes generationes saeculi saeculorum. Amen. **[4]** [1]Obsecro itaque vos ego vinctus in Domino,
ut digne ambuletis vocatione, qua vocati estis, [2]cum omni humilitate et mansuetudine, cum
longanimitate, supportantes invicem in caritate, [3]solliciti servare unitatem spiritus in vinculo pacis;
[4]unum corpus et unus Spiritus, sicut et vocati estis in una spe vocationis vestrae; [5]unus Dominus, una
fides, unum baptisma; [6]unus Deus et Pater omnium, qui super omnes et per omnia et in omnibus.
[7]Unicuique autem nostrum data est gratia secundum mensuram donationis Christi. [8]Propter quod dicit:
«*Ascendens in altum captivam duxit captivitatem, / dedit dona hominibus*». [9]Illud autem «ascendit»
quid est, nisi quia et descendit in inferiores partes terrae? [10]Qui descendit, ipse est et qui ascendit super
omnes caelos, ut impleret omnia. [11]Et ipse dedit quosdam quidem apostolos, quosdam autem prophetas,
alios vero evangelistas, alios autem pastores et doctores [12]ad instructionem sanctorum in opus ministerii,
in aedificationem corporis Christi, [13]donec occurramus omnes in unitatem fidei et agnitionis Filii Dei,
in virum perfectum, in mensuram aetatis plenitudinis Christi, [14]ut iam non simus parvuli fluctuantes
et circumacti omni vento doctrinae in fallacia hominum, in astutia ad circumventionem erroris;
[15]veritatem autem facientes in caritate crescamus in illum per omnia, qui est caput Christus, [16]ex quo
totum corpus compactum et conexum per omnem iuncturam subministrationis secundum operationem
in mensura uniuscuiusque partis augmentum corporis facit in aedificationem sui in caritate. [17]Hoc igitur
dico et testificor in Domino, ut iam non ambuletis, sicut et gentes ambulant in vanitate sensus sui
[18]tenebris obscuratum habentes intellectum, alienati a vita Dei propter ignorantiam, quae est in illis
propter caecitatem cordis ipsorum; [19]qui indolentes semetipsos tradiderunt impudicitiae in operationem
immunditiae omnis in avaritia. [20]Vos autem non ita didicistis Christum, [21]si tamen illum audistis et in
ipso edocti estis, sicut est veritas in Iesu: [22]deponere vos secundum pristinam conversationem veterem
hominem, qui corrumpitur secundum desideria erroris, [23]renovari autem spiritu mentis vestrae [24]et
induere novum hominem, qui secundum Deum creatus est in iustitia et sanctitate veritatis. [25]Propter
quod deponentes mendacium *loquimini veritatem unusquisque cum proximo suo*, quoniam sumus
invicem membra. [26]*Irascimini et nolite peccare*; sol non occidat super iracundiam vestram, [27]et nolite
locum dare Diabolo. [28]Qui furabatur, iam non furetur, magis autem laboret operando manibus bonum,
ut habeat unde tribuat necessitatem patienti. [29]Omnis sermo malus ex ore vestro non procedat, sed si
quis bonus ad aedificationem opportunitatis, ut det gratiam audientibus. [30]Et nolite contristare Spiritum
Sanctum Dei, in quo signati estis in diem redemptionis. [31]Omnis amaritudo et ira et indignatio et clamor
et blasphemia tollatur a vobis cum omni malitia. [32]Estote autem invicem benigni, misericordes,
donantes invicem, sicut et Deus in Christo donavit vobis. **[5]** [1]Estote ergo imitatores Dei sicut filii
carissimi [2]et ambulate in dilectione, sicut et Christus dilexit nos et tradidit seipsum pro nobis oblationem
et hostiam Deo in odorem suavitatis. [3]Fornicatio autem et omnis immunditia aut avaritia nec nominetur
in vobis, sicut decet sanctos, [4]et turpitudo et stultiloquium aut scurrilitas, quae non decent, sed magis
gratiarum actio. [5]Hoc enim scitote intellegentes quod omnis fornicator aut immundus aut avarus, id est
idolorum cultor, non habet hereditatem in regno Christi et Dei. [6]Nemo vos decipiat inanibus verbis;
propter haec enim venit ira Dei in filios diffidentiae. [7]Nolite ergo effici comparticipes eorum; [8]eratis
enim aliquando tenebrae, nunc autem lux in Domino. Ut filii lucis ambulate [9]—fructus enim lucis est
in omni bonitate et iustitia et veritate— [10]probantes quid sit beneplacitum Domino; [11]et nolite
communicare operibus infructuosis tenebrarum, magis autem et redarguite; [12]quae enim in occulto fiunt

ab ipsis, turpe est et dicere; [13]omnia autem, quae arguuntur, a lumine manifestantur, [14]omne enim, quod
manifestatur, lumen est. Propter quod dicit: «Surge, qui dormis, et exsurge a mortuis, et illuminabit te
Christus». [15]Videte itaque caute quomodo ambuletis, non quasi insipientes sed ut sapientes,
[16]redimentes tempus, quoniam dies mali sunt. [17]Propterea nolite fieri imprudentes, sed intellegite, quae
sit voluntas Domini. [18]Et nolite inebriari vino, in quo est luxuria, sed implemini Spiritu [19]loquentes
vobismetipsis in psalmis et hymnis et canticis spiritalibus, cantantes et psallentes in cordibus vestris
Domino. [20]Gratias agentes semper pro omnibus in nomine Domini nostri Iesu Christi, Deo et Patri,
[21]subiecti invicem in timore Christi. [22]Mulieres viris suis sicut Domino, [23]quoniam vir caput est
mulieris, sicut et Christus caput est ecclesiae, ipse salvator corporis. [24]Sed ut ecclesia subiecta est
Christo, ita et mulieres viris in omnibus. [25]Viri, diligite uxores, sicut et Christus dilexit ecclesiam et
seipsum tradidit pro ea, [26]ut illam sanctificaret mundans lavacro aquae in verbo, [27]ut exhiberet ipse sibi
gloriosam ecclesiam non habentem maculam aut rugam aut aliquid eiusmodi, sed ut sit sancta et
immaculata. [28]Ita et viri debent diligere uxores suas ut corpora sua. Qui suam uxorem diligit, seipsum
diligit; [29]nemo enim umquam carnem suam odio habuit, sed nutrit et fovet eam sicut et Christus
ecclesiam, [30]quia membra sumus corporis eius. [31]*Propter hoc relinquet homo patrem et matrem et
adhaerebit uxori suae, et erunt duo in carne una.* [32]Mysterium hoc magnum est; ego autem dico de
Christo et ecclesia! [33]Verumtamen et vos singuli unusquisque suam uxorem sicut seipsum diligat; uxor
autem timeat virum. **[6]** [1]Filii, oboedite parentibus vestris in Domino, hoc enim est iustum. [2]*Honora
patrem tuum et matrem*, quod est mandatum primum cum promissione, [3]*ut bene sit tibi et sis longaevus
super terram.* [4]Et, patres, nolite ad iracundiam provocare filios vestros, sed educate illos in disciplina
et correptione Domini. [5]Servi, oboedite dominis carnalibus cum timore et tremore, in simplicitate cordis
vestri sicut Christo [6]non ad oculum servientes quasi hominibus placentes, sed ut servi Christi facientes
voluntatem Dei ex animo, [7]cum bona voluntate servientes, sicut Domino et non hominibus, [8]scientes
quoniam unusquisque, si quid fecerit bonum, hoc percipiet a Domino, sive servus sive liber. [9]Et, domini,
eadem facite illis, remittentes minas, scientes quia et illorum et vester Dominus est in caelis, et
personarum acceptio non est apud eum. [10]De cetero confortamini in Domino et in potentia virtutis eius.
[11]Induite armaturam Dei, ut possitis stare adversus insidias Diaboli. [12]Quia non est nobis colluctatio
adversus sanguinem et carnem sed adversus principatus, adversus potestates, adversus mundi rectores
tenebrarum harum, adversus spiritalia nequitiae in caelestibus. [13]Propterea accipite armaturam Dei, ut
possitis resistere in die malo et, omnibus perfectis, stare. [14]State ergo *succincti lumbos* vestros *in veritate*
et *induti loricam iustitiae* [15]et calceati *pedes in praeparatione evangelii pacis*, [16]in omnibus sumentes
scutum fidei, in quo possitis omnia tela Maligni ignea exstinguere; [17]et *galeam salutis* assumite *et
gladium Spiritus*, quod est *verbum Dei*, [18]per omnem orationem et obsecrationem orantes omni tempore
in Spiritu, et in ipso vigilantes in omni instantia et obsecratione pro omnibus sanctis [19]et pro me, ut detur
mihi sermo in aperitione oris mei cum fiducia notum facere mysterium evangelii, [20]pro quo legatione
fungor in catena, ut in ipso audeam, prout oportet me loqui. [21]Ut autem et vos sciatis, quae circa me
sunt, quid agam, omnia nota vobis faciet Tychicus, carissimus frater et fidelis minister in Domino,
[22]quem misi ad vos in hoc ipsum, ut cognoscatis, quae circa nos sunt, et consoletur corda vestra. [23]Pax
fratribus et caritas cum fide a Deo Patre et Domino Iesu Christo. [24]Gratia cum omnibus, qui diligunt
Dominum nostrum Iesum Christum in incorruptione.

## EPISTOLA AD PHILIPPENSES

**[1]** [1]Paulus et Timotheus servi Christi Iesu omnibus sanctis in Christo Iesu, qui sunt Philippis, cum
episcopis et diaconis: [2]gratia vobis et pax a Deo Patre nostro et Domino Iesu Christo. [3]Gratias ago Deo
meo in omni memoria vestri [4]semper in omni oratione mea pro omnibus vobis cum gaudio
deprecationem faciens [5] super communione vestra in evangelio a prima die usque nunc, [6]confidens hoc
ipsum, quia, qui coepit in vobis opus bonum, perficiet usque in diem Christi Iesu; [7]sicut est mihi iustum
hoc sentire pro omnibus vobis, eo quod habeam in corde vos et in vinculis meis et in defensione et
confirmatione evangelii socios gratiae meae omnes vos esse. [8]Testis enim mihi Deus, quomodo cupiam
omnes vos in visceribus Christi Iesu. [9]Et hoc oro, ut caritas vestra magis ac magis abundet in scientia
et omni sensu, [10]ut probetis potiora, ut sitis sinceri et sine offensa in diem Christi, [11]repleti fructu
iustitiae, qui est per Iesum Christum, in gloriam et laudem Dei. [12]Scire autem vos volo, fratres, quia,
quae circa me sunt, magis ad profectum venerunt evangelii, [13]ita ut vincula mea manifesta fierent in

Christo in omni praetorio et in ceteris omnibus, [14]et plures e fratribus in Domino confidentes vinculis
meis abundantius audere sine timore verbum loqui. [15]Quidam quidem et propter invidiam et
contentionem, quidam autem et propter bonam voluntatem Christum praedicant; [16]hi quidem ex caritate
scientes quoniam in defensionem evangelii positus sum, [17]illi autem ex contentione Christum
annuntiant, non sincere, existimantes pressuram se suscitare vinculis meis. [18]Quid enim? Dum omni
modo, sive sub obtentu sive in veritate, Christus annuntietur, et in hoc gaudeo; sed et gaudebo, [19]scio
enim quia hoc mihi proveniet in salutem per vestram orationem et subministrationem Spiritus Iesu
Christi, [20]secundum exspectationem et spem meam quia in nullo confundar, sed in omni fiducia sicut
semper et nunc magnificabitur Christus in corpore meo, sive per vitam sive per mortem. [21]Mihi enim
vivere Christus est et mori lucrum. [22]Quod si vivere in carne, hic mihi fructus operis est, et quid eligam
ignoro. [23]Coartor autem ex his duobus: desiderium habens dissolvi et cum Christo esse, multo magis
melius; [24]permanere autem in carne magis necessarium est propter vos. [25]Et hoc confidens scio quia
manebo et permanebo omnibus vobis ad profectum vestrum et gaudium fidei, [26]ut gloriatio vestra
abundet in Christo Iesu in me per meum adventum iterum ad vos. [27]Tantum digne evangelio Christi
conversamini, ut sive cum venero et videro vos, sive absens audiam de vobis quia statis in uno Spiritu
unanimes concertantes fide evangelii [28]et in nullo perterriti ab adversariis, quod est illis indicium
perditionis, vobis autem salutis, et hoc a Deo; [29]quia vobis hoc donatum est pro Christo, non solum ut
in eum credatis, sed ut etiam pro illo patiamini [30]idem certamen habentes, quale vidistis in me et nunc
auditis in me. **[2]** [1]Si qua ergo consolatio in Christo, si quod solacium caritatis, si qua communio
spiritus, si quae viscera et miserationes, [2]implete gaudium meum, ut idem sapiatis, eandem caritatem
habentes, unanimes, id ipsum sapientes, [3]nihil per contentionem neque per inanem gloriam, sed in
humilitate superiores sibi invicem arbitrantes, [4]non, quae sua sunt, singuli considerantes, sed et ea, quae
aliorum. [5]Hoc sentite in vobis, quod et in Christo Iesu: / [6]qui cum in forma Dei esset, / non rapinam
arbitratus est esse se aequalem Deo, / [7]sed semetipsum exinanivit formam servi accipiens, / in
similitudinem hominum factus; / et habitu inventus ut homo, / [8]humiliavit semetipsum factus oboediens
usque ad mortem, / mortem autem crucis. / [9]Propter quod et Deus illum exaltavit / et donavit illi nomen,
/ quod est super omne nomen, / [10]ut in nomine Iesu *omne genu flectatur* / caelestium et terrestrium et
infernorum, / [11]*et omnis lingua confiteatur*: / «Dominus Iesus Christus!», / in gloriam Dei Patris.
[12]Itaque, carissimi mei, sicut semper oboedistis, non ut in praesentia mei tantum sed multo magis nunc
in absentia mea, cum metu et tremore vestram salutem operamini; [13]Deus est enim, qui operatur in vobis
et velle et perficere pro suo beneplacito. [14]Omnia facite sine murmurationibus et haesitationibus, [15]ut
efficiamini sine querela et simplices, filii Dei sine reprehensione in medio generationis pravae et
perversae, inter quos lucetis sicut luminaria in mundo, [16]verbum vitae firmiter tenentes ad gloriam
meam in die Christi, quia non in vacuum cucurri, neque in vacuum laboravi. [17]Sed et si delibor supra
sacrificium et obsequium fidei vestrae, gaudeo et congaudeo omnibus vobis; [18]idipsum autem et vos
gaudete et congaudete mihi. [19]Spero autem in Domino Iesu Timotheum cito me mittere ad vos, ut et
ego bono animo sim, cognitis, quae circa vos sunt. [20]Neminem enim habeo tam unanimem, qui sincere
pro vobis sollicitus sit; [21]omnes enim sua quaerunt, non quae sunt Iesu Christi. [22]Probationem autem
eius cognoscitis, quoniam sicut patri filius mecum servivit in evangelium. [23]Hunc igitur spero me
mittere, mox ut videro, quae circa me sunt; [24]confido autem in Domino, quoniam et ipse cito veniam.
[25]Necessarium autem existimavi Epaphroditum fratrem et cooperatorem et commilitonem meum,
vestrum autem apostolum et ministrum necessitatis meae, mittere ad vos, [26]quoniam omnes vos
desiderabat et maestus erat, propterea quod audieratis illum infirmatum. [27]Nam et infirmatus est usque
ad mortem, sed Deus misertus est eius; non solum autem eius, verum et mei, ne tristitiam super
tristitiam haberem. [28]Festinantius ergo misi illum, ut, viso eo, iterum gaudeatis, et ego sine tristitia sim.
[29]Excipite itaque illum in Domino cum omni gaudio et eiusmodi cum honore habetote, [30]quoniam
propter opus Christi usque ad mortem accessit in interitum tradens animam suam, ut suppleret id, quod
vobis deerat ministerii erga me. **[3]** [1]De cetero, fratres mei, gaudete in Domino. Eadem vobis scribere
mihi quidem non pigrum, vobis autem securum. [2]Videte canes, videte malos operarios, videte
concisionem! [3]Nos enim sumus circumcisio, qui Spiritu Dei servimus et gloriamur in Christo Iesu et
non in carne fiduciam habentes, [4]quamquam ego habeam confidentiam et in carne. Si quis alius videtur
confidere in carne, ego magis: [5]circumcisus octava die, ex genere Israel, de tribu Beniamin, Hebraeus
ex Hebraeis, secundum legem pharisaeus, [6]secundum aemulationem persequens ecclesiam, secundum
iustitiam, quae in lege est, conversatus sine querela. [7]Sed, quae mihi erant lucra, haec arbitratus sum
propter Christum detrimentum. [8]Verumtamen existimo omnia detrimentum esse propter eminentiam
scientiae Christi Iesu Domini mei, propter quem omnia detrimentum feci et arbitror ut stercora, ut
Christum lucri faciam [9]et inveniar in illo non habens meam iustitiam, quae ex lege est, sed illam, quae

per fidem est Christi, quae ex Deo est iustitia in fide, [10]ad cognoscendum illum et virtutem resurrectionis eius et communionem passionum illius, conformans me morti eius, [11]si quo modo occurram ad resurrectionem, quae est ex mortuis. [12]Non quod iam acceperim aut iam perfectus sim, persequor autem si umquam comprehendam, sicut et comprehensus sum a Christo Iesu. [13]Fratres, ego me non arbitror comprehendisse; unum autem: quae quidem retro sunt, obliviscens, ad ea vero, quae ante sunt, extendens me [14]ad destinatum persequor, ad bravium supernae vocationis Dei in Christo Iesu. [15]Quicumque ergo perfecti, hoc sentiamus; et si quid aliter sapitis, et hoc vobis Deus revelabit; [16]verumtamen, ad quod pervenimus, in eodem ambulemus. [17]Coimitatores mei estote, fratres, et observate eos, qui ita ambulant, sicut habetis formam nos. [18]Multi enim ambulant, quos saepe dicebam vobis, nunc autem et flens dico, inimicos crucis Christi, [19]quorum finis interitus, quorum deus venter et gloria in confusione ipsorum, qui terrena sapiunt. [20]Noster enim municipatus in caelis est, unde etiam salvatorem exspectamus Dominum Iesum Christum, [21]qui transfigurabit corpus humilitatis nostrae, ut illud conforme faciat corpori gloriae suae secundum operationem, qua possit etiam subicere sibi omnia.
**[4]** [1]Itaque, fratres mei carissimi et desideratissimi, gaudium et corona mea, sic state in Domino, carissimi! [2]Evodiam rogo et Syntychen deprecor idipsum sapere in Domino. [3]Etiam rogo et te, germane compar, adiuva illas, quae mecum concertaverunt in evangelio cum Clemente et ceteris adiutoribus meis, quorum nomina sunt in libro vitae. [4]Gaudete in Domino semper. Iterum dico: Gaudete! [5]Modestia vestra nota sit omnibus hominibus. Dominus prope. [6]Nihil solliciti sitis, sed in omnibus oratione et obsecratione cum gratiarum actione petitiones vestrae innotescant apud Deum. [7]Et pax Dei, quae exsuperat omnem sensum, custodiet corda vestra et intellegentias vestras in Christo Iesu. [8]De cetero, fratres, quaecumque sunt vera, quaecumque pudica, quaecumque iusta, quaecumque casta, quaecumque amabilia, quaecumque bonae famae, si qua virtus et si qua laus, haec cogitate; [9]quae et didicistis et accepistis et audistis et vidistis in me, haec agite; et Deus pacis erit vobiscum. [10]Gavisus sum autem in Domino vehementer quoniam tandem aliquando refloruistis pro me sentire, sicut et sentiebatis, opportunitate autem carebatis. [11]Non quasi propter penuriam dico, ego enim didici, in quibus sum, sufficiens esse. [12]Scio et humiliari, scio et abundare; ubique et in omnibus institutus sum et satiari et esurire et abundare et penuriam pati. [13]Omnia possum in eo, qui me confortat. [14]Verumtamen bene fecistis communicantes tribulationi meae. [15]Scitis autem et vos, Philippenses, quod in principio evangelii, quando profectus sum a Macedonia, nulla mihi ecclesia communicavit in ratione dati et accepti nisi vos soli; [16]quia et Thessalonicam et semel et bis in usum mihi misistis. [17]Non quia quaero datum, sed requiro fructum, qui abundet in rationem vestram. [18]Accepi autem omnia et abundo; repletus sum acceptis ab Epaphrodito, quae misistis odorem suavitatis, hostiam acceptam, placentem Deo. [19]Deus autem meus implebit omne desiderium vestrum secundum divitias suas in gloria in Christo Iesu. [20]Deo autem et Patri nostro gloria in saecula saeculorum. Amen. [21] Salutate omnem sanctum in Christo Iesu. Salutant vos, qui mecum sunt, fratres. [22]Salutant vos omnes sancti, maxime autem, qui de Caesaris domo sunt. [23]Gratia Domini Iesu Christi cum spiritu vestro. Amen.

## EPISTOLA AD COLOSSENSES

**[1]** [1]Paulus apostolus Christi Iesu per voluntatem Dei et Timotheus frater [2]his, qui sunt Colossis, sanctis et fidelibus fratribus in Christo: gratia vobis et pax a Deo Patre nostro. [3]Gratias agimus Deo Patri Domini nostri Iesu Christi semper pro vobis orantes, [4]audientes fidem vestram in Christo Iesu et dilectionem, quam habetis in sanctos omnes, [5]propter spem, quae reposita est vobis in caelis, quam ante audistis in verbo veritatis evangelii, [6]quod pervenit ad vos, sicut et in universo mundo est fructificans et crescens sicut et in vobis ex ea die, qua audistis et cognovistis gratiam Dei in veritate; [7]sicut didicistis ab Epaphra carissimo conservo nostro, qui est fidelis pro nobis minister Christi, [8]qui etiam manifestavit nobis dilectionem vestram in Spiritu. [9]Ideo et nos, ex qua die audivimus, non cessamus pro vobis orantes et postulantes, ut impleamini agnitione voluntatis eius in omni sapientia et intellectu spiritali, [10]ut ambuletis digne Domino per omnia placentes, in omni opere bono fructificantes et crescentes in scientia Dei, [11]in omni virtute confortati secundum potentiam claritatis eius in omnem patientiam et longanimitatem, cum gaudio [12]gratias agentes Patri, / qui idoneos vos fecit in partem sortis sanctorum in lumine; / [13]qui eripuit nos de potestate tenebrarum / et transtulit in regnum Filii dilectionis suae, / [14]in quo habemus redemptionem, / remissionem peccatorum; / [15]qui est imago Dei invisibilis, / primogenitus omnis creaturae, / [16]quia in ipso condita sunt universa in caelis et in terra, / visibilia et invisibilia, / sive throni sive dominationes / sive principatus sive potestates. / Omnia per ipsum et in

ipsum creata sunt, / [17]et ipse est ante omnia, / et omnia in ipso constant. / [18]Et ipse est caput corporis
ecclesiae; / qui est principium, primogenitus ex mortuis, / ut sit in omnibus ipse primatum tenens, /
[19]quia in ipso complacuit omnem plenitudinem habitare / [20]et per eum reconciliare omnia in ipsum, /
pacificans per sanguinem crucis eius, sive quae in terris sive quae in caelis sunt. [21]Et vos, cum essetis
aliquando alienati et inimici sensu in operibus malis, [22]nunc autem reconciliavit in corpore carnis eius
per mortem exhibere vos sanctos et immaculatos et irreprehensibiles coram ipso, [23]si tamen permanetis
in fide fundati et stabiles et immobiles a spe evangelii, quod audistis, quod praedicatum est in universa
creatura, quae sub caelo est, cuius factus sum ego Paulus minister. [24]Nunc gaudeo in passionibus pro
vobis et adimpleo ea quae desunt passionum Christi in carne mea pro corpore eius, quod est ecclesia,
[25]cuius factus sum ego minister secundum dispensationem Dei, quae data est mihi in vos, ut impleam
verbum Dei, [26]mysterium, quod absconditum fuit a saeculis et generationibus, nunc autem manifestatum
est sanctis eius, [27]quibus voluit Deus notas facere divitias gloriae mysterii huius in gentibus, quod est
Christus in vobis, spes gloriae; [28]quem nos annuntiamus, commonentes omnem hominem et docentes
omnem hominem in omni sapientia, ut exhibeamus omnem hominem perfectum in Christo; [29]ad quod
et laboro certando secundum operationem eius, quae operatur in me in virtute. **[2]** [1]Volo enim vos
scire qualem sollicitudinem habeam pro vobis et pro his, qui sunt Laodiciae, et quicumque non viderunt
faciem meam in carne, [2]ut consolentur corda ipsorum instructi in caritate et in omnes divitias
plenitudinis intellectus, in agnitionem mysterii Dei, Christi, [3]in quo sunt omnes thesauri sapientiae et
scientiae absconditi. [4]Hoc dico, ut nemo vos decipiat in subtilitate sermonum. [5]Nam etsi corpore absens
sum, sed spiritu vobiscum sum, gaudens et videns ordinem vestrum et firmamentum eius, quae in
Christum est, fidei vestrae. [6]Sicut ergo accepistis Christum Iesum Dominum, in ipso ambulate, [7]radicati
et superaedificati in ipso et confirmati fide, sicut didicistis, abundantes in gratiarum actione. [8]Videte,
ne quis vos depraedetur per philosophiam et inanem fallaciam secundum traditionem hominum,
secundum elementa mundi et non secundum Christum; [9]quia in ipso inhabitat omnis plenitudo
divinitatis corporaliter, [10]et estis in illo repleti, qui est caput omnis principatus et potestatis, [11]in quo
et circumcisi estis circumcisione non manufacta in exspoliatione corporis carnis, in circumcisione
Christi, [12]consepulti ei in baptismo, in quo et conresuscitati estis per fidem operationis Dei, qui
suscitavit illum a mortuis; [13]et vos, cum mortui essetis in delictis et praeputio carnis vestrae,
convivificavit cum illo, donans nobis omnia delicta, [14]delens, quod adversum nos erat, chirographum
decretis, quod erat contrarium nobis, et ipsum tulit de medio affigens illud cruci; [15]exspolians
principatus et potestates traduxit confidenter, triumphans illos in semetipso. [16]Nemo ergo vos iudicet
in cibo aut in potu aut ex parte diei festi aut neomeniae aut sabbatorum, [17]quae sunt umbra futurorum,
corpus autem Christi. [18]Nemo vos bravio defraudet complacens sibi in humilitate et religione angelorum
propter ea, quae vidit, ingrediens, frustra inflatus sensu carnis suae [19]et non tenens caput, ex quo totum
corpus per nexus et coniunctiones subministratum et compaginatum crescit in augmentum Dei. [20]Si
mortui estis cum Christo ab elementis mundi, quid tamquam viventes in mundo decretis subicimini:
[21]«Ne tetigeris neque gustaveris neque contrectaveris», [22]quae sunt omnia in corruptionem ipso usu
secundum praecepta et doctrinas hominum? [23]Quae sunt rationem quidem habentia sapientiae in
superstitione et humilitate, et non parcendo corpori, non in honore aliquo ad saturitatem carnis. **[3]** [1]Igitur
si conresurrexistis Christo, quae sursum sunt quaerite, ubi Christus est in dextera Dei sedens; [2]quae sursum
sunt sapite, non quae supra terram. [3]Mortui enim estis, et vita vestra abscondita est cum Christo in Deo!
[4]Cum Christus apparuerit, vita vestra, tunc et vos apparebitis cum ipso in gloria. [5]Mortificate ergo
membra, quae sunt super terram: fornicationem, immunditiam, libidinem, concupiscentiam malam et
avaritiam, quae est simulacrorum servitus, [6]propter quae venit ira Dei super filios incredulitatis; [7]in
quibus et vos ambulastis aliquando, cum viveretis in illis. [8]Nunc autem deponite et vos omnia: iram,
indignationem, malitiam, blasphemiam, turpem sermonem de ore vestro; [9]nolite mentiri invicem, qui
exuistis vos veterem hominem cum actibus eius [10]et induistis novum, eum, qui renovatur in agnitionem
secundum imaginem eius, qui creavit eum, [11]ubi non est Graecus et Iudaeus, circumcisio et praeputium,
barbarus, Scytha, servus, liber, sed omnia et in omnibus Christus. [12]Induite vos ergo sicut electi Dei,
sancti et dilecti, viscera misericordiae, benignitatem, humilitatem, mansuetudinem, longanimitatem,
[13]supportantes invicem et donantes vobis ipsis, si quis adversus aliquem habet querelam; sicut et
Dominus donavit vobis, ita et vos; [14]super omnia autem haec: caritatem, quod est vinculum perfectionis.
[15]Et pax Christi dominetur in cordibus vestris, ad quam et vocati estis in uno corpore. Et grati estote.
[16]Verbum Christi habitet in vobis abundanter, in omni sapientia docentes et commonentes vosmetipsos
psalmis, hymnis, canticis spiritalibus, in gratia cantantes in cordibus vestris Deo; [17]et omne,
quodcumque facitis in verbo aut in opere, omnia in nomine Domini Iesu gratias agentes Deo Patri per
ipsum. [18]Mulieres, subditae estote viris, sicut oportet in Domino. [19]Viri, diligite uxores et nolite amari

esse ad illas. 20Filii, oboedite parentibus per omnia, hoc enim placitum est in Domino. 21Patres, nolite ad indignationem provocare filios vestros, ut non pusillo animo fiant. 22Servi, oboedite per omnia dominis carnalibus, non ad oculum servientes, quasi hominibus placentes, sed in simplicitate cordis, timentes Dominum. 23Quodcumque facitis, ex animo operamini sicut Domino et non hominibus, 24scientes quod a Domino accipietis retributionem hereditatis. Domino Christo servite; 25qui enim iniuriam facit, recipiet id quod inique gessit, et non est personarum acceptio. **[4]** 1Domini, quod iustum est et aequum, servis praestate, scientes quoniam et vos Dominum habetis in caelo. 2Orationi instate, vigilantes in ea in gratiarum actione, 3orantes simul et pro nobis, ut Deus aperiat nobis ostium sermonis ad loquendum mysterium Christi, propter quod etiam vinctus sum, 4ut manifestem illud, ita ut oportet me loqui. 5In sapientia ambulate ad eos, qui foris sunt, tempus redimentes. 6Sermo vester semper sit in gratia, sale conditus, ut sciatis quomodo oporteat vos unicuique respondere. 7Quae circa me sunt, omnia vobis nota faciet Tychicus, carissimus frater et fidelis minister et conservus in Domino, 8quem misi ad vos ad hoc ipsum, ut cognoscatis, quae circa nos sunt, et consoletur corda vestra, 9cum Onesimo fideli et carissimo fratre, qui est ex vobis; omnia, quae hic aguntur, nota facient vobis. 10Salutat vos Aristarchus concaptivus meus et Marcus, consobrinus Barnabae, de quo accepistis mandata—si venerit ad vos, excipite illum—11et Iesus, qui dicitur Iustus, qui sunt ex circumcisione, hi soli adiutores in regno Dei, qui mihi fuerunt solacio. 12Salutat vos Epaphras, qui ex vobis est, servus Christi Iesu, semper certans pro vobis in orationibus, ut stetis perfecti et impleti in omni voluntate Dei. 13Testimonium enim illi perhibeo quod habet multum laborem pro vobis et pro his, qui sunt Laodiciae et qui Hierapoli. 14Salutat vos Lucas, medicus carissimus, et Demas. 15Salutate fratres, qui sunt Laodiciae, et Nympham et, quae in domo eius est, ecclesiam. 16Et cum lecta fuerit apud vos epistula, facite ut et in Laodicensium ecclesia legatur, et eam, quae ex Laodicia est, vos quoque legatis. 17Et dicite Archippo: «Vide ministerium, quod accepisti in Domino, ut illud impleas». 18Salutatio mea manu Pauli. Memores estote vinculorum meorum. Gratia vobiscum.

## EPISTOLA AD PHILEMON

1Paulus vinctus Christi Iesu et Timotheus frater Philemoni dilecto et adiutori nostro 2et Apphiae sorori et Archippo commilitoni nostro et ecclesiae, quae in domo tua est: 3gratia vobis et pax a Deo Patre nostro et Domino Iesu Christo. 4Gratias ago Deo meo semper memoriam tui faciens in orationibus meis, 5audiens caritatem tuam et fidem, quam habes in Dominum Iesum et in omnes sanctos, 6ut communio fidei tuae evidens fiat in agnitione omnis boni, quod est in nobis in Christum; 7gaudium enim magnum habui et consolationem in caritate tua, quia viscera sanctorum requieverunt per te, frater. 8Propter quod multam fiduciam habens in Christo imperandi tibi, quod ad rem pertinet, 9propter caritatem magis obsecro, cum sim talis ut Paulus senex, nunc autem et vinctus Christi Iesu; 10obsecro te de meo filio, quem genui in vinculis, Onesimo, 11qui tibi aliquando inutilis fuit, nunc autem et tibi et mihi utilis, 12quem remisi tibi: eum, hoc est viscera mea; 13quem ego volueram mecum detinere, ut pro te mihi ministraret in vinculis evangelii. 14Sine consilio autem tuo nihil volui facere, uti ne velut ex necessitate bonum tuum esset sed voluntarium. 15Forsitan enim ideo discessit ad horam, ut aeternum illum reciperes, 16iam non ut servum sed plus servo, carissimum fratrem, maxime mihi, quanto autem magis tibi et in carne et in Domino. 17Si ergo habes me socium, suscipe illum sicut me. 18Si autem aliquid nocuit tibi aut debet, hoc mihi imputa. 19Ego Paulus scripsi mea manu, ego reddam; ut non dicam tibi quod et teipsum mihi debes. 20Ita, frater! Ego te fruar in Domino; refice viscera mea in Christo! 21Confidens oboedientia tua scripsi tibi, sciens quoniam et super id, quod dico, facies. 22Simul autem et para mihi hospitium, nam spero per orationes vestras donari me vobis. 23Salutat te Epaphras, concaptivus meus in Christo Iesu, 24Marcus, Aristarchus, Demas, Lucas, adiutores mei. 25Gratia Domini Iesu Christi cum spiritu vestro.

# Explanatory Notes

*Asterisks in the text of the New Testament refer to these "Explanatory Notes" in the RSVCE.*

## THE LETTER OF PAUL TO THE EPHESIANS

1:1, *To the saints who are*: The addition "at Ephesus" is doubtful. The letter may have been a form of encyclical.
1:10, *to unite*: Or, "to sum up." This is one of the chief themes of the letter. Men are to be under Christ as head of the Mystical Body, and even irrational creatures must be in some way under him as the cornerstone of creation.
2:14, *dividing wall*: A metaphor taken from the wall that divided the court of the Gentiles from the court of the Israelites in the temple.
3:3, *the mystery*: i.e., that the Gentiles were to be admitted to the Church on a basis of equality.
5:14: Apparently a fragment of an early Christian hymn; cf. 1 Tim 3:16.

**Changes in the RSV for the Catholic Edition**

| | RSV | RSVCE |
|---|---|---|
| Eph 1:14 | which | who |
| Eph 5:32 | I take it to mean | I mean in reference to |

## THE LETTER OF PAUL TO THE PHILIPPIANS

1:14, *because of my imprisonment*: i.e., because I continue to preach in their midst, though in prison.
1:20, *honoured in my body*: i.e., through my sufferings.
2:6, *in the form of God*: The Greek shows that divine attributes and therefore nature are implied here. It is not the divine nature he set no store by, but equality of treatment and recognition of his divinity.
2:7, *emptied himself* of this external recognition which was his right.
3:12, *made me his own*: On the road to Damascus.
3:19: These Judaizers made holiness a question of distinction of foods and set great store by circumcision.

**Changes in the RSV for the Catholic Edition**

| | RSV | RSVCE |
|---|---|---|
| Phil 2:5 | you have | was |

## THE LETTER OF PAUL TO THE COLOSSIANS

1:15, *first-born*: Born of the Father before all ages. The reference here is to the divine person of the Word; see verse 16.

## Explanatory Notes

1:18: His human nature.

1:24, *what is lacking*: Christ's sufferings were, of course, sufficient for our redemption, but we may all add ours to his, in order that the fruits of his redemption may be applied to the souls of men.

3:18–4:5: The whole passage corresponds closely to Eph 5:22–6:9.

4:10: Mark, the evangelist, and, probably, the John Mark of Acts 12:25.

4:14: Luke, the evangelist.

# Headings added to the Biblical Text

## EPHESIANS

1. INTRODUCTION
Greeting 1:1
Christ, head of the Church and source of unity 1:3
Thanksgiving and prayer 1:15

2. SALVATION IN CHRIST

3. MEMBERSHIP OF THE CHURCH

4. PAUL'S MISSION
Revelation of the mystery of Christ 3:1
Prayer for the faithful 3:14
Doxology 3:20

5. UNITY IN THE CHURCH
Bases of unity 4:1
Building up Christ's body 4:11

6. NEW LIFE IN CHRIST AND IN THE CHURCH
Corruption, a thing of the past 4:17
The purity of life of God's children 5:1
Walking in the light 5:8
Marriage compared to Christ's union with the Church 5:21
Advice to children and parents 6:1
Advice to servants and masters 6:5
Weapons for spiritual combat 6:10
Conclusion and blessing 6:21

## PHILIPPIANS

1. INTRODUCTION
Greeting 1:1
Thanksgiving. Paul's affection and love 1:3
Paul's own circumstances 1:12

2. TEACHINGS
Appeal for steadfastness 1:27
Unity and humility 2:1
Hymn in praise of Christ's self-emptying 2:5
The children of God, the light of the world 2:12

3. PLANS AND NEWS
Timothy's mission 2:19
Epaphroditus' mission 2:25

4. THE CHRISTIAN LIFE
A warning about Judaizers 3:1
The righteousness of God exceeds that of the Law 3:7
The spiritual athlete 3:12
Citizens of heaven 3:17
Exhortation to perseverance and joy 4:1
Thanks for help received 4:10
Words of farewell 4:21

## COLOSSIANS

1. INTRODUCTION
Greeting 1:1
Thanksgiving for the Colossians' response to the Gospel 1:3
Hymn in praise of Christ, the head of all creation 1:15
The effect of Christ's saving action 1:21

2. PAUL'S MISSION
Proclamation of the Mystery 1:24
Paul's concern for the faithful 2:1

3. FIRMNESS IN THE FAITH
A warning about heresy 2:6
Rejection of false asceticism 2:16

4. NEW LIFE IN CHRIST
Seeking the things that are above 3:1
Avoiding sin 3:5
Progress in the spiritiual life 3:12
Morals in family life 3:18
Prayer and upright conduct 4:2
Conclusion 4:7

# Headings added to the Biblical Text

## PHILEMON

Greeting 1
Thanksgiving 4
A plea on behalf of Onesimus 8
Words of farewell 22

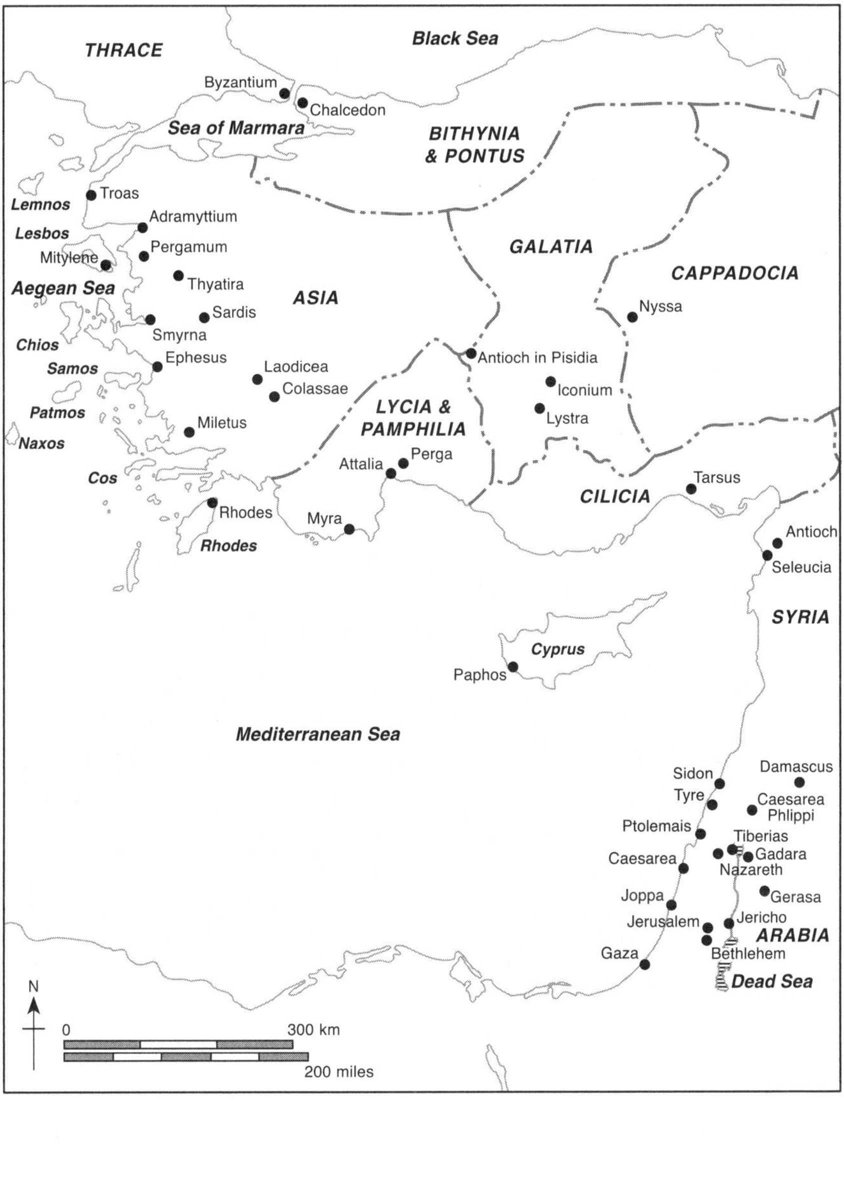


*The Eastern Mediterranean Sea in the first century* AD

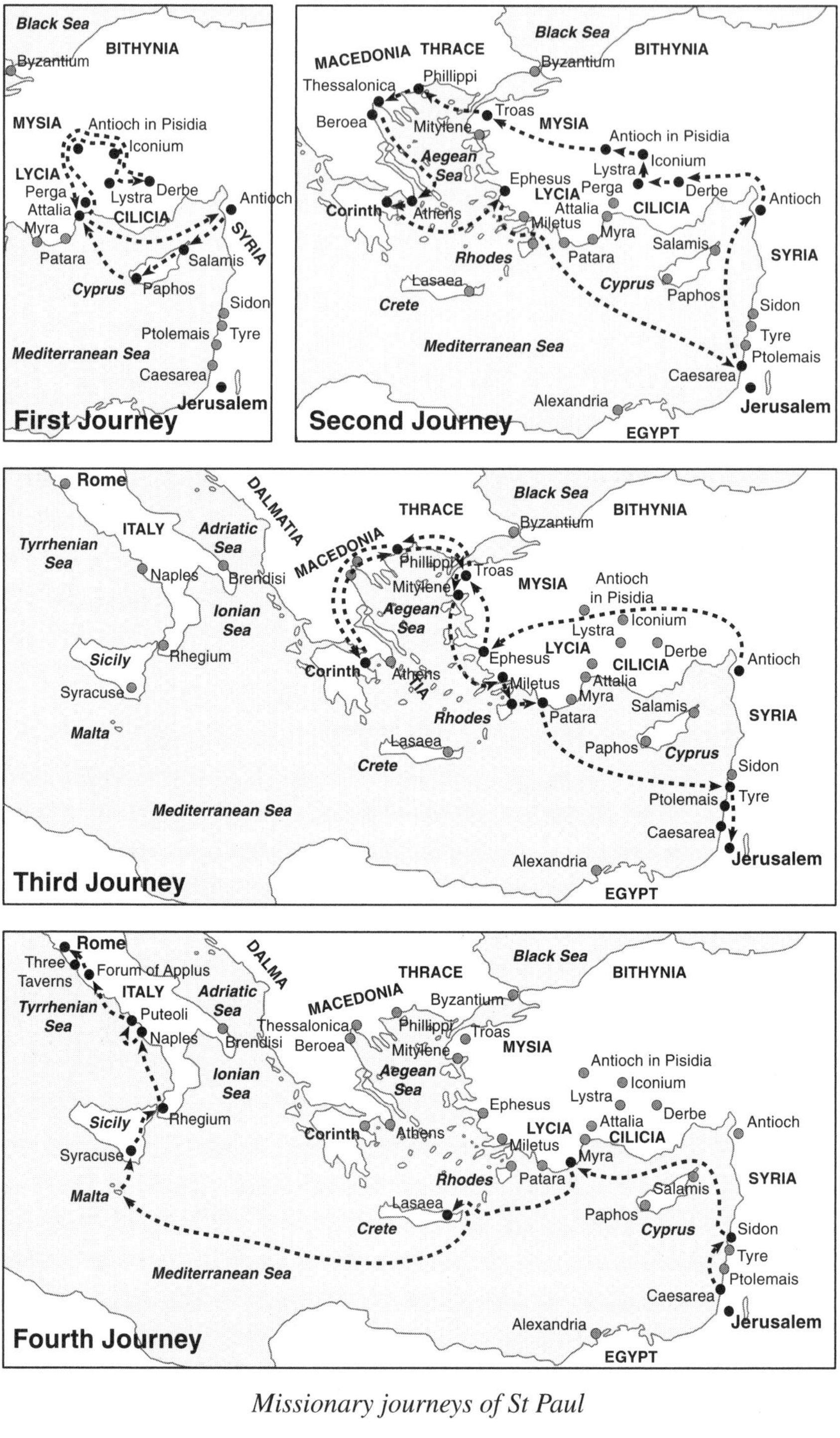


*Missionary journeys of St Paul*

# Sources quoted in the Navarre Bible New Testament Commentary

## 1. DOCUMENTS OF THE CHURCH AND OF POPES

**Benedict XII**
Const. *Benedictus Deus*, 29 January 1336
**Benedict XV**
Enc. *Humani generis redemptionem*, 15 June 1917
Enc. *Spiritus Paraclitus*, 1 September 1920
**Clement of Rome, St**
*Letter to the Corinthians*
**Constantinople, First Council of**
*Nicene-Constantinopolitan Creed*
**Constantinople, Third Council of**
*Definitio de duabus in Christo voluntatibus et operationibus*
**Florence, Council of**
Decree *Pro Jacobitis*
*Laetentur coeli*
Decree *Pro Armeniis*
**John Paul II**
Addresses and homilies
Apos. Exhort. *Catechesi tradendae*, 16 October 1979
Apos. Exhort. *Familiaris consortio*, 22 November 1981
Apos. Exhort. *Reconciliatio et paenitentia*, 2 December 1984
Apos. Letter. *Salvifici doloris*, 11 February 1984
Bull, *Aperite portas*, 6 January 1983
Enc. *Redemptor hominis*, 4 March 1979
Enc. *Dives in misercordia*, 30 November 1980
Enc. *Dominum et Vivificantem*, 30 May 1986
Enc. *Laborem exercens*, 14 September 1981
*Letter to all priests*, 8 April 1979
*Letter to all bishops*, 24 February 1980
**Gelasius I**
*Ne forte*
**Gregory the Great, St**
*Epistula ad Theodorum medicum contra Fabianum*
*Exposition on the Seven Penitential*
*Ne forte*
*In Evangelia homiliae*
*In Ezechielem homiliae*
*Moralia in Job*
*Regulae pastoralis liber*
**Innocent III**
Letter *Eius exemplo*, 18 December 1208
**John XXIII**
*Pacem in terris*, 11 April 1963
Enc. *Ad Petri cathedram*, 29 June 1959
**Lateran Council** (649)
Canons
**Leo the Great, St**
Homilies and sermons
*Licet per nostros*
*Promisisse mememeni*
**Leo IX**
*Creed*
**Leo XIII**
Enc. *Aeterni Patris*, 4 August 1879
Enc. *Immortale Dei*, 1 November 1885
Enc. *Libertas praestantissimum*, 20 June 1888
Enc. *Sapientiae christianae*, 18 January 1890
Enc. *Rerum novarum*, 15 May 1891
Enc. *Providentissimus Deus*, 18 November 1893
Enc. *Divinum illud munus*, 9 May 1897
**Lateran, Fourth Council of** (1215)
*De fide catholica*
**Lyons, Second Council of** (1274)
*Doctrina de gratia*
*Profession of faith of Michael Palaeologue*
**Orange, Second Council of** (529)
*De gratia*
**Paul IV**
Const. *Cum quorumdam*, 7 August 1555
**Paul VI**
Enc. *Ecclesiam suam*, 6 August 1964
Enc. *Mysterium fidei*, 9 September 1965
Apos. Exhort. *Marialis cultus*, 2 February 1967
Apos. Letter *Petrum et Paulum*, 27 February 1967
Enc. *Populorum progressio*, 26 March 1967
Enc. *Sacerdotalis coelibatus*, 24 June 1967
*Creed of the People of God: Solemn Profession of Faith*, 30 June 1968
Apos. Letter *Octagesima adveniens*, 14 June 1971

## Sources quoted in the Commentary

Apos. Exhort. *Gaudete in Domino*, 9 May 1975
Apos. Exhort. *Evangelii nuntiandi*, 8 Dec. 1975
Homilies and addresses
**Pius V, St**
*Catechism of the Council of Trent for Parish Priests* or *Pius V Catechism*
**Pius IX, Bl.**
Bull *Ineffabilis Deus*, 8 December 1854
*Syllabus of Errors*
**Pius X, St**
Enc. *E supreme apostolatus*, 4 October 1903
Enc. *Ad Diem illum*, 2 February 1904
Enc. *Acerbo nimis*, 15 April 1905
*Catechism of Christian Doctrine*, 15 July 1905
Decree *Lamentabili*, 3 July 1907
Enc. *Haerent animo*, 4 August 1908
**Pius XI**
Enc. *Quas primas*, 11 December 1925
Enc. *Divini illius magistri*, 31 December 1929
Enc. *Mens nostra*, 20 December 1929
Enc. *Casti connubii*, 31 December 1930
Enc. *Quadragesimo anno*, 15 May 1931
Enc. *Ad catholici sacerdotii*, 20 December 1935
**Pius XII**
Enc. *Mystici Corporis*, 29 June 1943
Enc. *Mediator Dei*, 20 November 1947
Enc. *Divino afflante Spiritu*, 30 September 1943
Enc. *Humani generis*, 12 August 1950
Apost. Const. *Menti nostrae*, 23 September 1950
Enc. *Sacra virginitas*, 25 March 1954
Enc. *Ad caeli Reginam*, 11 October 1954
Homilies and addresses
**Quierzy, Council of** (833)
*Doctrina de libero arbitrio hominis et de praedestinatione*
**Trent, Council of** (1545–1563)
*De sacris imaginibus*
*De Purgatorio*
*De reformatione*
*De sacramento ordinis*
*De libris sacris*
*De peccato originale*
*De SS. Eucharistia*
*De iustificatione*
*De SS. Missae sacrificio*
*De sacramento matrimonio*
*Doctrina de peccato originali*
*Doctrina de sacramento extremae unctionis*
*Doctrina de sacramento paenitentiae*
**Toledo, Ninth Council of** (655)
*De Redemptione*
**Toledo, Eleventh Council of** (675)
*De Trinitate Creed*
**Valence, Third Council of** (855)
*De praedestinatione*
**Vatican, First Council of the** (1869–1870)
Dogm. Const. *Dei Filius*
Dogm. Const. *Pastor aeternus*
**Vatican, Second Council of the** (1963–1965)
Const. *Sacrosanctum Concilium*
Decree *Christus Dominus*
Decl. *Dignitatis humanae*
Decl. *Gravissimum educationis*
Decl. *Nostrae aetate*
Decree *Optatam totius*
Decree *Ad gentes*
Decree *Apostolicam actuositatem*
Decree *Perfectae caritatis*
Decree *Presbyterorum ordinis*
Decree *Unitatis redintegratio*
Dogm. Const. *Dei Verbum*
Dogm. Const. *Lumen gentium*
Past. Const. *Gaudium et spes*

### Liturgical Texts

*Roman Missal: Missale Romanum, editio typica altera* (Vatican City, 1975)
*The Divine Office* (London, Sydney, Dublin, 1974)

### Other Church Documents

**Code of Canon Law**
*Codex Iuris Canonici* (Vatican City, 1983)
**Congregation for the Doctrine of the Faith**
*Declaration concerning Sexual Ethics*, December 1975
*Instruction on Infant Baptism*, 20 October 1980
*Inter insigniores*, 15 October 1976
*Letter on certain questions concerning Eschatology*, 17 May 1979
*Libertatis conscientia*, 22 March 1986
*Sacerdotium ministeriale*, 6 August 1983
*Libertatis nuntius*, 6 August 1984
*Mysterium Filii Dei*, 21 February 1972
**Pontifical Biblical Commission**
Replies
**New Vulgate**
*Nova Vulgata Bibliorum Sacrorum editio typica altera* (Vatican City, 1986)

# Sources quoted in the Commentary

## 2. THE FATHERS, ECCLESIASTICAL WRITERS AND OTHER AUTHORS

**Alphonsus Mary Liguori, St**
*Christmas Novena*
*The Love of Our Lord Jesus Christ reduced to practice*
*Meditations for Advent*
*Thoughts on the Passion*
*Shorter Sermons*
*Sunday Sermons*
*Treasury of Teaching Material*
**Ambrose, St**
*De sacramentis*
*De mysteriis*
*De officiis ministrorum*
*Exameron*
*Expositio Evangelii secundum Lucam*
*Expositio in Ps 118*
*Treatise on the Mysteries*
**Anastasius of Sinai, St**
*Sermon on the Holy Synaxis*
**Anon.**
*Apostolic Constitutions*
*Didache*, or *Teaching of the Twelve Apostles*
*Letter to Diognetus*
*Shepherd of Hermas*
**Anselm, St**
*Prayers and Meditations*
**Aphraates**
*Demonstratio*
**Athanasius, St**
*Adversus Antigonum*
*De decretis nicaenae synodi*
*De Incarnatio contra arianos*
*Historia arianorum*
*Oratio I contra arianos*
*Oratio II contra arianos*
*Oratio contra gentes*
**Augustine, St**
*The City of God*
*Confessions*
*Contra Adimantum Manichaei discipulum*
*De Actis cum Felice Manicheo*
*De agone christiano*
*De bono matrimonii*
*De bono viduitatis*
*De catechizandis rudibus*
*De civitate Dei*
*De coniugiis adulterinis*
*De consensu Evangelistarum*
*De correptione et gratia*
*De doctrina christiana*
*De dono perseverantiae*
*De fide et operibus*
*De fide et symbolo*
*De Genesi ad litteram*
*De gratia et libero arbitrio*
*De natura et gratia*
*De praedestinatione sanctorum*
*De sermo Domini in monte*
*De spiritu et littera*
*De Trinitate*
*De verbis Domini sermones*
*Enarrationes in Psalmos*
*Enchiridion*
*Expositio epistulae ad Galatas*
*In I Epist. Ioann. ad Parthos*
*In Ioannis Evangelium tractatus*
*Letters*
*Quaestiones in Heptateuchum*
*Sermo ad Cassariensis Ecclesiae plebem*
*Sermo de Nativitate Domini*
*Sermons*
**Basil, St**
*De Spiritu Sancto*
*Homilia in Julittam martyrem*
*In Psalmos homiliae*
**Bede, St**
*Explanatio Apocalypsis*
*In Ioannis Evangelium expositio*
*In Lucae Evangelium expositio*
*In Marci Evangelium expositio*
*In primam Epistolam Petri*
*In primam Epistolam S. Ioanis*
*Sermo super Qui audientes gavisi sunt*
*Super Acta Apostolorum expositio*
*Super divi Iacobi Epistolam*
**Bernal, Salvador**
*Monsignor Josemaría Escrivá de Balaguer*, Dublin, 1977
**Bernard, St**
*Book of Consideration*
*De Beata Virgine*
*De fallacia et brevitate vitae*
*De laudibus novae militiae*
*Divine amoris*
*Meditationes piissimae de cognitionis humanae conditionis*
*Sermons on Psalm 90*
*Sermon on Song of Songs*
*Sermons*
**Bonaventure, St**
*In IV Libri sententiarum*
*Speculum Beatae Virgine*
**Borromeo, St Charles**
*Homilies*

## Sources quoted in the Commentary

**Catherine of Siena, St**
*Dialogue*
**Cano, Melchor**
*De locis*
**Cassian, John**
*Collationes*
*De institutis coenobiorum*
**Clement of Alexandria**
*Catechesis III, De Baptismo*
*Commentary on Luke*
*Quis dives salvetur?*
*Stromata*
**Cyprian, St**
*De bono patientiae*
*De dominica oratione*
*De mortalitate*
*De opere et eleemosynis*
*De unitate Ecclesiae*
*De zelo et livore*
*Epist. ad Fortunatum*
*Quod idola dii non sint*
**Cyril of Alexandria, St**
*Commentarium in Lucam*
*Explanation of Hebrews*
*Homilia XXVIII in Mattheum*
**Cyril of Jerusalem, St**
*Catecheses*
*Mystagogical Catechesis*
**Diadochus of Photike**
*Chapters on Spiritual Perfection*
**Ephrem, St**
*Armenian Commentary on Acts*
*Commentarium in Epistolam ad Haebreos*
**Eusebius of Caesarea**
*Ecclesiastical History*
**Francis de Sales, St**
*Introduction to the Devout Life*
*Treatise on the Love of God*
**Francis of Assisi, St**
*Little Flowers*
*Reflections on Christ's Wounds*
**Fulgentius of Ruspe**
*Contra Fabianum libri decem*
*De fide ad Petrum*
**Gregory Nazianzen, St**
*Orationes theologicae*
*Sermons*
**Gregory of Nyssa, St**
*De instituto christiano*
*De perfecta christiana forma*
*On the Life of Moses*
*Oratio catechetica magna*
*Oratio I in beatitudinibus*
*Oratio I in Christi resurrectionem*
**Hippolytus, St**
*De consummatione saeculi*
**Ignatius of Antioch, St**
*Letter to Polycarp*
*Letters to various churches*
**Ignatius, Loyola, St**
*Spiritual Exercises*
**Irenaeus, St**
*Against Heresies*
*Proof of Apostolic Preaching*
**Jerome, St**
*Ad Nepotianum*
*Adversus Helvidium*
*Comm. in Ionam*
*Commentary on Galatians*
*Commentary on St Mark's Gospel*
*Contra Luciferianos*
*Dialogus contra pelagianos*
*Expositio in Evangelium secundum Lucam*
*Homilies to neophytes on Psalm 41*
*Letters*
*On Famous Men*
**John of Avila, St**
*Audi, filia*
*Lecciones sobre Gálatas*
*Sermons*
**John Chrysostom, St**
*Ante exilium homilia*
*Adversus Iudaeos*
*Baptismal Catechesis*
*De coemeterio et de cruce*
*De incomprehensibile Dei natura*
*De sacerdotio*
*De virginitate*
*Fifth homily on Anna*
*Hom. De Cruce et latrone*
*Homilies on St Matthew's Gospel, St John's Gospel, Acts of the Apostles, Romans, Ephesians, 1 and 2 Corinthians, Colossians, 1 and 2 Timothy, 1 and 2 Thessalonians, Philippians, Philemon, Hebrews*
*II Hom. De proditione Iudae*
*Paraeneses ad Theodorum lapsum*
*Second homily in praise of St Paul*
*Sermon recorded by Metaphrastus*
**John of the Cross, St**
*A Prayer of the Soul enkindled by Love*
*Ascent of Mount Carmel*
*Dark Night of the Soul*
*Spiritual Canticle*
**John Damascene, St**
*De fide orthodoxa*
**John Mary Vianney, St**
*Sermons*

## Sources quoted in the Commentary

**Josemaría Escrivá, St**
*Christ Is Passing By*
*Conversations*
*The Forge*
*Friends of God*
*Furrow*
*Holy Rosary*
*In Love with the Church*
*The Way*
*The Way of the Cross*
**Josephus, Flavius**
*Against Apion*
*Jewish Antiquities*
*The Jewish War*
**Justin Martyr, St**
*Dialogue with Tryphon*
*First and Second Apologies*
**à Kempis, Thomas**
*The Imitation of Christ*
**Luis de Granada, Fray**
*Book of Prayer and Meditation*
*Guide for Sinners*
*Introduccíon al símbolo de la fe*
*Life of Jesus Christ*
*Sermon on Public Sins*
*Suma de la vida cristiana*
**Luis de Léon, Fray**
*Exposición del Libro de Job*
**Minucius Felix**
*Octavius*
**Newman, J.H.**
*Biglietto Speech*
*Discourses to Mixed Congregations*
*Historical Sketches*
**Origen**
*Contra Celsum*
*Homilies on Genesis*
*Homilies on St John*
*In Exodum homiliae*
*Homiliae in Iesu nave*
*In Leviticum homiliae*
*In Matth. comm.*
*In Rom. comm.*
**Philo of Alexandria**
*De sacrificio Abel*
**Photius**
*Ad Amphilochium*
**Polycarp, St**
*Letter to the Philippians*
**del Portillo, A.**
*On Priesthood*, Chicago, 1974
**Primasius**
*Commentariorum super Apocalypsim B. Ioannis libri quinque*
**Prosper of Aquitaine, St**
*De vita contemplativa*
**Pseudo-Dionysius**
*De divinis nominibus*
**Pseudo-Macarius**
*Homilies*
**Severian of Gabala**
*Commentary on 1 Thessalonians*
**Teresa of Avila, St**
*Book of Foundations*
*Exclamations of the Soul to God*
*Interior Castle*
*Life*
*Poems*
*Way of Perfection*
**Tertullian**
*Against Marcion*
*Apologeticum*
*De baptismo*
*De oratione*
**Theodore the Studite, St**
*Oratio in adorationis crucis*
**Theodoret of Cyrrhus**
*Interpretatio Ep. ad Haebreos*
**Theophylact**
*Enarratio in Evangelium Marci*
**Thérèse de Lisieux, St**
*The Autobiography of a Saint*
**Thomas Aquinas, St**
*Adoro te devote*
*Commentary on St John = Super Evangelium S. Ioannis lectura*
*Commentaries on St Matthew's Gospel, Romans, 1 and 2 Corinthians, Galatians, Ephesians, Colossians, Philippians, 1 and 2 Timothy, 1 and 2 Thessalonians, Titus, Hebrews*
*De veritate*
*Expositio quorumdam propositionum ex Epistola ad Romanos*
*On the Lord's Prayer*
*On the two commandments of Love and the ten commandments of the Law*
*Summa contra gentiles*
*Summa theologiae*
*Super Symbolum Apostolorum*
**Thomas More, St**
*De tristitia Christi*
**Victorinus of Pettau**
*Commentary on the Apocalypse*
**Vincent Ferrer, St**
*Treatise on the Spiritual Life*
**Vincent of Lerins, St**
*Commonitorium*
**Zosimus, St**
*Epist. Enc. "Tractoria" ad Ecclesias Orientales*